D1597948

"Collecting Stamps Would Have Been More Fun"

"Collecting Stamps Would Have Been More Fun"

Canadian Publishing and the Correspondence
of Sinclair Ross, 1933–1986

Selected and with an Introduction by Jordan Stouck
Annotations by David Stouck

THE UNIVERSITY OF ALBERTA PRESS

Published by

The University of Alberta Press

Ring House 2

Edmonton, Alberta, Canada T6G 2E1

Copyright © 2010 Jordan Stouck and David Stouck

LIBRARY AND ARCHIVES CANADA CATALOGUING IN PUBLICATION

Ross, Sinclair, 1908–1996

   "Collecting stamps would have been more fun" : Canadian publishing and the correspondence of Sinclair Ross, 1933–1986 / edited by Jordan Stouck, with David Stouck.

Includes bibliographical references and index.

ISBN 978-0-88864-521-0

   1. Ross, Sinclair, 1908–1996—Correspondence. 2. Ross, Sinclair, 1908–1996—Interviews. 3. Publishers and publishing—Canada. 4. Authors, Canadian (English)—20th century—Correspondence. I. Stouck, Jordan, 1970- II. Stouck, David, 1940- III. Title.

PS8535.O79Z87 2010   C813'.54   C2009-906599-1

All rights reserved.

First edition, first printing, 2010.

Printed and bound in Canada by Houghton Boston Printers, Saskatoon, Saskatchewan.

Copyediting and proofreading by Jean Wilson.

Indexing by Elizabeth Macfie.

The University of Alberta Press is committed to protecting our natural environment. As part of our efforts, this book is printed on Enviro Paper: it contains 100% post-consumer recycled fibres and is acid- and chlorine-free.

The University of Alberta Press gratefully acknowledges the support received for its publishing program from The Canada Council for the Arts. The University of Alberta Press also gratefully acknowledges the financial support of the Government of Canada through the Book Publishing Industry Development Program (BPIDP) and from the Alberta Foundation for the Arts for its publishing activities.

This book has been published with the help of a grant from the Canadian Federation for the Humanities and Social Sciences, through the Aid to Scholarly Publications Program, using funds provided by the Social Sciences and Humanities Research Council of Canada

Contents

Acknowledgements

PROFESSIONAL ASSISTANCE has been crucial for this project.
We thank first of all Carl Spadoni, McMaster University Library,
for assisting us in using the Macmillan and McClelland & Stewart
Archives, and for his advice about publishing items from these collec-
tions. His facilitating skills and professional goodwill are a constant
boon to Canadian researchers. We are also grateful to librarians else-
where who have assisted us to find letters and arrange permissions.
They include Suzanne Dubeau, York University Library; Linda Fritz,
University of Saskatchewan Library; Anne Goddard and Ghislain
Malette, Library and Archives Canada; Jennifer Toews, Thomas Fisher
Rare Book Library; and Marlys Chevrefils, University of Calgary Library.

Permission to publish his letters ("selections from my unpublished
writings") was granted by Sinclair Ross in August 1992. For permis-
sion to reproduce here letters to Sinclair Ross and others, we thank
Margaret Atwood, Toronto; Sheila Kieran, Toronto; Jocelyn Laurence,
Toronto (Margaret Laurence Estate); Wailan Low, Toronto (Earle
Birney Estate); Ken Mitchell, Regina; Guy Vanderhaeghe, Saskatoon;

and Robert Weaver, Toronto. (We have made every effort to locate and secure a permission from Andrew Suknaski, without success.)

   Equally important has been the generosity of Sinclair Ross's correspondents who provided us with copies of his letters for this volume. We thank Christine Bissell, Toronto; Wilfred Cude, West Bay, Nova Scotia; Laurenda Daniells, Vancouver; Keath Fraser, Vancouver; Alvin Goldman, Montreal; Myrna Kostash, Edmonton; John Moss, University of Ottawa; John Whitefoot, Ontario; and David Williams, University of Manitoba. We acknowledge gratefully past assistance from Jo Marriott, Lorraine McMullen, Audrey O'Kelly Peterkin, Doris Saunders, Winnifred Stouck and Mary-Ann Stouck (illustrations), and Roy St. George Stubbs. We are especially grateful to Earle Toppings, Toronto, for permission to publish his 1971 interview with Sinclair Ross.

Introduction

SINCE THE EARLY 1970S, Sinclair Ross's novels and short stories have been widely recognized as classics of Canadian literature that continue to inspire lively and diverse critical interpretations. Born on a homestead in northern Saskatchewan in 1908, Ross was one of the first authors to describe life on the Canadian prairies, giving artistic voice to experiences dissimilar from those described in the works of Eastern contemporaries such as Hugh MacLennan or Morley Callaghan. As Margaret Laurence writes in her New Canadian Library introduction to Ross's short fiction, "most of his writing [was] done out of the background of the prairie drought and depression of the Thirties, and as a chronicler of that era, he stands in a class by himself."[1] Certainly, his first novel, *As for Me and My House*, is an originary text in western Canadian literature, while his fourth novel and his short stories have inspired numerous younger writers through their perceptive treatment of characters and landscape. Major prairie authors such as Margaret Laurence, Robert Kroetsch, and Guy Vanderhaeghe have credited Ross with enabling their fiction, while writer-critics Robertson Davies and Margaret Atwood have used Ross's writing to identify archetypal themes for a Canadian literary canon. Today, a wide range of critics turns to Ross's work to explore issues of sexuality, ethnicity, genre, and regionalism in Canadian literature, and scholars are likely to turn again to his stories of drought and depression to study the effects of climate change and economic recession from a cultural perspective.

Yet despite Ross's status as a founder of Canadian literature, he perceived his literary career as a failure. In a letter dated 12 September 1970 to one of his editors at McClelland & Stewart, he wrote that his life was a lesson in how not to be a writer: many of his projects had failed to find publishers, he had been paid just $25 each for his short stories, and after thirty years his only novel in print had earned less than $3,000.[2] Elsewhere he wryly observed that "collecting stamps or butterflies would have been more fun."[3] He sometimes quoted Pearl S. Buck, only half in jest, that a writer should be careful where he is born.[4] He was referring to his Saskatchewan origins and his childhood and youth spent in a series of small prairie towns where opportunities for a young artist were meagre. With a grade eleven education, he had worked as a clerk at the Royal Bank of Canada to support himself and his mother and had remained an employee of the bank for forty-three years. He was never in a financial position to leave his job and consequently wrote fiction sporadically in the evenings and on weekends. Like the now celebrated painter Emily Carr, he found an audience only late in his life. The question arises as to why such an important Canadian author had to struggle so hard for recognition and remuneration. What do his difficulties say about the development and preoccupations of Canadian culture during the mid-twentieth century, and what do they reveal about publishing in Canada?

One of the resources available for approaching these questions is the correspondence engaged in by several of Canada's most accomplished writers, editors, and publishers that spans more than fifty years. At the centre is Ross; a reclusive man who almost invariably refused interviews and never gave public readings, but who always answered his mail. Accordingly, there are substantial collections of letters to friends such as Doris Saunders and Alvin Goldman, to editor-publishers such as John Gray, Robert Weaver, and Jack McClelland, and to fellow writers such as Margaret Atwood, Margaret Laurence, Ken Mitchell, and Keath Fraser. Ross himself kept only a small selection of letters because he seldom lived in one place very long, but the ones he did keep reflect important events in his writing life. There are, however, significant gaps in the correspondence. A particularly unfortunate hiatus is the correspondence between Ross and the first publisher of *As for Me and My House*, Reynal and Hitchcock of New York. Ross himself kept none of the letters and the Reynal and Hitchcock archive, part of the Harcourt Brace Library in Orlando, Florida, contains no record of the Ross correspondence. At other points, as for instance during the early 1960s when he was writing little, Ross kept practically no letters, feeling that his everyday affairs were of little consequence. However, the letters that do remain and have been selected here for publication constitute a valuable record of Canadian culture and mark the key periods in Ross's life as a writer. Given the organization to Ross's own collected letters and the replies they engendered, the letters here are loosely categorized according to the five major periods of Ross's writing life: the early short stories and *As for Me and My House*, the mid-career short stories and *The Well*, *Whir of Gold*, *Sawbones Memorial*, and his final period of reflection and correspondence as a literary mentor and forefather.

Ross's early career, which culminated in the publication of *As for Me and My House* in New York, is marked by the often chilly and indifferent publishing climate he encountered in Canada. The first documented evidence of Ross writing fiction appears in a letter dated 8 January 1933 from his English uncle, Sir John Foster Fraser, a popular writer who was knighted for his political journalism and travel writing. Fraser refers to a story that Ross has sent him in manuscript form. He does not give its title but describes it as something with "real power," and though he thinks it is "a little sombre," he suggests trying the *Atlantic Monthly* because it publishes, in his estimate, the best stories in the English-speaking world. Ross's dream, of course, was to leave the bank and earn his living as a writer and that meant breaking into the

British or American markets. But his attempts to place stories with high-paying American magazines including *Liberty*, *Atlantic Monthly*, and the *New Yorker* were not successful. Editors wanted stories with strong plot whereas Ross's stories, as he knew himself, were strongest in terms of mood, setting, and character.

The first and only international acclaim Ross ever received for his work came when he won third prize in *Nash's-Pall Mall Magazine* story contest in 1934. Judges for this prestigious British competition included Somerset Maugham and Rebecca West, and third prize included twenty pounds and the magazine publication of the winning story, "No Other Way." A leg up had not come from his uncle, however, but from Ernest Court, the leader of an amateur writers' group in Winnipeg known as the Phoenix Club. Before the advent of creative writing classes, writers' groups like the Phoenix Club were the chief venue in Canada for aspiring writers to try out their works, reading aloud to each other, offering praise and suggesting improvements. When Ross had no further success in placing his stories with popular magazines, having tried Canadian as well as American publishers, Court suggested *Queen's Quarterly*, whose editors in fact were quick to recognize the craft and power of Ross's writing and, paying an honorarium of $25 each, published most of the stories he wrote between 1935 and 1952. There is no extant archive for *Queen's Quarterly* until the late 1940s. Ross remembered genial letters from the chairman of the editorial board, Alexander Macphail, commending his stories but making almost no suggestions for revisions. Of greater interest were letters from the latter's brother, Sir Andrew Macphail, professor of medicine at McGill and an essayist and fiction writer of some distinction. Two of these letters have survived, both written in 1935. With their references to other magazines and writers, they represent Ross's first substantial connection to a world of literary talk, and they reveal that this talk in Canada was chiefly academic.

By September 1939, Ross had completed the manuscript for *As for Me and My House* but, outside the Phoenix Club and *Queen's Quarterly*, he had not established any connections for marketing his writing.[5] This changed in the fall of 1939 when he met Kathleen Strange, the

Winnipeg author whose best-selling autobiography, *With the West in Her Eyes*, had recently won the McLeod-Dodge Prize and was published by Dodge in New York. Ross gave her a manuscript copy of *As for Me and My House* to read and she soon urged him to contact her American agent, Maximilian Becker of the AFG (American-French-German) Literary Agency in New York. Becker agreed to act as his agent and sent the manuscript of *As for Me and My House* to Reynal and Hitchcock with significant consequences for Canadian literary history.

Independently wealthy, Eugene Reynal chose for publication manuscripts that personally appealed to him, with little concern for their commercial possibilities.[6] According to the author's account, *As for Me and My House* was accepted for publication within two days of being sent to Reynal for consideration. Unfortunately, the correspondence between Ross and Reynal has been lost on both sides; only a fragment survives in three paragraphs that Ross incorporated into an application for a Guggenheim Award.[7] Nonetheless, from Ross's conversation we know that the publishers did not ask for any changes to the manuscript. The only publication problems were technical ones: when the galley proofs arrived, Ross noticed at once that the running head on each page read "As for Me and My Home" and so it was omitted; when the blueline proof arrived for the dust jacket copy, Ross was more than annoyed to find that it included disparaging remarks about the backward nature of Canadian society. He had taken pains, in order to find an American publisher, not to identify the setting of his novel as Canadian, and so he protested and an advertisement for other Reynal and Hitchcock titles was substituted instead. In spite of these irritations, Ross would look back on his correspondence with Eugene Reynal as the most encouraging and helpful that he ever received from a publisher during his career as a writer.

Ross's dream of making his living as a writer had quickened with the American publication of *As for Me and My House*, but it would not last very long. When the novel was published in the U.S. in February 1941 it received a handful of notices in which the reviewers praised the book's style, but found little to commend in its gloomy subject matter. There was a scattering of positive reviews from the academic community in Canada and then the book dropped from sight, earning its author no more than the $270, which had been paid in advance royalties. But the dream died hard. In the fall of 1941 Ross put together an application to the Guggenheim Foundation for support to write a story about the life of Louis Riel, a figure in Canadian history whose hybrid identity as a Métis and as a rumoured bisexual held special fascination. And he was completing a novel about a prairie boy growing up to be a musician, with the projected title "Day Coach to Wagneria," which he would submit to Reynal and Hitchcock in the spring of 1942. He felt especially optimistic about this project because, as a letter written more than thirty-five years later makes fairly clear, it was a *Bildungsroman* built around stories such as "A Day with Pegasus" and "Cornet at Night," which had already received some praise.[8] Max Becker, in the meantime, was trying to find a New York publisher for an earlier novel manuscript titled "The Wife of Peter Guy." But in the summer of that year, Ross learned he had not won a Guggenheim, that Becker was having no luck with the Peter Guy manuscript, and that Reynal and Hitchcock had turned down "Day Coach to Wagneria." In late July he enlisted in the army, and on 27 August entrained for Ottawa as a member of the Canadian forces ready for service in the Second World War.

The first substantial collections of Ross letters are the result of his departure for war. Concerned about the welfare of his mother, for whom he had full responsibility, he wrote fairly often to two women friends who visited her regularly and saw to her needs. One of these was Audrey O'Kelly, an aspiring writer who lived with her sister and mother in the same building as the Rosses. The other was Doris Saunders, a professor of English at the University of Manitoba, who, impressed with Ross's fiction, sometimes taught his stories in her classes. To both women he gave a vivid account of what it was like to go through basic training, to travel to eastern Canada for the first time, and then to make the voyage across the Atlantic and take up his duties with the Ordnance Corps. In these letters the reader glimpses the excitement the prairie "boy" felt in London where bombs were falling but where, for the first time in his life, theatre and concerts and art galleries were an everyday possibility. He writes of attending performances of Turgenev, Ibsen, Shaw, and Shakespeare, and of hearing lectures by Charles de Gaulle and T.S. Eliot. In his letters to O'Kelly and Saunders he also discusses some of the thematic concerns of his fiction. For example, to O'Kelly on 18 March 1943 he writes about the ambiguous mixture of good and bad he sees at work in the world, as well as his realistic, thoroughly unromantic view of human nature. In portraying obliquely these unfashionable, less palatable attitudes in his work, Ross of course was establishing himself as both experimentally prescient and commercially problematic.

During the war he was also engaged in correspondence for the first time with other Canadian writers. Although *As for Me and My House* sold very few copies, Ross had acquired a reputation among fellow Canadian writers as a skilled craftsman and poignant illustrator of prairie life. Poets Ralph Gustafson and Earle Birney were both editing volumes of Canadian writing for international markets and they asked Ross if he would submit a story for their collections. In his letters to them he shares the frustration he experiences trying to write honestly and at the same trying to revise his manuscripts to meet market expectations. Especially indicative of his plight is when he laments to Earle Birney that he cannot plot a story to suit what he calls "slick magazines" like *Saturday Evening Post* and that he is probably "doomed" to write what no one wants to read.[9] He tells both Saunders and Gustafson that he was also engaged in a lengthy revision of "Day Coach to Wagneria," expanding the story to give his protagonist the experience of being in the war. Probably his two war stories, "Barrack Room Fiddle Tune" and "Jug and Bottle," were originally part of the expanded "Day Coach" manuscript. From the letters he wrote and from a form he filled out at the end of the war for the Department of Veterans Affairs detailing his future plans, we know that he was still working on the manuscript in 1945–1946. In an exchange with W.A. Deacon, book reviewer for the *Globe and Mail*, Ross explains that he is supporting his mother and that this sense of duty conflicts with his desire to "take the plunge" and devote himself exclusively to writing; but "I hope," he says, that "this novel will give me an answer."[10] There is no further information about his submitting it for publication, though one can justifiably assume that he did so and that the commercial and formulaic publishing climate after the war decided against it. There is a haunting aspect to the "Day Coach" manuscript: given the high quality of stories like "A Day with Pegasus," "Cornet at Night," and "One's a Heifer," it is very possible that, if it had been published in the 1940s or 1950s, it might have achieved the stature of a book like Sherwood Anderson's *Winesburg, Ohio,* or Alice Munro's *Lives of Girls and Women,* episodic rural narratives of the young artist awakening to vocation. In the late 1940s Ross turned away from the lure of American markets, resigned apparently to placing his stories with *Queen's Quarterly.* But in 1948 artist Grant Macdonald proposed to Ross the idea of a story collection for which he would prepare illustrations, and he simultaneously persuaded John Gray at Macmillan to give the idea serious consideration. Letters between Ross and Macdonald in 1948–1949 describe the preparation of a manuscript including two new stories, but Gray finally turned the project down, explaining with regret that economically at that time in Canada a collection of short stories was just not feasible.[11]

The correspondence between Ross and Macdonald is interesting on another level in its failure to acknowledge, even hint at, their sexual relationship. Ross's letters never describe his homosexual experiences, but they do record some of his relationships with men and therein reflect the social prohibitions that inform the encoded patterns of desire in his writings. Those patterns now form the basis of many of the recent critical approaches to Ross in which critics explore the unconventional permutations of sexual desire in his novels and short stories.[12] Andrew Lesk has suggested that Ross's refusal to publicly acknowledge his homosexuality, even in personal correspondence, was likely the result of his desire to retain a socially legitimate subjectivity vis-à-vis his readers.[13]

Disappointment continued to dog Ross's writing projects for the next twenty years. His professional correspondence reveals that the publishing of his second novel, *The Well* (1958), was especially fraught. Through a confusing series of failed negotiations, bad advice, and ill-conceived editorial demands, the writing and publication of *The Well* was a nightmare for the author and a commercial fiasco for Macmillan. But it began differently. From conversation we know that Ross had read a translation of Albert Camus' *The Stranger* at some point in the early 1950s.[14] He had been shaken by it, recognizing certain points of resemblance between his own life and that of Meursault; he especially saw himself, in Camus' words, as "a taciturn, rather self-centred person, resigned to the benign indifference of the universe."[15] Ross felt exhilarated by the idea that he, too, could write openly about young men who experienced the alienation he felt and could act at times with little moral restraint, young men wanting no connection to life beyond the existential recognition of its essential meaninglessness. He felt, as well, that the Canadian West was just as likely a decentred locale for such fiction as Algeria.

In the original version of the novel, Chris Rowe, a self-absorbed protagonist on the run from the law, finds work on a Saskatchewan farm where he seduces the farmer's young wife, Sylvia, eventually kills the elderly farmer, Larsen, and leaves without a trace. Ross submitted the manuscript to Macmillan Canada, but Frank Upjohn, one of the editors, observed that "[Chris] disappears into the thin prairie air, and without even a hint of any sort of justice ever catching up with him."[16] This reader's assumptions about character, moral order, and closure in fiction were completely at odds with those of the author, who was steeped in the works of Sartre and Camus. Ross complained years later that from the beginning his editors and publishers "just didn't get it."[17] Upjohn was also concerned about the reader's feelings for Chris, who is present for most of the story, but Ross did not intend readers to have sympathy for him. The letters reveal how, as Ross negotiated with Macmillan and with a series of agents and editors, he found himself in subsequent revisions pressured to refashion Chris into something like a sympathetic hero. Whereas Chris originally kills the old man because of his entanglement with Sylvia, indifferent to the moral implications of his act and purely responsive to the situation, in a second version, while he still participates in hammering the old man to death, he is made unsure of his actions and experiences guilt. In the third and final version, the murder is committed by Sylvia alone—she shoots Larsen—and in revulsion Chris feels "it was as if *he* had done it"[18] and the phrase "as if guilty" and the adverb "guiltily" recur again and again. Ross later observed that "*The Well* was so much rewritten according to the popular psychological formula of the day that the book was no longer mine in the end."[19] In other words, an existential novel had been turned into a more fashionably Oedipal one. The letters negotiating all these changes over a two-year period are a striking instance of an author coerced to meet the expectations of the moral, psychological, and aesthetic standards of the day, standards for serious fiction in Canada represented by leading writers such as Morley Callaghan and Hugh MacLennan.

Correspondence from the Macmillan archive reveals that Ross's problems with *The Well* did not end with revising the manuscript for Macmillan. John Gray encouraged him to prepare a shorter version of the manuscript to be considered for *Maclean's* Novel Award, worth $5,000 to the author, and worth a good deal in advertising for the publisher of the novel. Especially interesting, though lamentable, are the confusing signals from the magazine's fiction editor Janice Tyrwhitt who, before Ross began shortening the novel, wrote 9 September 1955 saying it was "an extraordinarily fine book" but that the tastes and prejudices of their million readers could not be ignored; "the tricky sex relationship" would require "a good deal of condensation." Ralph Allen, another editor at *Maclean's*, advised Ross to imply the sexual relationship between Chris and Sylvia without naming or detailing it, and to make it clear to the reader that Chris will pay for any crimes. Ross produced a condensed version of the novel, with an ending that fulfilled conventional moral paradigms, but early in 1956 he learned that *Maclean's* had decided against it. The novel *Maclean's* published that year was titled *The Face at the Window*, an early version of *A Dance in the Sun* by South African novelist Dan Jacobson. The story has similarities to *The Well* in that it tells of two students at a deserted farmhouse who discover a family's dark secrets, but unlike the original version of *The Well* the story involves a clear moralistic ending.

Ross also had negative news from his American agent, W.K. Wing. For Macmillan Canada, it was important financially to find a U.S.

co-publisher for their books and John Gray recommended W.K. Wing as a more enterprising and successful agent than Max Becker. Wing initially expressed considerable enthusiasm for *The Well* manuscript, but Ross explains to John Gray, with uncharacteristic anger, that Wing has changed his opinion and that he feels the agent has acted in bad faith.[20] Ross speculates in this letter that American agents may feel Canadian standards are inferior. The letters between Ross and Gray in this period also reveal the financial pressures affecting Canadian publishing. In his letter of 11 April 1956, responding to Ross's indignation over Wing, Gray says he fears Canadian publication alone would represent failure to Ross and, despite the latter's polite response, both men accepted the fact that publication solely in Canada would almost certainly preclude commercial success.

Amidst all the discouraging revisions and negotiations for *The Well*, Ross received a letter 10 April 1957 from McClelland & Stewart editor Hugh Kane, who wrote for permission to include *As for Me and My House* in the first series of New Canadian Library paperbacks. Kane's letter is of particular interest because it suggests that Ross might have submitted some of his early manuscripts to McClelland & Stewart for publication, or at least broached the matter with the country's leading publisher. Kane, who, according to this letter, had met Ross a few times in Winnipeg in 1941, writes: "I have some hesitation about reminding you of those days for at that time the policy of this firm was being influenced by people who were more interested in the distribution of imported books than the publication of Canadian ones." Ross's cautious and dispirited reply—that "*As for Me and My House* is something that happened a long time ago in which I am now not very interested"—suggests a tinge of bitterness about relations with McClelland & Stewart in the early 1940s and the subsequent neglect of his novel.[21] Ross nonetheless cleared publication rights with Harcourt Brace and the novel made its popular debut on 17 January 1958. Twenty years later it had sold over 100,000 copies, but at 3 per cent royalty until 1973, it earned its author very little money.[22] Nonetheless its reputation as a classic Canadian text and its commercial value were firmly established by this 1958 paper reprint; by 1979 only Margaret Laurence's *The*

Stone Angel, Gabrielle Roy's *The Tin Flute*, and Stephen Leacock's *Sunshine Sketches of a Little Town* exceeded *As for Me and My House* in sales.

The big shift in publishing that put Canadian books in the forefront for the first time took place in the late 1960s, as a new nationalism made the country zealously self-conscious about its own culture and government support accordingly became substantial. As so often, that shift is especially visible in the publishing fortunes of a Ross text. In 1964, encouraged by the adoption of *As for Me and My House* as a text in colleges and universities, Ross proposed an edition of his collected short stories to McClelland & Stewart. The idea was unceremoniously rejected, but just three years later the company was pursuing the idea. Because Ross had been offended by the earlier rebuff and the long gaps in communication with the company, on 26 September 1967 Jack McClelland wrote a brief but carefully worded apology to Ross, which succeeded in putting the project in place. It was followed on 15 October 1967 by an effusive, if "belated fan letter" from McClelland, praising *As for Me and My House* as "a superb novel and certainly one of the finest that has ever been written in this country." Thus author and publisher established cordial relations, Ross perhaps thinking about eventually sending McClelland & Stewart his next novel manuscript, and McClelland clearly anxious to firm up the deal for *The Lamp at Noon and Other Stories* and continue royalty payments at 3 per cent.[23]

But Ross's next manuscript, published as *Whir of Gold* in 1970, was already running into trouble. Despite both the commercial and critical failure of *The Well*, John Gray, true to form in championing Canadian writers, sent Ross a note 19 October 1962 wondering if he would have another manuscript for Macmillan. Ross eventually sent him the manuscript for *Whir of Gold* in 1966, a novel with a particularly long history. In a letter he wrote to Roy Daniells as far back as 10 December 1954 he says that in 1952 he had finished a novel about crime and delinquency in an urban setting, that it had received some good readers' reports, but had been turned down because of its pessimism.[24] That he was referring to *Whir of Gold*, the story of Sonny McAlpine, is supported by the fact that he had published a story about this character titled "The Outlaw" in *Queen's Quarterly* (Summer 1950) and that this magazine had turned down a second one titled "Sonny and Mad" in 1952.[25] At Macmillan in 1966, the future novelist Richard B. Wright, with some reluctance, recommended rejecting the novel on the grounds that it seemed dated; the other readers more or less concurred and this brought to a close Ross's long and troubled connection with John Gray's publishing house.

Jack McClelland, eager to publish Canadian authors of note and to secure a paperback edition of Ross's stories for the New Canadian Library, had encouraged him to let his editors look at any other works he might have, and so Ross eventually sent McClelland & Stewart the Sonny and Mad manuscript.[26] There was enthusiasm at McClelland & Stewart, and McClelland wrote in a memo to one of his employees that "[t]he day we can't publish Sinclair Ross is the day we shouldn't be in publishing,"[27] although two readers of the manuscript for McClelland & Stewart were cautious about the book's chances, and Robert Weaver suggested the book be published in a "modest" edition, with "modest hopes" for sales.[28] Ross became acquainted with Pamela Fry, a senior employee at McClelland & Stewart, who proved to be an astute editor and sympathetic correspondent; their extant letters stand as the happiest exchange Ross had with anyone in the publishing industry. Nonetheless, the publication of *Whir of Gold* was beset by huge problems, this time of a mechanical nature. With *Whir of Gold*, McClelland & Stewart experimented with a new method of computer printing and it generated numerous spelling errors, omissions, and repetitions in the text that were never completely eradicated, no matter how many times Ross proofread galleys. Again his work was on the rough edge of the future. As the correspondence reveals, Ross lost patience in spite of Pamela Fry's tactful encouragement, and when he had the book in hand, the unattractive cover, poor quality paper, small type, and narrow leading made Ross feel that this book, twenty years in the making, had not been worth all the effort. A majority of negative reviews, some faulting Ross for abandoning the prairie setting, compounded that feeling, even though the story itself remained his favourite.[29]

Ross describes his frustrations as a writer in a twelve-year correspondence with Margaret Laurence that began in 1966. He was introduced to Laurence in person in May 1967 by their mutual friend, Adele Wiseman, and the letters he wrote to her have the special ring of two equals in conversation about their craft, the publishing world, and the times they are living in. Ross, for instance, comments humorously in his 4 December 1966 letter on one critic's speculation that it was his devotion to his work at the Royal Bank that hindered his development as a writer: "Of all the reasons critics and biographers trot out to account for an artist's failure to mature—drinks, drugs, sex, neglect, ill-health—this one is surely unique." Their friendship was reinforced at an early stage when Laurence was asked by McClelland & Stewart to provide the introduction for *The Lamp at Noon* stories; this gave Laurence an opportunity to identify and praise Ross as one of Canada's literary forefathers.

The emergence of major writers like Margaret Laurence consolidated the shift in Canadian publishing, which was no longer dependent on American tastes and financial considerations. By the early 1970s, Canadians were becoming interested in fiction from their own country; large numbers of university and college students were reading Sinclair Ross in the New Canadian Library paperbacks and critics were exploring the regional, religious, and psychological dimensions of his writings.[30] In *Survival*, an immensely popular overview of Canadian literature, Margaret Atwood identified Ross as writing the archetypal Canadian novel in *As for Me and My House*. Atwood's book gave voice to an emerging nationalism and, like Laurence's introduction to *The Lamp at Noon and Other Stories*, established Ross's writing as central to this new perspective on Canada and Canadian literature. The letters between Atwood and Ross collected here gave Ross renewed confidence in his work and set the scene for the publication of his fourth and final novel, *Sawbones Memorial*, in 1974.

As the letters reveal, the writing, editing, and production of *Sawbones Memorial* went smoothly and reviews of the book for the most part were excellent. Conditions were finally right for Ross: Canada's leading publisher was eager to bring his work forward and there was a reading public eager to admire a new piece of fiction from this literary icon. McClelland & Stewart files indicate the press was optimistic about the book's success and as early as April 1974 (the book was not published until 26 October) were sending galley proofs to Robert Weaver at the CBC and Judith Finlayson at *Maclean's* to stimulate some advanced publicity. In their "publishing plan" form, under promotion and publicity, they designated this book for "major author special treatment," gave "prestige" as the reason for publishing *Sawbones*, and under author's record entered "one of the most important writers in Canada." From this same form we learn that the first printing was boosted from 3,500 copies to 5,500 (based on projected Literary Guild sales) and the estimated long-range sales was set at 15,000.[31] But in two ways Ross taxed his public and brought disappointment to both his readers and publisher. His new book was set on the prairie, as his readers expected, but it was experimental in form, consisting solely of dialogue and stream-of-consciousness reflections, without connecting narrative. Critics liked the challenge posed by the book's form, but general readers found it difficult and more often than not set the book aside, not recommending it to others. Further, Ross refused to do publicity for the book, even finding it difficult, as is evident in his May 1974 letter to Martin O'Malley, to give an interview to a book reviewer prepared to fly to Spain to meet him.[32] Accordingly, *Sawbones Memorial* was a critical "succès d'estime" rather than the bestseller Ross had dreamed of, and McClelland & Stewart declined the sequel, titled "A Price above Rubies."

Nonetheless, by the late 1970s Ross's position as a forefather and mentor of Canadian, and particularly western Canadian, literature was firmly established. The final selection of letters in this volume records the widening academic interest in Ross and his role in encouraging younger western writers. The correspondence between Ross and Lorraine McMullen, author of the first book-length critical study on Ross and his work, includes the author's reflections on his writing career and those writers who influenced him, while his replies to the inquiries of other literary critics such as John Moss, Wilfred Cude, and David Williams reveal him engaged in academic debates surrounding his first novel, offering valuable insights on his creative process. The 29 January 1984 letter to Ross from Guy Vanderhaeghe eloquently sums up the feelings of numerous western creative writers, including Ken Mitchell, Robert Kroetsch, and Lorna Crozier, who wrote to or about Ross during this period, identifying him as a specific inspiration for their work. On a national level, Margaret Laurence's endeavour in 1978 to get a Canada Council grant for Ross in the Senior Arts Award category was endorsed by twenty of the country's leading writers. Ultimately, this section reveals a community of writers and informed readers who constituted a select and sophisticated audience for his work. However, the identification of this audience came late and Ross, by then in his seventies and suffering physically and psychologically from the onset of Parkinson's disease, was unable to write for that discriminating audience he had so painstakingly won. In the last twenty-two years of his life he published a fourteen-page memoir of his mother titled "Just Wind and Horses." The interest and recognition documented by this final period of Ross correspondence continues in the critical industry that surrounds his work, for it has always proved hospitable to a variety of ways to read literature.

To return to the question of Ross's belated recognition, the correspondence gathered here suggests some preliminary answers by revealing the meagre artistic and financial resources available for a serious writer in western Canada in the first half of the twentieth century. Ross wrote without the artistic affirmation of a professional literary community until the 1970s and his literary pursuits were steadily curtailed by the practical demands of making a living. For most of Ross's career, from the Great Depression through to the 1960s, the limited to non-existent financial support for Canadian authors simply precluded professional writing, particularly given Ross's personal obligation to support his mother as well as himself. Perceptions of the U.S. market as the only financially and artistically legitimate publishing venue also complicated the initial placement and reception of his work. Letters from the 1950s reveal how writers in a country with such small markets were constrained by the popular formulas for fiction and the moral assumptions of the day. The letters further reveal how the emergence of Canadian literature as a cultural phenomenon in the late 1960s altered the career of a writer whose best work seemed to have been done by 1941. Robert Lecker has argued that Ross's early work fulfilled academic and nationalist ideas about Canadian literature and this, in part, led to his canonization.[33] Ross's belated success was, in this sense, an issue of social concerns being applied or catching up to a particular artistic form and, while this undoubtedly and finally validated Ross's accomplishment, critical response to *Whir of Gold* also suggests that it placed constraints on Ross's settings and subject matter—that is, Ross became viewed only within a certain western context and subject. More recent readings of Ross in terms of race, gender, and sexuality reveal that the scope of Ross's work reaches beyond the nationalist paradigms of regional setting and history which initially interested critics.[34] Ultimately, these letters to, from, and about Sinclair Ross reveal important shifts within Canadian publishing history and expose the crucial roles that community and audience can play in the reception of fiction.

In preparing the correspondence, we have selected letters of literary and biographical interest, and made exclusions to avoid repetition and long discussions of purely practical matters. When letters have been abridged to avoid repetition or when part of a letter is missing, ellipses are used accompanied by an explanatory note. Ross's use of ellipses is left without commentary. Because he made very few mistakes in his writing, we have silently corrected any spelling or punctuation errors. These occurred chiefly in the late letters when Parkinson's disease made typing difficult. We have regularized dates and the format of book and story titles. Addresses are only used at the point when Ross changed residences.

To close this volume we have transcribed from audiotape the one formal, previously unpublished interview Ross ever gave—a conversation with Earle Toppings at the Ontario Institute for Studies in Education. Especially in light of the missing correspondence with his American publisher, this is an important resource because in the interview he talks about *As for Me and My House* and some of the conditions that produced it. Similarly, the collection of letters allows Sinclair Ross to speak for himself—to negotiate with his publishers, confide in his friends, encourage his admirers, and respond to his critics. These interactions convey Ross's remarkable humour and humility, aspects of his personality which public shyness often concealed. The collection is also designed to reveal what correspondents had to say about Ross, whereby a case study of one writer's experience becomes both an intimate and collective view of Canadian literary history.

NOTES

1. Margaret Laurence, introduction to *The Lamp at Noon and Other Stories*, 7.

2. Ross wrote to Pamela Fry: "I'm resolutely not thinking about that damned interview on tape which is bringing me to Toronto in November. What the hell have I to say which might be useful to students? Unless to serve as a good example of how *not* to do it." MUL, M&SA, CC1.

3. See letters dated 10 January 1972 and 5 February 1978.

4. Earle Toppings, *Canadian Writers on Tape: Mordecai Richler / Sinclair Ross*.

5. Ross remembered vividly that when he had finished final revisions to the manuscript he was boarding a train at Lake Winnipeg at the end of a holiday, and over the loudspeaker at the station came the announcement that Canada was at war.

6. Reynal's special interest was in art books, but the company's list was varied, including works as diverse as Antoine de Saint Exupéry's *Wind, Sand, and Stars* and Adolph Hitler's *Mein Kampf*.

7. Reynal and Hitchcock was sold to Harcourt Brace in 1947 after the early death of Curtice N. Hitchcock in 1946. The company's files form part of the Harcourt Brace Library in Orlando, Florida, but letters exchanged during the publication of *As for Me and My House* were apparently not preserved. The three paragraphs that Ross incorporated into the Guggenheim application were from a letter of advice he received from the company about writing a historical novel. They can be found with the Roy Daniells Papers, UBCL, box 4, folder 1.

8. See letter from Ross to Lorraine McMullen, 15 January 1979.

9. See letter to Earle Birney dated 26 July 1943, TFRBL, Earle Birney Papers, box 16, file 18.

10. See letter from Ross to Deacon, 15 April 1946.

11. See letter from John Gray to Ross, 2 May 1949.

12. See Keath Fraser, *As for Me and My Body*, 44–66, Valerie Raoul, "Straight or Bent: Textual/Sexual T(ri)angles in *As for Me and My House*," *Canadian Literature* 156 (Spring 1998); Andrew Lesk, "Something Queer Going on Here: Desire in the Short Fiction of Sinclair Ross," *Essays in Canadian Writing* 61 (Spring 1997): 129–41, and "On Sinclair Ross's Straight(ened) House," *English Studies in Canada* 28 (March 2002): 65–90; Timothy R. Cramer, "Questioning Sexuality in Sinclair Ross's *As for Me and My House*,"

ARIEL 30 (April 1999): 49–60; Peter Dickinson, "Sinclair Ross's 'Queers,'" in *Here is Queer: Nationalisms, Sexualities, and the Literature of Canada,* 17–21; and Terry Goldie, "Not Precisely Gay in Tone" in *Pink Snow: Homotextual Possibilities in Canadian Fiction,* 39–56.

13. Andrew Lesk, "Getting Ross not so Straight," *Books in Canada* 34, no. 6 (September 2005): 21–22.

14. Ross in conversation with David Stouck, 17 March 1991 and 18 May 1994.

15. Albert Camus, *The Stranger,* 70.

16. Reader's report prepared for Macmillan by editor Frank Upjohn, 30 September 1955. M U L, Macmillan Company Collection, box 130, file 10.

17. Ross in conversation with David Stouck, 18 May 1994.

18. *The Well* (Edmonton: University of Alberta Press, 2001), 222.

19. Ross in conversation with David Stouck, 24 January 1993.

20. See letter to John Gray dated 8 April 1956.

21. Ross's letter to Hugh Kane is dated 16 April 1957 and along with Kane's letter to Ross is held at M U L, M&SA, Series A, box 47, file 3.

22. By 1979 the novel had sold 116,906 copies. Sales figure for the New Canadian Library from 1958 to 1979 are in M U L, M&SA, Series A, box 93, file 14.

23. In a note to Geoff Fielding dated 9 November 1967, Jack McClelland says he is afraid "Ross may well want 10%—or at least more than our normal 4%," but in a 20 November 1967 reply Fielding writes "I can't see us getting away with a 3% royalty to Ross, but this is Malcolm [Ross]'s suggestion." Ross continued to receive 3 per cent for both books until royalties were increased in 1973 to 7 per cent.

24. See the Roy Daniells Papers, U B C L, box 6, folder 19.

25. G.H. Clarke, the editor, wrote to Ross 18 March 1952 saying the story did not suit the journal's needs. This letter is held in the *Queen's Quarterly* Archive, Q U A.

26. Ross refers to a meeting with McClelland in a letter to Margaret Laurence dated 9 December 1967. See the Margaret Laurence Collection, York University Library. He didn't actually send a revised version of the *Whir of Gold* manuscript to McClelland & Stewart until May 1969.

27. Quoted by Pamela Fry in a letter to Sinclair Ross 12 June 1969, M U L, M&SA, CC1.

28. See Weaver's report dated May 1969, M U L, M&SA, CC1.

29. See, for example, Malcolm Foster, "Sinclair Ross's Latest Lost in New Locale," *Gazette* [Montreal], 12 December 1970, 43, and Harvard Dahlie, "Maybe Sinclair Ross Should Have Stayed in His Small Prairie Town," *The Albertan* [Calgary], 6 March 1971, 8.

30. Some examples of these approaches include Laurie Ricou's "The Prairie Internalized: The Fiction of Sinclair Ross" in *Vertical Man/Horizontal World: Man and Landscape in Canadian Prairie Fiction,* 81–94; Dick Harrison's *Unnamed Country: The Struggle for a Canadian Prairie Fiction;* Sandra Djwa's "No Other Way: Sinclair Ross's Stories and Novels," *Canadian Literature* 47 (Winter 1971): 49–66; and Wilfred Cude, "Beyond

Mrs. Bentley: A Study of *As for Me and My House*," *Journal of Canadian Studies* 8 (February 1973): 3–18. Reprinted in *A Due Sense of Differences: An Evaluative Approach to Canadian Literature*, 31–49.

31. Publication details for *Sawbones Memorial*, including the author's royalty set at 10 per cent on the first 5,000 copies, are located in MUL, M&SA, CC54, box A.

32. The interview was eventually conducted by William French in July, but unfortunately his article appeared in the *Globe and Mail* more than two months before the novel's appearance in bookstores.

33. See Robert Lecker, *Making It Real: The Canonization of English-Canadian Literature*, 173–87.

34. See, for example, "Sinclair Ross's 'Foreigners,'" *From the Heart of the Heartland: The Fiction of Sinclair Ross*, ed. John Moss, 91–101, in which Marilyn Rose applies the cultural sensitivity of postcolonial theory to representations of East European and Chinese immigrants in *As for Me and My House* and *Sawbones Memorial*.

Abbreviations

LAC: Library and Archives Canada
MUL: McMaster University Library
QUA: Queen's University Archives
TFRBL: Thomas Fisher Rare Book Library, University of Toronto
UBCL: University of British Columbia Library, Rare Books and Special
    Collections
UCL: University of Calgary Library
URL: University of Regina Library
USL: University of Saskatchewan Library
YUL: York University Library

Chronology

1908 | James Sinclair Ross is born January 22 to Peter Ross and
   Catherine Foster Fraser Ross on a homestead in northern
   Saskatchewan, twelve miles from Shellbrook and twenty-six miles
   northwest of Prince Albert. He is the youngest of three children.

1915–1924 | Ross's parents separate and he lives with his mother,
   who works as a housekeeper for a series of widowed and bachelor
   farmers. In 1924 he completes grade eleven high school at Indian
   Head, Saskatchewan, and in Abbey, Saskatchewan, begins working
   for the Union Bank (shortly thereafter absorbed by the Royal Bank
   of Canada). He remains an employee of the Royal Bank until his
   retirement in 1968.

1928–1933 | Ross works for the bank at Lancer in 1928–1929, is trans-
   ferred to Arcola, Saskatchewan. He makes a concerted effort to
   become a musician but only achieves second-place standings in
   pianoforte examinations. Begins writing fiction and submitting
   his work to American and Canadian magazines.

1933 | In April he is transferred by the bank to Winnipeg, Manitoba,
   where he continues to live with his mother.

1934 | Joins the Phoenix Club, a creative writers' group, and its leader, Ernest Court, convinces Ross to keep sending out his stories for publication. Ross's first published piece, "No Other Way," wins third prize of twenty pounds in an English short story competition. The story was published in *Nash's-Pall Mall Magazine* in October 1934.

1935 | "A Field of Wheat" is published in *Queen's Quarterly* (Spring 1935), the first of twelve stories to be published in that journal. All attempts to be published in other Canadian and American magazines are met with failure.

1941 | *As for Me and My House* is published by Reynal and Hitchcock in New York. The book sells only a couple hundred copies and drops out of sight.

1942–1946 | Ross joins the Canadian Army and goes overseas with the Ordnance Corps, and serves at Army Headquarters in London until March 1946.

1946 | Ross returns briefly to Winnipeg and to living with his mother, and then is transferred to Royal Bank headquarters in Montreal. From that point he lives alone for the rest of his life.

1946–1958 | Ross publishes five stories in this period. At least two novels and a collection of short stories that he completed do not find publishers.

1957 | *As for Me and My House* is published by McClelland & Stewart in the first series of the New Canadian Library.

1958 | After a series of revisions, *The Well* is published by Macmillan Canada to disappointing reviews.

1968 | In January Ross retires from the Royal Bank after 43 years of service and in March moves to Athens, Greece, where he lives for three years. *The Lamp at Noon and Other Stories* is published in the New Canadian Library series.

1970 | *Whir of Gold* is published by McClelland & Stewart, again to disappointing reviews.

1971–1973 | Ross moves to Spain, first Barcelona, then Málaga.

1974 | *Sawbones Memorial* published to excellent reviews. Ross works at a sequel.

1978 | *Sawbones Memorial* published in the New Canadian Library and *As for Me and My House* is brought out by University of Nebraska Press, but the sequel to *Sawbones Memorial*, after being rejected by McClelland & Stewart, is abandoned.

1980 | Ross is diagnosed with Parkinson's disease and returns to Canada to live in Montreal.

1982 | Ross moves to Vancouver, where his health steadily deteriorates. A second collection of his stories is brought out by University of Ottawa Press with the title *The Race and Other Stories*.

1985 | After recovering from a broken hip, Ross goes to live at Brock Fahrni veterans' hospital in Vancouver.

1988 | Ross publishes a short memoir titled "Just Wind and Horses." It was his last publication.

1990 | Ross and his work are the subject of a three-day conference at the University of Ottawa in April.

1992 | Ross is made a member of the Order of Canada

1996 | Dies February 29 at Brock Fahrni Pavilion, Vancouver. His ashes are interred at Indian Head, Saskatchewan, where members of his sister's family live.

2001 | With paperback publication of *The Well*, *Whir of Gold*, and *Sawbones Memorial* by University of Alberta Press, all Ross's books are in print.

ONE

American Dream | *Letters 1933–1945*

THE LETTERS IN THIS SECTION contain some first words of
encouragement and advice offered to Sinclair Ross by his English
uncle, a popular writer in Britain, and by a few contemporary
Canadians, most of whom were academics. The question of
American markets weighs heavily in the background in these letters. In terms of Canadian publishing history there is a great gap
here: Ross's early correspondence with his short story publisher,
Queen's Quarterly, and his editors at Reynal and Hitchcock, has not
survived. The only record of his transactions with the New York
company is a few paragraphs written by Eugene Reynal that Ross
quoted in an application for a Guggenheim Award. Included here
for their historical as well as literary interest are some of Ross's
letters written when he enlisted with the Canadian army and was
stationed in London during the Second World War.

From John Foster Fraser[1]
Princes Risborough, England

To James Sinclair Ross
Arcola, SK[2]

8 January 1933

My dear Jimmie
You will have heard from your mother how she is getting on in the old
country.[3] My wife and I were very glad to have her and so far she has
been with us just over three weeks. Soon she is going to London to stay
at some small comfortable hotel and toddle round on her own, before
going to Edinburgh to revisit places she knew as a child and I think her
plans are to sail from Glasgow for Canada on March 4th. Unfortunately
before Christmas I was bowled over with influenza and a touch of
bronchitis so I have not been able to give her as much attention as I
would have liked — we've been down here alone for a few days getting
some sunshine and sea air. Forty-five years is a long time since I saw
your mother. I didn't expect to recognize her and yet when we met I
knew her by her eyes. She has certainly led a brave life and she is so
frank and cheerful that I am filled with admiration. Of course her life
and outlook has been circumscribed by her long years in Saskatchewan.
It could not be otherwise. Everything, even in London, is judged by the
ways of Arcola, the size of the hotel at Regina and the thickness of the
carpet in the Hudson's Bay stores at Winnipeg! She is terribly loyal,
amusingly so at times. This is all a new world to her, but everybody she
meets she has to tell about the way things are done in Arcola and about
"my Jimmie." I've chaffingly told her that the folk she talks to don't
really care a damn about Arcola and that other mothers have sons of
their own of whom they think a heap — and this she thinks is criticism.
To me she is a very loveable and interesting study, but mentally there
is a great and impenetrable space between us — for my life has been
spent in the world and hers has been spent in Saskatchewan. I'm afraid
she must have bored the people in Arcola — Arcola has a bigger bank

Sir John Foster Fraser, Sinclair Ross's journalist uncle in London.

[Library and Archives Canada]

than we have in the village of Princes Risborough—with talk about her brother Jack. I chaffingly tell her she is a real snob, pestering people about her titled relatives. When she gets home and she starts talking about this country you must restrain her wearying people. My experience of untravelled western Canadians is that they really do not want to know that there is anything better on earth than they have. Years ago when your uncle Theodore was here he did an intelligent round of both England and Scotland. Before he returned to Prince Albert I casually observed he would have a lot to tell his pals about London. He replied "No, I've got to live with them and I don't want to make myself unpopular and be told I'm a liar because I say London is more interesting than Winnipeg. They won't and can't believe it." And I can't stop your mother talking—as she threatens to talk—about Constance and myself. Personally I hate that kind of adulation and I want my sister to be extremely happy with the good and genial souls of Arcola.

I ought to have written you long ago acknowledging some manuscript of a story and some short poems. First let me say, have nothing to do with any institute which in return for dollars will teach you to become a novelist or poet. These concerns are mostly fraudulent, tickling the vanity of people with qualified praise in order to get their money. There is only one school, natural aptitude, the careful study of other people's work and keeping at it. Quite freely let me say—and I'm not given to gush—you have not only the artistic temperament but have something near genius. I gathered from your mother about your music and heard that your favorite composer was Chopin. Good! The landscape you sent your aunt Constance is an amazing piece of work for one who has, I suppose, never been in touch with the great artists. The story you sent me has real power—a little sombre in treatment, but that is your present nature. I'm told the *Atlantic Monthly*—certainly the best story magazine in the English-speaking world—is holding a story of yours. Splendid.[4] Well Jimmie you've got it in you—and I'm an old and experienced bird in the game of writing for the public. Something must be done to get you away from the cramp of Arcola—notwithstanding I've been told I'll meet my intellectual superiors there!! Nothing however must be done rashly, because I know your financial situation and what a good son you have been to your mother. What a great and delightful and amusing story there is to be written about Arcola—as I've gathered from asides in conversation—but you have got your face so slap up against the picture you can't see it. If you could live for a year in Montreal, Toronto, or Ottawa you'd get perspective then see it. I could now map you out a real seller about the city of Arcola; but I don't know the background. Tell me what is in your mind that you have ambition to do—and we will see if some ropes can be pulled.[5] I've not a shilling in the world I have not earned, but I think I could help you a bit if you need funds. And keep on reading and be "a sedulous ape" as R.L. Stevenson was when he taught himself writing. Read some artistic writers—Henry [Harland] (now forgotten); read his "Cardinal's Snuff Box"; Maurice [Heroletts] "Little Novels of Italy" and give yourself a good dose of Leonard Merrick's novels—all artists in writing as well as storytellers.[6] All luck to you.

John Foster Fraser

1. Sir John Foster Fraser was Sinclair Ross's maternal uncle. When Ross's mother's family emigrated to Canada from Britain, John Fraser, in his late teens, remained in England and established himself as a popular journalist, travel writer, and lecturer. He was the author of more than twenty books, but was especially celebrated for *Round the World on a Wheel* (1899), an illustrated account of a trip he made across three continents on a bicycle. Knighted while still in his fifties, he represented to Ross the possibilities of fame and fortune for a writer.
2. Hereafter, Ross's address will only be given when he has moved to a new location.
3. Fraser is referring to an extended visit by his sister (Ross's mother, Catherine) from December 1932 to March 1933.
4. For several years Ross sent stories to the *Atlantic Monthly*, which was regarded as the best of the American magazines. Although his stories were refused, he persisted with submissions because one of the editors initially sent a handwritten note saying he liked the story very much, explaining apologetically that every year thousands were received and only ten or fifteen were printed.
5. John Fraser was a personal friend of Sir Herbert Holt, the head of the Royal Bank in Montreal, and the latter arranged for Ross to be transferred from Arcola to the Portage Avenue branch of the bank in Winnipeg in April 1933.
6. Popular British writers of the late nineteenth and early twentieth centuries.

From C.P.C. Downman

Editor, *The Royal Bank Magazine*

Montreal, PQ

18 June 1935

Dear Mr. Ross:

Many thanks indeed for sending me the *Queen's Quarterly* containing your story "A Field of Wheat." I have read this with intense interest and I should like to offer you my sincerest congratulations on the manner in which you have handled this "saga of the soil."

I am delighted to hear that *Queen's* will take more of your stories. I don't know whether they pay anything for them, but I would suggest that you try magazines like the *Atlantic Monthly* who, if they accepted a story, would pay a good price.

I have taken the liberty of writing to the Principal of Queen's for permission to reprint your story in the *Magazine*. This he has very kindly given to me and if you have no objections I should like to run your story in one of the autumn issues.

My sincerest thanks and best wishes for your further success.

Yours very truly,
C.P.C. Downman

From Sir Andrew Macphail[1]

Montreal, PQ
27 January 1936

Dear Mr. Ross,

I read with great admiration your "Field of Wheat," and "September Snow," in *Queen's Quarterly*; even at this late moment I cannot refrain from saying so.[2] The lamented Kipling[3] could not have done better. My hope is that you will continue. May I suggest that you look again at page 459, last paragraph, and ask yourself if the first three lines might not, or should not, have been omitted, for the reason that a woman in that situation is entitled to a certain secrecy.[4] Those lines lack beauty, and I thought them the only flaw in an otherwise perfect writing. I am sure you will not take this comment amiss; what we lack most in Canada is criticism.

Ever yours faithfully
Andrew Macphail

---

1. Sir Andrew Macphail (1864–1938) taught medicine at McGill, but was also a man of letters, best known for his *Essays in Puritanism* (1905) and a family narrative set in Prince Edward Island titled *The Master's Wife*, published posthumously in 1939. His brother Alexander Macphail was chairman of the editorial board of *Queen's Quarterly*.
2. The stories had been published the year before.
3. British novelist and short-story writer Rudyard Kipling had just died on 18 January 1936 at age 70.
4. Macphail objects here to the realistic glimpse of childbirth in "September Snow." The lines read: "There was a little moaning sound in answer, and he sprang across the kitchen and into the bedroom. She was on the bed, half-undressed, her face twisted into a kind of grin, the forehead shining as if the skullbones were trying to burst through the skin." Macphail's puritanical attitude reflects the common opinion and taste of the time.

Postcards, 1938 and 1941, to Harriett Duff-Smith, one of Ross's close friends in Winnipeg. The 1938 card from New York is the earliest extant piece of writing in Ross's hand. [Private collection; John Whitefoot]

From J.C. Nelson

Editor, *The Royal Bank Magazine*
Head Office, Montreal, PQ
29 July 1938

Dear Mr. Ross:

Just a note to let you know how much I enjoyed reading your story "Lamp at Noon." I do not wish to seem fulsome but I cannot help saying in all sincerity that it is one of the finest things of its kind I have ever read. Others with whom I have talked feel the same way about it and I am sure you will receive, 'ere this, many letters of congratulations from readers both of our magazine and *Queen's Quarterly*.

Might I make a suggestion although this may have occurred to you already? Why not submit your material to the publishers of magazines such as the *Atlantic Monthly*: your story "Lamp at Noon" is very definitely in the style of this publication and I cannot help but feel that they would buy articles of that type from you—and incidentally, I believe they pay very well.

I hope you do not mind my making this suggestion but there is no question whatever that you have exceptional gifts as a writer and it seems a shame not to capitalize on them.

To revert to a subject a little closer to our own interests we would be delighted if you could find time, in the course of a busy year, to write an occasional short story for our magazine.[1]

I hope you liked the way we handled your article. I am sending you a few extra copies under separate cover.

With kind regards,
Yours sincerely,
J.C. Nelson

P.S. As this is somewhat personal I should be glad if you would consider it as confidential.

1.   Ross declined this often-repeated invitation until 1958 when he acceded to an editor's request and sent a Christmas piece titled "The Unwilling Organist."

To Roy Daniells[1]
University of Manitoba, Winnipeg, MB
April 27, 1941

Dear Dr. Daniells:

I returned from my holidays just this morning, which explains my delay in acknowledging your letter. It was good of you to write so enthusiastically of my book. There's no use pretending that a word of praise isn't sweet. I find my appetite for it enormous.

I was sorry to learn you have been unwell this winter, and hope that you are yourself again. I hope too I will be able to see you before you leave for the summer. Perhaps you would be free some day to join me for lunch. You could reach me by telephone—906754.

Yours sincerely,
Jimmy S. Ross

1.   Roy Daniells was a professor of English at the University of Manitoba from 1937 to 1946. He first became aware of Ross as the author of several short stories being published by *Queen's Quarterly* in the late 1930s and began extending him invitations for dinner and for social gatherings with students. He became one of Ross's most ardent supporters and after reading *As for Me and My House* wrote to him in an excited mood: "You should be able to produce that phenomenon we've been waiting for since Confederation: the great Canadian novel. *As for Me and My House* is very close to it." In 1957 Daniells wrote the introduction to the first paperback issue of the novel and his opinion that Mrs. Bentley was "pure gold" would be contested by critics for many years to come.

One of the first enthusiastic readers of As for Me and My House:
Professor Roy Daniells. [Private Collection; Laurenda Daniells]

Sinclair Ross publicity photo for As for Me and My House, *1941.*

[Royal Bank Archives, Ross, Sinclair James, 1941]

To the John Simon Guggenheim Foundation

[New York City]

Autumn 1941

[In a letter to the Foundation applying for an award, Ross identified his subject as "a biography, in novel form, of Louis Riel."]

My intention is a fictional *treatment* of the subject, based on and adhering closely to all available factual material. There will be, for instance, invented dialogue, soliloquies, etc., also perhaps, invented incident and situation, insofar as this will aid the narrative, make the scene and characters convincing, etc., and insofar as it will not distort or throw a false light on the historical and biographical facts.

It will not be an historical study, but simply an attempt to tell the story of Louis Riel, to think with and reveal the man.

In such a treatment, however, certain historical issues will be implicit, and therefore, perhaps, I ought to state that at the present time I do not see Riel as he is usually depicted in history textbooks. (I make this qualification "at the present time" because the reading and research still to be done before undertaking the actual writing may modify or alter my point of view.) I may not be able to agree with certain groups of his admirers who look upon him as a patriot-martyr; on the other hand I feel there is a strong case to be made in his defense. Misguided, undisciplined, "psychotic" perhaps, but no mere renegade or adventurer. I would repeat, however, that any revisions of historical attitudes which might result from the successful completion of the book would be by the way. My interest in Riel is more psychological than political.[1]

A biography of Riel, I feel, is long overdue. While the Red River and Saskatchewan Rebellions, seen in historical perspective, are perhaps not very important, Riel himself is one of the most colorful and tragic figures in Canadian history. His career is in itself a drama that requires neither addition nor distortion, but only telling.

I am now working on a second novel, on which the publishers of my first book have an option, and which they would like to have in their hands not later than May, 1942.[2] At my present rate of progress I should have it ready by that time. If awarded a Fellowship I would begin work on this project (Riel) towards the end of May, 1942, devoting a few months to research, and the rest of the time to the writing and preparation of the manuscript. Some travel would be necessary, to Saskatchewan, and perhaps to Ottawa and Montana, but I believe that most of the required data is available in Manitoba. While engaged in the actual writing I would remain in Winnipeg.

As to the likelihood of publication when the book is finished, I know that Reynal & Hitchcock Inc., New York, will at least give the manuscript their favourable consideration. They are a reputable, well-established firm, with several important writers on their list. One of the partners, Curtice Hitchcock, was in Winnipeg recently, and he thought that if I could find time for the necessary research, Riel would be a good third venture. The following extracts from a letter written by Eugene Reynal, principal of the firm, shortly after acceptance of my first novel last November, will perhaps serve as a practical estimate of my prospects as a writer:

"We are extremely enthusiastic about your present novel, *As for Me and My House*, and particularly impressed with the fluency of your style. It seems to all of us here that you have great promise as a writer, and that if you do not try to push yourself too fast, you have a real future ahead of you."

"Your agent, Mr. Becker, tells us that you are anxious to give up your job and devote your entire time to writing. This does not seem to us a wise decision at the moment....Building up a reputation as a novelist is a slow, laborious job unless you happen to get the very special breaks that come perhaps once in a thousand times. You have a whole lifetime ahead of you and a promising writing career. Because it is so promising, it is all the more important to take it slowly and let it develop as you yourself develop."

"What we have in the back of our minds is the possibility that your real field might be in the historical background of the Canadian northwest. So far as we know, nobody has done in that area what Walter Edmonds[3] and Kenneth Roberts[4] have done in northeastern America, and it seems to us there is a very wide field of endeavor for someone with talent such as yours."

[Signed] James Sinclair Ross

1. Ross was particularly interested in exploring the possibility of Riel's bisexual nature.
2. The manuscript Ross refers to here was titled "Day Coach to Wagneria" and told the story of a young musician growing up on the prairie. It never found a publisher, but fragments of the original manuscript survive in *Whir of Gold*. It was actually the third novel manuscript that Ross completed, preceded by *As for Me and My House* and an earlier manuscript titled "The Wife of Peter Guy."
3. In popular novels such as *Drums along the Mohawk*, 1936, Walter Edmonds (1903–1998) recreated the history of upper New York state in the eighteenth century.
4. In his Arundel series, Kenneth Roberts (1885–1957) wrote fictional histories of the period around the American Revolution. *Northwest Passage*, 1938, was an immensely popular novel in this series.

To Earle Birney[1]
Toronto, ON
29 January 1942

Dear Mr. Birney:
I have read and reread "David"[2] — and unqualified as I am to pass an
opinion on poetry, I would like to let you know how deeply it
impressed me. I thought it a moving, sensitively-handled piece of
work. Some of your lines, particularly "into valleys the moon could be
rolled in," and "the last of my youth, on the last of our mountains,"
made me really envious.

I hope you will be publishing more poems like this one — and soon.

With kindest regards,
Sinclair Ross

---

1. Ross first met the distinguished Canadian poet Earle Birney (1904–1995) at Hart
    House in April 1941.
2. Birney's famous poem is a narrative about a mountain-climbing accident. It is the
    central piece in *David and Other Poems*, which won the Governor General's Award for
    poetry in 1942.

From Earle Birney
Toronto, ON
24 February 1942

Dear Sinclair Ross,
It was very good of you to write so appreciatively of "David." That
letter gave me real pleasure, for I value the judgment of someone who
writes as well as you do very much. I would have replied sooner but
I was waiting for more definite word on a matter I want to broach to
you. A.J.M. Smith[1] has been in touch with me by letter for some time

concerning a project for a special Canadian issue of *Story* magazine.[2] Whit Burnett is out of New York at the moment, finishing a book, and it seems to be difficult to get a final decision from him. But in Smith's last letter he said that Burnett had given the go-ahead signal, and, since I am apparently going to be a joint guest editor with Smith, I'm writing you, first of all, to ask that you save a story for submission for the projected number.[3] Until Burnett comes back to NYC, everything is tentative, but I think the issue will come out late in the summer,[4] will be devoted to some Canadian verse, which Smith will edit, and stories by representative Canadians. The stories presumably must be hitherto unpublished. I take it that the pay will be the usual *Story* pay, $25–35 a story. I am approaching Callaghan this week, as I consider him a "must,"[5] and I shall be writing Bob Ayre in Montreal,[6] and speaking to Mrs. Innis[7] and one or two others here. At the moment I won't go beyond that, and this note to you. I certainly wouldn't want to go ahead with it if I couldn't get something from both yourself and Callaghan. Also, I would be very grateful if you would turn over in your mind other possible contributors, particularly west of the Lakes.[8] Don't, of course, noise the matter abroad too much or both you and I will be plagued with ambitious young pulp writers. The idea is to present as good a literary face to the Americans as possible. I will be writing an introduction on the Canadian story.

In this latter connection, I would be glad if you could let me have, sometime, a bibliography to your published short stories—if it isn't too much of a chore. I've been reading a number of them with pleasure, and would like to read them all, or at least know where they all are.

Let me hear from you soon, and thanks again for your very heartening note.

Sincerely,
Earle Birney

1. A.J.M. Smith (1902–1980) was a Canadian poet who made his living teaching literature at the University of Michigan.

2. *Story* magazine was founded in 1931 by Whit Burnett and his first wife, Martha Foley, and remained under Burnett's editorship until 1967. By the late 1930s it had a circulation of over 20,000 copies per issue and was an early publisher of such famous American writers as Richard Wright, Carson McCullers, William Saroyan, and J.D. Salinger, to name a few. Birney was right to be excited by the prospect of editing a Canadian issue of this influential magazine.

3. Ross sent Birney a copy of a new story he had written titled "One's a Heifer." Birney liked the story but felt the boy's age should be changed from eleven to thirteen, a suggestion which Ross agreed to.

4. In a letter to Ross dated 21 May 1942 Birney wrote to say that he had joined the army and that *Story* had dropped the idea of a Canadian issue. Ross subsequently sent "One's a Heifer" to Ralph Gustafson for a collection of stories he was editing. See letters to Ralph Gustafson beginning 17 April 1942.

5. Canadian fiction writer Morley Callaghan (1903–1990) was considered a "must" because he had already established himself in the U.S. when his first book, *Strange Fugitive*, was published there by Scribner's in 1928. In Canada he was also popularly identified as a friend of Ernest Hemingway.

6. Robert Ayre was a public relations officer with the CNR, and a part-time journalist living in Montreal in the 1940s. He published critical pieces on art and poetry in the Montreal *Standard* and in *Canadian Forum*. (In 1944 he became co-editor, with Donald Buchanan, of *Canadian Art*.)

7. Mary Quayle Innis (1899–1972), economist, editor, and wife of political economist Harold Innis, published some forty-five short stories between 1938 and 1947 in magazines like *Saturday Night* and *Canadian Forum*. Some of these stories were shaped into the autobiographical "novel," *Stand on a Rainbow* (1943).

8. In a reply to Birney dated 9 March 1942, Ross writes that he is mentioning the project to Roy Daniells in Winnipeg and to Desmond Pacey at Brandon College, Manitoba.

To Doris Saunders[1]

University of Manitoba, Winnipeg, MB

25 March 1942

Dear Doris:

It was awfully kind of you to pass on your friend's comment on *As for Me...* I did appreciate it. Especially because at the present moment I am up to my eyes in revision of my next one, and hating every damned word of it.[2] What stupid tripe you write sometimes, convinced at the moment it's not bad. I come to a particularly inane paragraph, slash it out, then realize that at least part of it is necessary for continuity. The only comfort I can find is that I felt exactly the same about *As for Me...* and actually grudged the postage it took to mail it out. Anyway, it should be out of the way sometime in May, and then perhaps I shall be able to find my way back to the ways and moods of normal men. (Way-way-ways—and in a letter to a professor of English!)

Mother says "hello" to you and Miss Riley,[3] and still is looking forward to having you over. (1) If you will come. (2) When she gets some spring-cleaning done.

My thanks again—and kindest regards,

Jimmy Ross

1. Doris Saunders (1900–2000) was a professor of English at the University of Manitoba. When she read *As for Me and My House* in 1941 she introduced herself to the author and thereafter encouraged him in his work. She remained a lifelong friend.
2. Ross is referring here to the manuscript titled "Day Coach to Wagneria" that was never published.
3. Edna Riley was a close friend to Doris Saunders and accompanied Saunders when she first introduced herself to Ross.

Another of the first enthusiastic readers of As for Me and My House: *Professor Doris Saunders at the University of Manitoba.*

[Private Collection]

To Ralph Gustafson[1]

New York City

17 April 1942

Dear Mr. Gustafson:

My apologies for the long delay in answering your letter. I have been busy, groggy with the 'flu—and also waiting word from Earle Birney about a short story I sent him for a Canadian issue of *Story* magazine that they plan to bring out this summer. I thought it might not be suitable for him, and intended, in that case, to let you see it for your forthcoming Penguin volume. He plans to use it, however—provided the magazine comes out—and as I am extremely busy finishing a novel I regret that I cannot submit to you anything at present. The publishers want to see the novel next month, so I'm giving it every minute of my spare time. When is the deadline for your material? If later on in the summer I might manage something. Or would you consider anything that has already been published? *Queen's*, I am sure, would give permission to reprint any of my stories that they have used, provided that their name is mentioned.

I am sorry that I know no one in the armed forces able to turn out the sort of thing you want. I have spoken to some of the men at the University here, but they can suggest no names either.

With best wishes for the success of this and "Canadian" Penguins,

Yours sincerely,
Sinclair Ross

---

1.   Ralph Gustafson (1909–1995) was a highly esteemed poet, anthologist, and music critic. He was a Canadian but lived in New York City for a number of years before returning to his home in Quebec's Eastern Townships. A prolific poet, he won a Governor General's Award in 1974.

To Ralph Gustafson
New York City

Fort Osborne Barracks, Winnipeg
2 August 1942

Dear Mr. Gustafson:
Thank you for your letter and the return of the manuscript of "One's a Heifer." I was awfully pleased that you liked it. The approval of someone with taste and standards is real encouragement. The second novel that I mentioned in a previous letter has been turned down by Reynal & Hitchcock — "too thin in plot" — and while the agent is trying it on some other people I'm not very hopeful. It's about a farm boy from the age of 14 to 18, and there's not much action or drive to it.[1] I feel there is some good writing in it — but it's better in spots than as a whole. Perhaps after an interval I may see it in clearer perspective, and succeed in shaking it into firm form. A disappointment — yes — but at least this is a very bad time for a novel, and perhaps I may ultimately gain by the delay. In the meantime I'm pretty well absorbed by the Army.

I have been in a week, and can Right Turn — Left Turn — and fold my blankets. No small achievement, the last, either. I'm with the Ordnance — and after four months Basic Training will likely go overseas. I hope so — since I'm in it I might as well get as much experience out of it as possible. I'm not finding it so difficult to get adjusted as I expected. The first two days I couldn't get the food down, but now I'm ravenous. The lads seem a decent sort. Farmers, mechanics, tradesmen, clerks — all nationalities — but there is a curious blending, a paring down to masculine essentials. We get along. I begin to like it.

I have your *Anthology of Canadian Poetry*[2] and offer my sincere congratulations. I hadn't realized before the scope of Canadian poetry. To me it seems you have done a splendid job of selection. I run through the pages and all at once Canada becomes mature.

Naturally I read with particular interest the poems by Ralph Gustafson. Interest and pleasure and increasing respect. Frankly I didn't know much about you. When your first letter came the name registered, and that was about all. I imagined you an oldish, professorial sort—your poetry uplifting and Edwardian. What a delightful surprise to read your poems and meet the attractive young man of the frontispiece. I do hope the opportunity will present itself before too long for me really to meet you. In the meantime my thanks again for your interest in my work.

Sincerely,
J.S. Ross

1.   See letter to Doris Saunders, 15 February 1945.
2.   Ralph Gustafson's *Anthology of Canadian Poetry* was published by Penguin Books in England in 1942.

From Ralph Gustafson

[New York City]
11 August 1942

Dear Sinclair Ross:
Many thanks for your letter that arrived this morning. I was glad to hear you liked *The Anthology of Canadian Poetry.* It has done remarkably well, I am glad to say—in fact, I remain startled that a book of poems, by anyone about anything, can sell 500 a day. There seems to me reason for good hope within such news. I think Wm Lyon Phelps' broadcast about it was the boost that exhausted the first edition (15,000).[1] Another is on the way.

Particularly, I'm glad you liked my own stuff. I am not too good at knowing about my own stuff but perhaps the selection is all right. A.J.M. Smith persuaded me to "Dedication" which I thought might be too long.[2] I'm also glad not to remain oldish and professorial!

The typescript of *Contemporary Canadian Writing* is taking shape. I am way over contract time with the publishers[3]—but I can only snatch time for it from work at the B.I.S.[4] However, by the first of next month I hope to have the ms on the way to England. It promises well; I have pieces from E.K. Brown, Leon Edel, L.A. MacKay, Smith, Klein, Pratt, et al. I hope for pieces from Leacock, MacLennan, and others.[5] There is a dearth of good imaginative prose in close contact with the war. It is my one disappointment. The poets seem to write out of the struggle—but no short stories that I am aware of.

I am hoping your new novel gets a publisher. I have a feeling that "too thin in plot" means little and smacks of the commercial viewpoint. Do let me know of your writing when you can.

Meanwhile, good fortune...

Sincerely,
Ralph Gustafson

1. William Lyon Phelps (1865–1943) was an American educator and literary critic whose opinions were highly regarded by the public at large.
2. An anthologizer himself, A.J.M. Smith (1902–1980) was a distinguished Canadian writer whose early imagist poem, "The Lonely Land," is probably anthologized more than any other Canadian poem. "Dedication" is the title of a two-page war poem written by Gustafson.
3. The anthology Gustafson was editing was retitled *Canadian Accent* and was not published until November 1944. The two-and-a-half-year delay persuaded Ross he should withdraw the story in favour of a request from English editor John Lehmann, but Gustafson largely ignored his letters. Ross received payment of just $17.85 for "One's a Heifer."
4. Gustafson was employed in New York at the British Information Services.
5. E.K. Brown (1905–1951) and Leon Edel (1907–1997) were Canadian-born critics and scholars who established international reputations working at American universities. L.A. MacKay (1901–1982), A.M. Klein (1909–1972), and E.J. Pratt (1882–1964) emerged as leading poets in the 1920s and 1930s, Klein and Pratt becoming major figures in Canadian literature. Stephen Leacock (1869–1944) and Hugh MacLennan (1907–1990) were writers who enjoyed the wide popularity that eluded Ross, Leacock as a humorist and MacLennan as a novelist who made national identity his central theme.

To Audrey O'Kelly[1]
Winnipeg, MB

Ottawa, ON
1 September 1942

Dear Audrey:
I hope you're surprised at a letter from me so soon because I'm
really surprised myself. And if you saw — or even better, heard — the
writing-room! A juke-box with a cowboy yodelling — some of the boys
tap-dancing, some of them playing ping-pong — everybody drinking
Coca-Cola and eating raisin pie — my neighbour at the table determined to tell me about the car and girl he gave up to join the Army.

Ottawa, however, is an improvement on Fort Osborne. The food is
much better — more taste, more variety — and there are neither kitchen
smells nor fatigues. We don't even have to mop the floor — such things
are done by the "defaulters." There are about 2000 men here, mostly
Ordnance and Army Service, all barracked in the exhibition buildings. (We're in "Horticulture"; the dining room is "Horse Show.")
Discipline is good, but the atmosphere is more relaxed and leisurely
than at Winnipeg. We don't get up till six, and aren't chased so hard
on the parade ground. Officers friendly — they talk with the men
during break-offs, and even make jokes on parade. The Ordnance's
Sergeant-Major is from Winnipeg — almost the double of Gary
Cooper, except that he's a bit bow-legged — and because he's from
Winnipeg too he's been around both yesterday and today to drill us
himself. (Incidentally, they think we're pretty good. They stepped
us out today to show the Easterners in our platoon how the turns
"ought" to be done.) This evening we had a route march with a Piper
Band along the Rideau Canal. Trees and grounds so beautiful it was
almost like a story-setting — weeping willows, Balm of Gilead, rowan,
and evergreens — ornamental shrubs that I had never seen before.[2]
Saturday I had dinner with Charlie Clay[3] (he used to be with the *Free
Press*, and is now here freelancing) and afterwards he walked me
around the Parliament Buildings and pointed out the best views: Hull

across the river, with the "flèche" of its cathedral silhouetted against the sunset, and the Parliament Buildings from behind, on a cliff that rises almost sheer out of the river. I'm looking forward to hearing the famous carillon—they say it plays three or four times a week—and this Saturday we plan to go up in the town.

I'm still plodding through *The Brothers Karamazov*—almost 300 pages to go—and am nearly through *To the Lighthouse* a second time.[4] Having to concentrate on what I'm reading—frequently the boys throw a pillow or magazine at me to bring me back. No more books in my pack though—it was as much as I could do to make it down here, and for the next move there will be still more equipment. However, it apparently isn't going to be for two months, and by that time I may be brawnier. They say that all troops now, regardless of what unit they belong to, have to take *commando* training when they get overseas. Boy, that took the wind out of my sails for a few minutes. Can't you see me swimming rivers or climbing walls with full pack—the way they do in the newsreels?

I hope you find time soon to give me the office news. Please say "hello" to the staff for me—to Alice, however, only on the condition that she's now thrown over that big blond chump of a movie star... "Hello" and good wishes, too, to Mrs. O'Kelly, Pat and Bernard.[5]

Does deciphering this remind you of the home Return?

As ever,
Jimmy Ross

1. Audrey O'Kelly worked with Ross at the Royal Bank in Winnipeg, but also lived with her mother and sister in the same apartment building as the Rosses. She aspired to be a writer and eventually was an influential member of The Penhandlers, a society of largely amateur writers.

2. This was Ross's first trip to eastern Canada and his first glimpse of Quebec province, which would eventually be his home from 1946 to 1968.

3. Charles Clay (1906–1980), in addition to working at the *Winnipeg Free Press* in the 1930s, was the author of adventure and historical novels for boys. During the war he published a weekly syndicated column called the *Listening Post*, which informed

readers of Canada's work at war. He was national secretary of the Canadian Authors Association from 1942 to 1946.

4. Major novels by Fyodor Dostoevsky (1821–1881) and Virginia Woolf (1882–1941) respectively.

5. All members of the O'Kelly family.

To Doris Saunders
University of Manitoba, Winnipeg, MB
23 October 1942

Dear Doris:

Forgive my long delay in answering your kind and interesting letter. Truthfully, I was waiting for a quiet hour to give it the reply it deserved. Here, however, quiet hours are rare, so I ask your indulgence for a few scribbled lines.

I have been in Ottawa eight weeks tomorrow—and now stand clicking my heels with bags all packed and waiting for the word to go. Tomorrow perhaps, or the next day, or in a week's time—waiting is one of the things the Army teaches us.

It's been an uneventful stay here—the usual infantry basic training course, drill, route marches, rifle practice etc. The Ordnance aren't a "combatant unit," but in modern mobile warfare, when they are likely to be isolated, they have to be able to look after their own defence. Not being very "hefty," I've found it hard in places, but have managed to grunt and grumble through. Mechanically I'm the most useless person alive, so you can imagine the fun I've had learning to take a Bren gun apart and put it together again.

Through Charlie Clay (formerly with the *Wpg Free Press*, now free-lancing here) I met Eric Gaskell[1] recently. A sincere, intelligent fellow—I warmed to him instantly. We went together for dinner to a Madge Macbeth's,[2] an elderly lady who has written a number of short stories and a couple of travel books. Do you know of her? Her reputation seemed to be taken for granted, and I had a tough time trying to conceal my ignorance of who she was and what she had done. Gaskell is leaving in a day or two to join the Navy, so we didn't have as much time together as we (at least I) would have liked.

Apart from Charlie, they are the only congenial contacts I have made here, and the satisfaction they have brought makes me realize how much I am "putting up" with, and only pretending not to mind. But then it's good for me. Because I had come close to farmers and white collars I thought I knew men, but how I was "kidding" myself. A good deal of what you discover is disappointing, very little of it is to be altogether condemned. And how self-sufficient they are, how indifferent to "us" with our books and theories. Working in a bank and smiling at all the customers has made me a fair hypocrite; consequently I get along with them. They infuriate you one day, and the next do the opposite. Sometimes, watching and listening—plus doing a little self-analysis— I think that you could define humanity as good ideals and noble resolves without the necessary strength and will to carry them out.

All of which means, I hope, that I am learning something. In writing, vanity is the most difficult thing to overcome—and there are a hundred forms that vanity can take. It seems if I could only be genuinely humble, that then I could turn out worthwhile work. Between the conceptions and the executions there is always this self-seeking "me" pushing forward. You say you have been reading Dostoyevsky, so you will know what I mean. I have just finished *The Brothers Karamazov* for the second time, and I have been feeling that the writer has almost completely effaced himself. I have done nothing since joining the Army except notes and rough drafts for short stories—the barrack room doesn't give one much opportunity—but a great many ideas are presenting themselves, and I'm inclined to believe that an enforced fallow period may be good for me.[3] I suspect I have been trying to do too much too fast. As to the novel I finished last spring, I've pretty well forgotten about it for the present.[4] The agent is holding the manuscript, and the copy is hardly in condition for anyone else to read—corrections in pencil etc. that I jotted down so I could [mail out] the original. The publishers said the plot wasn't strong enough, that I depended too much on style and characterization. They want more suspense in the last hundred pages—the reader, they say, suspects the ending, that the boy is going to [desert] the girl and escape from the farm. Well, I wasn't even trying to conceal it. I feel convinced that there's a lot of fair work in it, but wonder now if it may not be better in parts than as a whole. A little later, perhaps, I may see it in clearer perspective, and whip it into more satisfactory story form. Right now it seems remote and unimportant.

Thank you for giving me the address of your friend—if I have the opportunity I shall certainly get in touch with her. I'm looking forward to England, though it will likely be monotonous except for the occasional leaves. We are to be in the country, about two hours from London—some of the boys already gone from here say living conditions for us will be good.

Sorry I write such a scrawl—using my knee as a desk doesn't improve it. I did appreciate your letter, and hope you find time—soon—for another. The address you have will reach me. Remember me please to Miss Riley and Chester[5]—I'm going to write him a little later.

Yours sincerely,
Jimmy Ross

Mother is still in the Boyce Apts. She would be awfully pleased to see you.

---

1. Eric Gaskell was national secretary of the Canadian Authors Association from 1938 to 1942.
2. Madge Macbeth (1878–1965) was a popular and prolific fiction writer best known for two satirical novels about Ottawa and parliament, *The Land of Afternoon* (1924) and *The Kinder Bees* (1926), published under the pseudonym of "Gilbert Knox." She has gathered critical attention more recently for an early feminist novel titled *Shackles* (1926). She had been president of the CAA from 1939 to 1941.
3. Five years later Ross published a story with the title "Barrack Room Fiddle Tune" in the spring 1947 issue of *Manitoba Arts Review*.
4. Ross is again referring to the manuscript titled "Day Coach to Wagneria." See letter to the John Simon Guggenheim Foundation dated Autumn 1941.
5. Chester Duncan (1913–2002) was a musician friend and professor of English at the University of Manitoba.

To Audrey O'Kelly
Winnipeg, MB

London, England

18 March 1943

Dear Audrey:

I'm sorry to have been so long answering your two letters, but London has made me an even worse correspondent than usual. And then, truthfully, the course has kept us jumping, study every evening except over the weekend, when I went out for a play or a concert and a little sightseeing. We are just finishing up now, and leave the day after tomorrow—destination unknown. I have done fairly well, and understand I am getting a good report, though 80 words a minute shorthand seems to be my limit at present. It is the speed required for a pass out, but as I made good progress up to 70 I was hoping to reach 90 or 100. My cramped, screwed-up way of writing—*you* remember—doesn't lend itself to speed, but I think I can do better when I have had time to develop a style to suit me. I turned in my final typewriting test yesterday, 68 words a minute with .4% errors, which is well over the required speed. I still have the bad habit, though, of taking a squint every now and then at the keys.

I think I told you in my last letter that I had hopes of coming to work here, but there is such need now of typing-shorthand clerks in the field that there isn't much chance that I will. I don't mind now, however, having satisfied my curiosity about London in the last three months. If anything, I'm looking forward to a change—and it will moreover be better experience than up here.

London, of course, is interesting, and has a fascination that is impossible to describe or define—the fog and rain and blackouts notwithstanding. I should like to spend a few months here in peacetime—with money in my pocket. I haven't seen a great deal of it at that—the fog and rain again, and so many places closed for the duration—but know my way pretty well around the West End. It is really a difficult place to find your way in, the streets do so much twisting and chopping and changing. They also have the amazing habit of changing their names without warning, and the directions that the citizens give you—"Bear right, then left, then right, then left again"—leave you dizzy. The Londoner's idea of distance, too, seems to be different from ours. "Just a step," he will say, and you cover a mile before you're there. There is fine transportation, though, buses, trams and the underground, but Saturday night, when you want to be out late, everything stops a little after eleven, and you can either take a taxi or a park bench.

There have been a few raids, but all small. The barrage is terrific, though—if you can imagine a hundred thunder storms all at once, and even inside you can feel the air giving convulsive little jerks. They dropped incendiaries on the Common right in front of our billets one night, and another time I was up town when the sirens went and had to slip into an underground at Piccadilly (the chief danger is our own shrapnel coming down). The crowd was unbelievable, but everybody was in high spirits, and jubilant because it was such a small raid after what Berlin had got a few nights before.

There is a great deal of symphony and theatre this winter, and I managed a concert nearly every Sunday afternoon. I also saw several plays, Shaw's *Heartbreak House*, Noel Coward's *Blithe Spirit*, Turgenev's *A Month in the Country* (by the way, if you haven't already done so, read his *Fathers and Sons*, I think you'll get it in the library), *The Merchant of Venice*—was bored stiff—and Ibsen's *Hedda Gabler*. As these titles themselves tell you, almost everything is revival—in wartime, I suppose, no one is writing plays—though England has been turning out some good movies lately. Particularly *In Which We Serve*[1]—I suppose it has reached Winnipeg by now—if not, don't miss it when it does come.

I was glad to hear you are working at a story, and sorry that it wasn't working out as you wanted. You'll get used to that. You mention that you shrink from writing about people just as they are, because just as they are most of them aren't worth writing about. Yes—that's the hard part, ánd one to which you'll have to find your own solution.

Interruption

Continued at Borden, March 23–26, 1943

Now—where were we? We nearly all begin as Romantics, then swing the other way, to what we think is Realism, but which is as far away in one direction from the mean of *real* reality as Romanticism is in the other, then arrive, usually with some reluctance, at that mean. With reluctance because it is so undramatic, so ordinary—nothing very good, nothing very bad—everything just so-so. It becomes increasingly difficult to admire humanity. You may go "sour" on it for a while, but then, if you are honest, and see "straight," you will pity it. You may even become fascinated by the mixture of good and bad, noble and base, exalted and petty. But it's no use shutting your eyes and pretending that it's *not* a mixture. The best way, I suppose, to understand humanity, is to understand yourself. Really understand yourself. An unflinching examination of your deepest thoughts and motives, all the ugly little things as well as the finer ones. The hard part is that we have such an intense desire to think well of ourselves that despite our firm resolve to be "honest" we cover up, twist, rationalize. The differences between a conscientious citizen and a criminal, a sane and an insane man, are of degree, not kind. The little flare of anger you have sometimes felt—instantly "sat upon," passed off without harm—becomes, when uncontrolled, or when aggravated, the rage that strikes a man down. The foolish and illogical "feeling" you have sometimes had that people don't like you, that they notice this or that about you, becomes, in a certain kind of mind, and in certain circumstances, a maniacal "persecution complex" (Hitler's got it). And when you have discovered all these things about yourself you will no doubt be sorry that life is that way, but you will not be impatient with or intolerant of it. But in any case, as I said before, you'll have to work out your own solution. Be honest—there's nothing harder—and, unafraid. And always—dropping to the practical—keep writing, so that you develop a feeling for words, and skill and precision in expressing yourself.

To return to myself for a minute—incidentally it's now March 26—I came back to camp last Saturday, and am waiting to be posted. They gave me my leave on Wednesday and then at the last minute—I was almost out the gate—cancelled it. This morning I was put on draft—destination still unknown—and I was nearly through the preparations, medical, dental, etc., when *that* was cancelled. But word is I'm going back to London to H.Q.—working on the staff of a Brigadier General, and, probably, "scared" doesn't half describe my condition—but judging the future from the past it will be time enough to worry when I get there. In the meantime I'm relieving in one of the camp offices, and having a rather easy time of it. I'm only going to be here a few days anyway, so there's no point in teaching me much. I'll be glad, though, when I get settled, and down to working seriously. It's 8 months tomorrow, by the way, since I joined. Some veteran, eh!

Forgive this messy, rather disreputable looking letter, and my long delay in writing it. "Hello" to the family for me—I wish I could drop in sometimes to see you. There are moments when I feel an awfully long way from home—almost as if I had landed on the moon.

And "Hello" please too to all my old friends on the Staff. I'm writing Riddie and Bess perhaps tomorrow—and will you, till I do it myself, thank Alice for her Air-Graph.[2]

Letters are always welcome.

As ever,
Jimmy Ross

1. This popular naval picture of 1942, directed by Noel Coward and David Lean, is an outstanding example of the propaganda films made by Britain and the U.S. during the Second World War.
2. Ross is referring here to fellow employees at the Portage Avenue branch of the Royal Bank in Winnipeg.

To Earle Birney
London, England

Headquarters, No 1 CBOD, UK
26 July 1943

Dear Earle:

Was awfully glad to hear from you again, and do hope you can get over some afternoon or evening. However, it looks right now as if I am going to London shortly—I am going up tomorrow for an interview—and if I do we should be able to arrange a weekend—perhaps several.[1]

I know how you feel about writing and then not knowing what to do with it. I am really in the same position—it sounds all right to say I have a New York agent—but he is always chasing me for "slick" magazine material, and I just can't turn it out. I get horribly depressed at times—being "doomed" to write what no one wants to read.[2] There is so much about the Army that I want to do—and, eventually, I suppose will—but damned if I can "plot" it to suit the *Saturday Evening Post*. But bad enough to afflict editors with my gloom—I ought to spare my friends. I am looking forward to seeing some of the things you are doing now—curious to find out what the reactions of another member of the tribe are to the War—or at least the Army.

Will write again as soon as I learn more about what is to happen to me. Do write again when you have a spare minute—and don't notice the "write again"—no wonder editors don't get enthusiastic.

Sincerely,
Jimmy Ross

1. Ross and Birney met in mid-August, but both men were disappointed in the meeting, Ross feeling intimidated by Birney's rank, and bearing, Birney finding Ross withdrawn and uninteresting.
2. Ross also tried to place some of his stories with English publications. On 12 January 1943 he sent a "few" of his published stories and the manuscript of a "recently

completed" one to John Lehmann, editor of the *New Writing* series. The new story
might have been "Barrack Room Fiddle Tune," since he was working to turn his army
experiences into fiction. Lehmann, however, did not use any of the stories in his
anthologies.

To Audrey O'Kelly
Winnipeg, MB
27 November 1944

Dear Audrey:

Slow as usual — my face is really red as I start to send off a few greetings and realize how many of my friends I haven't written a line to
since last Christmas. It doesn't seem like Christmas over here. So
many had hoped that the lights would be on and the war would be up
this year, and as another dark winter sets in people find themselves
apathetic and despondent. And besides there are the rockets — and they
do make a mess.[1] Speaking from experience — though I was wonderfully lucky and escaped without a scratch. Had just walked away from
my desk, and so by about ten seconds missed the glass of the window.
It wasn't a pretty sight, but everyone behaved splendidly — no panic
or hysterics, and over and over you heard "Mine's not serious — I'll
wait till the doctors get around the others." There is no warning of
any kind — perhaps a blessing, at least for your nerves — just a sudden,
terrific explosion that sounds on your doorstep when it's 3 or 4 miles
away. They actually can factor their sound, and you hear them coming
after they have come. There is the explosion, and then a swishing
rumbling sound, something like distant thunder — though we hadn't
ears left to hear the rumble after "ours."

However, to be a little brighter, London has a fine season of music
and theatre under way — the best in some ways, it has ever had,
according to the critics. At present, for instance, Olivier is playing
Richard III, Ralph Richardson *Peer Gynt*, and John Gielgud *Hamlet*, and all
performances sold out weeks ahead. It's the same in the provinces —

Shaw and Shakespeare where there used to be thrillers and musical hall entertainment. The government has a hand in it—and apparently a very intelligent hand, though everything in London—ballet, symphony, serious theatre—is more than getting by on its own. I wonder after the war will there be a similar development in Canada.

You know, I suppose, that mother had a cataract removal this month. Apparently the operation is successful—I have just had a letter—but I think she is still upset and weak. If you have seen her you likely know that my nephew lost an arm in Normandy and is back in Canada.

Myself, I keep well and busy. I am trying to get on with a novel, though in these times, especially in the Army, it's hard to concentrate on creative work—hard to see straight and keep your values. I have written a number of short stories—all bad—but I hope they have at least served as exercises in handling the people and atmosphere of the novel. It's not an easy switch from western Canada to wartime Europe.[2] I find myself approaching my material self-consciously, almost gingerly—as if I had gloves on. I have met some writing people in London, and they are rather encouraging.[3] Have you read Louis Golding's novels? He was especially famous for *Magnolia Street*.[4] I spent an evening with him recently, and was somewhat embarrassed because I hadn't read a line by him. But he was very charming and friendly—not a bit "great authorial," and I have an invitation to go again.

And you Audrey? I hope so. Canada—especially western Canada—has need of writers. To the outside world, except for snow and wheat, we're just non-existent.

I have put a Spanish novel in the mail for you—I saw a large shelf of them in a shop the other day, and I thought it likely that in Wpg. you would get only textbooks. But I don't read Spanish so have no idea what kind of book it is. Therefore you must be indulgent if it's not all it ought to be. If there's any title you particularly want I might be able to get it for you. Don't hesitate to let me know.

Hello and best wishes to all the O'Kellys—including Bernard. I hope he was able to get home for Christmas, and that he is happy in his new work.

A few lines sometime will be appreciated—however little I deserve them.

As ever,
Jimmy Ross

1. During the latter part of the war, Ross was posted in London, working as a clerk for the Ordnance Corps at Fairfax House.
2. This appears to be another reference to "Day Coach to Wagneria," the manuscript about a farm boy who becomes an artist. At this point he was extending the narrative to give his protagonist experience in the war.
3. Chief among these literary contacts were the poets John Lehmann (1907–1987), general manager of the Hogarth Press but especially well known for founding and editing the *New Writing* series (see note 2 of letter to Earle Birney dated 26 July 1943), and Oscar Williams (1900–1964), an American writer who had grown up in the west, but was living in London during the war and was widely known for his *New Poems* anthology and later for the *Little Treasury* series.
4. Louis Golding (1895–1958) was an interpreter of Jewish life in England, best known for his novel *Magnolia Street*, 1932.

To Doris Saunders
University of Manitoba, Winnipeg, MB
15 February 1945

Dear Doris:
Just in case this hasn't already reached you, copies are scarce over here, and I don't know whether there have ever been any available for shipment to Canada.[1]

Thank you for the Air Mail—just arrived—and the encouraging way you write—almost to make me believe myself that as a writer I matter. However, only time will settle that point. Over here, somehow, it doesn't seem to make much difference. London in wartime tends to diminish your belief in the importance of humanity—or even of the individual. It isn't a matter of becoming disillusioned or cynical because of the "*licence*" bred by war, the "*harmless*" little sins of the flesh, but rather a sense of overall helpless aimlessness. If ever-poor humanity needed religion she needs it now, and the religions left us, I'm afraid, are not of much avail. We have absolutely nothing but ourselves, and when we stop and take an honest look at ourselves the picture is not too encouraging. To me it seems that the world's tragedy today is poor timing: the crutch has grown rotten before we are strong enough to do without it. All of which comes to my pen because it is hovering over what I am at work on just now; and perhaps, I'm afraid a *long* way off, you may read it formulated and expressed more clearly. Perhaps you remember after *As for Me*—I wrote about a farm lad and his struggle for music. Well, instead of going to New York he spends four years as a music teacher in Winnipeg—much more probable I think—and then finds himself in the Canadian Army, which was what all along, even while writing, I knew *ought* to happen, though at the time I wouldn't admit it. All the essentials of the first part I think I can weave in, as a sort of foil to his Army stay, which is the top-layer narrative. I have made three long false starts, finally (I think) am under way. (All this just between ourselves.)[2] And you smile, no doubt, at the contradiction: saying it doesn't matter, yet proceeding so busily with my plans. I know—and yet—it isn't really a contradiction. I write as someone else might grow a garden or play golf. If the result is a hole in one, prize cabbages or a good novel so much the better. If not—well, it's been a way of putting the time in, anyway.

Despite the above, however, I don't go round with a glum face brooding over the futility of existence. London, when you sit back and think about it, is depressing enough, but just casually rubbing shoulders with it you find plenty to interest and stimulate. (It's in *Howard's End*, I think, that Forster says it only stimulates—it can't nourish.) Last night, for instance, I saw a magnificent *Lear*—and earlier this winter Olivier's *King Richard III* and Gielgud's *Hamlet*. I know far too many people, but they too interest and stimulate, and I don't always have such an opportunity. (The difficulty of living in the world and out of it—walking a tight-rope is surely easier!) But the paper says stop chattering and let the poor soul get on with what she's doing. A few lines are always welcome.

As ever,
Jimmy Ross

1. Most likely this refers to a copy of *Canadian Accent* where "One's a Heifer" was published (see note 3 of letter to Ralph Gustafson dated 11 August 1942), because Ross regularly provided Doris Saunders with copies of his fiction.
2. Ross is again referring to "Day Coach to Wagneria." Although the manuscript never found a publisher, it contained some of Ross's finest short stories such as "A Day with Pegasus," "Cornet at Night," and "The Outlaw." By the author's account, some parts of the manuscript were also used in *Whir of Gold* (1970).

TWO

Canadian Failure | *Letters 1946–1960*

THE LETTERS IN THIS SECTION focus on two projects that occupied Ross for several years. The first was a collection of his short stories, with illustrations by Grant Macdonald; the second was the long drawn-out procedure of publishing *The Well* (1958). Both projects vividly demonstrate how difficult it was for a serious writer to be published in Canada in the 1950s. Most of the letters are from the Macmillan Company Canada Archive at McMaster University.

From W.A. Deacon[1]
Globe and Mail, Toronto, ON

To Sinclair Ross
c/o Department of National Defence
Ottawa, ON
4 April 1946

Dear Sinclair Ross,

Where in hell are you? Your friends and admirers want to know, and that includes me. Please come clean.[2]

Are you going back to the bank or what? Have you written another novel? If so, is it placed yet? (If not, I strongly urge upon you the advisability of a separate Canadian contract. Publishing conditions have changed out of recognition since you left and you ought to look into the business end of writing before signing any new contract. See me or one of the more commercially successful of the new novelists.)[3]

Did you get married?

You were kind enough to send me a couple of cards while you were in the army. I appreciated them but I took on a difficult and arduous war job and could not keep up with anybody. I reverted to civil life Jan. 1. Records tell me you were discharged March 22 but that it is against the rule for them to tell me where you are. I therefore send this letter in their care to forward, hoping you will materialize from somewhere.

Pardon me not writing you in wartime, and do now, please, give me an address and basic information, such as "Were you wounded or incapacitated? What are your plans—1. literary; 2. occupational?"

If you happen to be in these parts, my phone number is Mohawk 7068 at home and Waverley 7851 at *The Globe and Mail*, where you once called.

Hope all is well with you and that another novel is completed or well on the way.

Sincerely,
[W.A. Deacon]

1. William Arthur Deacon (1890–1977) was book reviewer for the *Globe and Mail* from 1928 to 1960 and was regarded as the most influential literary critic in the country. *As for Me and My House* met Deacon's nationalist expectation that a good novel interpreted contemporary Canadian life, but in his review, 26 April 1941, he predicted that Ross's faithfulness to the "dreary monotony of the once-hopeful West almost kills any chance of popularity."

2. Ross was demobilized from the Canadian Army on 22 March 1946 and returned to Winnipeg shortly thereafter. Deacon had written to the Department of National Defence and was told that that it was against the rules to reveal civilian addresses, but that mail would be sent forward if he directed a letter to Ross care of Department of Records.

3. Reynal and Hitchcock had sole rights to *As for Me and My House* and McClelland & Stewart simply distributed some copies in Canada for the American publisher. After the war, exclusive joint publication became a more frequent practice.

To W.A. Deacon
Toronto, ON

7 Lancaster Apartments
Winnipeg, MB

15 April 1946

Dear Mr. Deacon:
My sincere thanks for your letter, which found its way to me just this morning. It's awfully nice—and encouraging—to learn that someone remembers and takes an interest in me. I deserve neglect, for apart from family letters I didn't write half a dozen during my three and a half years overseas.

No, I didn't get married. Afraid I'm destined to be a grumpy, solitary old bachelor. The ones I want don't want me—though I will say I don't work very hard on it.

No, I wasn't wounded or—at least to my knowledge—incapacitated. Stayed in England—London, most of the time—experienced nothing more dramatic than the flying bombs. Enjoyed London thoroughly.

No, I haven't a novel completed but am hard at work on one.[1] A long one—perhaps too long. I find myself with an abundance of material, and am going straight ahead with it. About 100,000 words done—first draft—and at least that many more to go. I will do some whittling and tightening, of course, when I get to the revision.

Yes, so far as I know now I am going back to the Bank, but not until July 1—I'm taking as much time off as I may and working on the novel.[2] I write slowly, though, and won't have the first draft done in that time, but should have its back pretty well broken.

I don't look forward to going back, but I don't see how I can better myself. I think I would take the plunge if I were alone, but my mother is 70, nearly blind and dependent upon me. We live comfortably now, and naturally I don't want to expose her to the hazards of a free-lance's income. Besides, being practical about it, I'm not at all sure that my commercial possibilities as a writer amount to much. I hope this novel will give me an answer.

I appreciate your suggestion of looking into the possibility of a Canadian publisher. Reynal & Hitchcock have the option on this one, of course, but as you say a separate Canadian contract might be arranged. Especially as what I am doing this time is all-out Canadian—Americans might not be interested. Incidentally I have just had a letter from Bernard McEvoy of Longmans Green, and an invitation to submit a novel to them for consideration if and when I have it completed.[3]

I'm afraid it will be the end of the year anyway before I get East; when I do arrive, though, I shall certainly drop in and say hello. Thanks again for your letter and interest.

As ever,
Sinclair Ross

1. Ross was still at work on a revision of "Day Coach to Wagneria." See letters to Audrey O'Kelly, 27 November 1944, and Doris Saunders, 15 February 1945.
2. Encouraged by Roy Daniells and Doris Saunders, Ross was interviewed in April 1946 at University of Manitoba for a teaching position that resembled something like the writer-in-residence programs developed in the late 1960s. He was probably

waiting for the results of that interview when he wrote this letter. His unstated
hopes, however, were disappointed when he was eventually told that he didn't know
enough about Canadian literature to hold the position. Consequently he did return
to work at the Royal Bank.

3. Ross apparently never acted on this invitation. Rejection of the "Wagneria" manuscript by American publishers persuaded him that the novel was deeply flawed and
he abandoned the project.

From W.A. Deacon

Globe and Mail, Toronto, ON
24 April 1946

Dear Sinclair Ross:

Congratulations on getting safely through the war and being so far
along with your next novel. I'm indeed glad to know where to lay hands
on you in an emergency.

On the whole I believe in the principle of professionalism. A man
working all his time and living by it may master his craft more fully.
But the artist has advantages in amateur status. He can write what he
likes, not just what will sell. The succès d'estime of your first novel indi-
cates that earnings may be moderate for some time. Only time will tell.
Public taste is unaccountable.

Reynal and Hitchcock are the No.1 publishers in English at present.
They are decent and honest men, even generous. They may permit you
to make a separate Canadian contract and it is highly desirable from
your standpoint.

Longmans here are first rate and anxious to build a Canadian
list. They are acquiring some excellent native talent. Theodore Pike,[1]
Canadian manager and also manager for the U.S., is my oldest friend in
the trade. Extremely shrewd and ditto honorable. He won't look at you
unless you have obtained a release of your Canadian rights. He will not
negotiate with R&H. You'll have to do that; and I should do it—when
you send ms just say you desire a separate contract for Canada. No
point in concealment of your plans. They may say yes or no. Or, as you

hint, your novel may be too Canadian and they will reject, in which case Longmans here are in splendid position to place it with one of their related firms — say Coward-McCann. I'm glad you have no disabilities or awkward problems. It is good to see a Canadian novelist who can just go ahead and write without complications.

Confidentially, anticipating my presidency of Canadian Authors,[2] I hope you will join that outfit. They are weak out there and need you. We have become very practical with the new success for Canadian books. We are at work on copyright, income tax, standard contracts, and are already of real help to our members, if they are authors. You should be in touch via membership, get our literature and throw in your own weight and prestige. A lot is going to happen at the Toronto Convention June 27–29.

Give me notice when you make plans to come East and some arrangements can be made to introduce you. December is my peak but there is a let-up after 25th.[3]

Regards and good luck — W.A. Deacon

---

1.   Theodore Pike (1886–1953) established Longman's Toronto branch in 1922 and served as its president until his death in 1953.
2.   W.A. Deacon was the optimistic and energetic president of the Canadian Authors Association from 1946 to 1948.
3.   There is no evidence that Ross ever followed up this invitation.

To Grant Macdonald[1]
Kingston, ON

3551 Durocher St.
Montreal, PQ

21 September 1948

Dear Grant:

Yes—I think it's a splendid idea, and I look forward to an opportunity to discuss it at length with you.[2] The first question, of course, is have you read any of my short stories? They are pretty grim, and abound with horses, wistful small boys and poverty-stricken farmers. Do you think you could come to terms with such subjects—I mean artistically?

I do hope the Thanksgiving weekend will work out—I *think* there will be no hitch at this end. I enjoyed our being together.[3] To be frank, you turned out to be much more approachable than I had always imagined you to be. More of this, however, at a later date. For now sincere thanks and crossed fingers.

Sincerely,
Jimmy Ross

1. Grant Macdonald (1909–1987) was an artist and illustrator of note in Ontario. He and Ross met through a mutual English friend, possibly John Lehmann, the poet and anthologizer to whom Ross had submitted some stories (see note 2 of letter to Earle Birney dated 26 July 1943) and whom he eventually met in London.
2. Macdonald proposed that they find a publisher for Ross's stories and that he would illustrate them.
3. Ross a few weeks later took a train from Montreal and spent Thanksgiving weekend with Grant Macdonald and his father at their home in Kingston. The trip to Kingston gave Ross an opportunity to visit Queen's University where most of his stories had been published. Grant Macdonald was gay and the two men spent the nights together.

Grant Macdonald, Kingston illustrator. [Queen's University Archives]

To Grant Macdonald

Kingston, ON
31 October 1948

Dear Grant:

First of all, I hope you won't mind too much the typewriter. It is much easier for me, and you too, I think, will be relieved not to have to decipher my scrawl. Years ago Mother was in England for a few months, and in reply to my first typewritten letter she wrote, "You should be ashamed of yourself, using the typewriter for your mother." Dutifully I wrote the next one, and in reply to it I received a postcard bearing three words: "In future type."

I'm sorry to have taken so long to answer, but as you know I have been under the weather with the 'flu and some minor complications. Haven't been to work all week with the exception of Monday morning, and I'm not looking forward exactly to tomorrow. The doctor put me on a diet of milk—which I loathe—and soup, so you can imagine what my disposition is like.

Thank you Grant for your letter. You have the stimulating effect of making me feel important, that I really amount to something, and while, as I have already told you, I have a compulsive tendency to reject all such [praise], I am none the less grateful and encouraged. I can't tell you how gratifying it is that you respond to my stories as you do. Since my return from England there has been a kind of hopelessness taking possession of me; now I ask myself if there is still time for fresh beginnings.

I am especially pleased that you liked "Jug and Bottle."[1] I am not sure about it yet, but I put a great deal into it, and would like it some day to see the light of print. Not much has happened to "Old Chippendale"[2] since I saw you—the lady is still hanging—but I think I know what to do. Just this morning I finished the first draft of "And All the Diamonds Too,"[3] which I am rather pleased with, though there is an enormous amount of chopping and changing and polishing to be done. It has a fair story, and I am hopeful that I may find an American market for it.

As to your drawings, Grant, don't worry about whether or not I shall be satisfied. Your response to the stories, it seems to me, is almost a

OLD CHIPPENDALE

1.

It was worse when there was a wind. The eaves sawed and the windows rattled, and the dust-dark sky filled air and mind alike with thick, oppressive gloom. Whatever you touched, towel, spoon or book, felt gritty and soiled. There was a constant singing whine in the air which, decoy-like, drew fear and loneliness into the open from their hiding-places. When you looked up the street the dust was a curtain. Landscape and future were alike obscured.

The wind always roused her. From room to room she would be pacing, charging herself with grievance and scorn till the discontent that was habitual had become a slashing, hot-eyed rage.

As he stood at the window and went up and down the counter with his duster Paul could see her. The aggressive cheek-bones and the deep, flashing eyes, the shoulders hunched together broodingly, the big hips and breasts that at such times seemed

Typescript for the unpublished story, "Old Chippendale."
[Queen's University Archives]

50

guarantee, quite apart from the quality of your work. And I go back and apologize for the word "almost."

I hope you are feeling better now, and finished with the carpenters and plasterers. They are a trial but you won't mind when you have your studio to your satisfaction. Even as it was when I saw you I thought it extremely desirable. And I hope too that you enjoy your weekend in Peterborough, and that there will be no more delays or interruptions.

I listened to the radio version of *Fortune, My Foe*[4] and thoroughly enjoyed it. Some of the characters, I felt, were caricatures rather than people, but no doubt the cuts were responsible, and in a play of ideas I suppose that is to some extent inevitable anyway. The important thing is that he has ideas, and that he puts them across with such skill and courage. I wish, though, that it roused more indignation. I should like to think that the Canadian acceptance of it was an indication of maturity, but I wonder if it isn't really apathy—a smug, two-dimensional self-satisfaction which is not to be ruffled by anything a mere writing-man or intellectual may have to say. However, that is just an uncalled for pride. I don't really know.

Shortly after my visit with you I saw Olivier's *Hamlet*.[5] Many fine things—Olivier's lines are especially beautiful, a strange quality of voice at once sweet and virile—but I came away not altogether satisfied. Too much of the poetry cut, and that larger-than-life, rather mysterious something completely gone. But well worth seeing. If the admission price were not $1.50 I should go a second time.

I don't know yet what weekend I can come again to Kingston. I was to have gone to Ottawa this weekend, but being under the weather had to put it forward two weeks. Perhaps the weekend after that—but I will let you know in plenty of time. And as you too have your plans to be considered, you mustn't hesitate to *suggest* when to come.

Remember me again to your father, and tell him I look forward to seeing him again soon. As to my greetings, messages, etc. to you—embroider them according to your fancy and imagination.

Sincerely,
Jimmy

1. This wartime story, the only fiction Ross set outside of Canada, was published in *Queen's Quarterly* the following year (Winter 1949).
2. "Old Chippendale" was never published in the author's lifetime, but was preserved in manuscript form with the Grant Macdonald Papers at Queen's University Archives.
3. This story was eventually titled "The Runaway" and was published in *Queen's Quarterly* 59 (Autumn 1952).
4. *Fortune, My Foe*, a play by Robertson Davies, is the story of an immigrant from Prague who wants to start a puppet theatre in Canada. The importance of art to civilization was always central and compelling for Ross.
5. Ross is referring here to Laurence Olivier's very popular 1948 film version of Shakespeare's play.

To Grant Macdonald

Kingston, ON

13 January 1949

Dear Grant:

I was delighted to receive your letter and learn that John Gray[1] is interested. At your suggestion I am keeping my fingers crossed *and* putting in all my spare time at the typewriter.

Both "Old Chippendale" and "The Diamonds and the Mills of the Gods"[2] will need more work on them but, as they are, the important things come through, I think, and I am typing them out and sending them along. And I am not forgetting copies for you.

As to the stories you have already handed Gray, please let me know whether the following list is correct: "A Field of Wheat," "The Lamp at Noon," "A Day with Pegasus," "Cornet at Night," "One's a Heifer," "The Outlaw," "Jug and Bottle." There are three stories published in *Queen's* of which I have no copies: "The Painted Door," "Not by Rain Alone," "Circus in Town." I think they belong with the others, and I should like John to see them. Would you be able to find a typist who could go to the library and run them off—and of course send me the bill? If not let me know, and I will drop a line to *Queen's*. There is a possibility, rather remote, though, I'm afraid, that they might have extra copies.

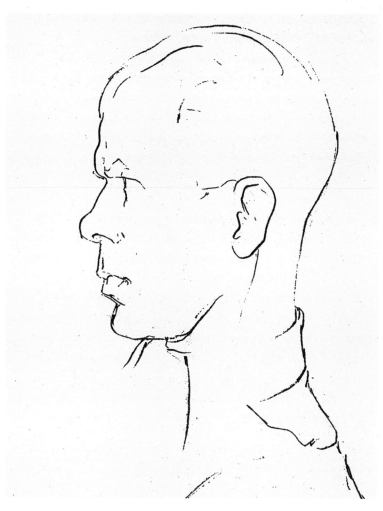

Sketch of Sinclair Ross by Grant Macdonald, 1948. [Queen's University Archives]

Needless to say, Grant, that I am grateful for your efforts on my behalf, and I do hope your work will not be wasted.

Since my visit to Kingston I have had a fairly miserable time — a number of painful visits to the dentist before Christmas, and now a mouth infection, which makes me like a bear with a sore head. The day after New Year's I was at Dorothy Klyn's for dinner — the lady from the *Standard* who "does" art — and she proved to be a very charming, genuine person. The conversation didn't get around to art, however, so I don't know. Perhaps I warmed to her because she is from a small town in Saskatchewan.[3]

I was beginning to be afraid Grant that you thought I had treated your invitation to Kingston for Christmas somewhat casually. I hope not, for I was appreciative, however undemonstrative. The truth was that I knew that Christmas, whatever the intentions, never passes without visiting and good cheer; and even if your friends don't mind you feel rather out of things when you are sitting back sober as a judge and everybody else is feeling convivial. I think I have told you that I am forbidden even a polite glass, and a few sly lapses have convinced me that my doctor knows what he is talking about.

You will be hearing from me in a few days. In the meantime the best to your father and yourself.

As ever,
Jimmy

1.   John Gray (1907–1979) was editor-in-chief at Macmillan Canada for more than two decades. Though not a particularly astute literary critic, he was keen nonetheless to promote serious literature in Canada and gave crucial encouragement to such writers as Morley Callaghan, W.O. Mitchell, and Ethel Wilson.

2.   Another working title for "The Runaway."

3.   Dorothy Klyn (known as Doyle) was born in Oxbow, Saskatchewan, just south of Arcola where Ross lived from 1929 to 1933. She was a columnist for the Montreal *Standard* and women's editor for *Weekend Magazine*. Her column was titled "According to Doyle" and it gave advice on food, fashions, and entertaining. In the 1960s she hosted her own CBC television program, which included interviews with famous personalities. The Klyns and Ross remained good friends for the rest of their lives.

To Grant Macdonald

Kingston, ON
16 February 1949

Dear Grant:

I shouldn't be writing to you tonight—I feel tired, depressed and irritable, and some of it I daresay will seep through and make you wish I would keep my low spirits at home in hiding. However, perhaps you have a drop of scotch at hand with which to wipe the unpleasant taste out of your mouth when you have finished reading.

It's a disgracefully long time, isn't it, since I last wrote—such a long time that I feel a little strange, not knowing exactly where to pick up the ends. The days tick off and I can't believe the winter is nearly over. At Christmas, as I wrote you, it was teeth and gums. Then it was more teeth and gums, then my old sinus trouble again, then, the other still keeping it company, it's this wretched fit of depression, the blame for which, in large part anyway, I lay on "Old Chippendale." A filthy story—and I wrote and rewrote and *rewrote* it—and even now it still clings to me.[1]

Your reaction to "The Diamonds and the Mills of God" did me good, and I only hope, though not too hopefully, that after longer acquaintance with it you remain as enthusiastic. I haven't looked at it since I mailed it to you, for I find that I return to a ms after a few weeks' interval better able to criticize it. Yes—I *would* like to see your drawings, but my curiosity and eagerness is quite free of concern. I know that when I do see them they will be right. Indeed, the one for "A Field of Wheat" impressed me as much more than right. It was, I felt, a deepening and extension of the story.

This, I know, is counting our chickens before they are hatched—and it is also, I know, a piece of presumption for which I won't mind a good stiff rap over the knuckles—but it occurred to me while typing out "The Diamonds" that *if* the book should materialize, the runaway scene, with the blazing load of straw and the boy racing alongside on his pony, might make a vivid and exciting jacket. But if it doesn't strike you as a good suggestion, or if you have something else in mind, please don't give it a second thought.

I had a letter from John Gray a few days ago. He sounds interested in the project, but makes it clear he isn't at all sure that it can be done.[2] He doesn't like "Jug and Bottle," so if you haven't already done so, don't spend time on a drawing for it. His criticism is sound—essentially the one I passed on it myself—that the Jug and Bottle incident at the end is not related to the story. He thinks, incidentally, that it is a poor title.

And now, just between ourselves, and all my low spirits and lack of confidence notwithstanding, I think I am about to begin a novel. It has been shaping up for a long time, and now I see my way clear. To say as much is premature, of course, for the amount of work involved frightens me, and I may falter before I get properly started—but still I say it. I think I told you something of the conflict that has involved me—a dissatisfaction with the prairie as a background and milieu, a feeling that it cramps me, a desire to escape to where issues are larger, and at the same time the impossibility of feeling at home, rooted, confident anywhere else. Well, I'm going back. It's retreat, in a way, but better retreat, I tell myself, than no novel. And while the background is a little prairie town again, the principal characters, I think, have possibilities. It's the old triangle theme. A solid, small-town, community-minded husband, the bride he brings home from overseas, sophisticated, cultured—I'm throwing in adjectives slap-stick style to give a rough quick picture—the young doctor who comes back to practice in his home-town. Foreign born—Ukrainian perhaps—proud, sensitive, who suffered cruelly as a boy among other boys, one of the ringleaders being the husband, whom he has always hated, and on his return hates more intensely than ever. An affair with the young English wife develops, not so much from love for her, as hatred for her husband. But there is no real satisfaction, no revenge, unless the husband *knows* he is having his wife. She begins to see and feel this, fears that the doctor, because of his neurotic compulsions, may try to make the husband suspicious in order to torment him, and seized by panic kills the doctor.[3] Not a very original theme, but properly handled it *could* be interesting psychologically. We'll see. I'll try to keep good hours and eat lots of spinach.

Poor Grant—what a terrible muddle that last paragraph is, and how weary you must be. Sorry. If you feel confused don't go back, whatever you do, trying to get it straight.

I should like to come to Kingston again—I take my welcome for granted—but there's always something. I thought we were probably going to have Saturday morning off this year, but nothing more has developed, and I keep waiting for a chance to ask for it some weekend when everything is clear. And then, quite frankly, I have to budget carefully, and doctor and dentist bills have been taking their toll. But perhaps three weeks from now—even if only for the day. Again, we'll see.

Forgive the gloom and the rambling and the long delay. Remember me to your father, and tell him I'm looking forward to another visit.

As ever,
Jimmy

1. "Old Chippendale," the story of a quarrelling family, can be read as heavily autobiographical.
2. This letter has not survived. The first note of caution to survive appears instead in a letter from John Gray to Grant Macdonald dated 15 March 1949 where he reports a conversation with Ross in which he was "frank and not too optimistic" about the market possibilities of the collection.
3. Readers of Ross's fiction will recognize a connection between this plot for a novel and *Sawbones Memorial* published in 1974. The novel as written in the late forties and early fifties failed to find a publisher, but when Ross came to write a sequel to *Sawbones* he developed the story exactly as outlined here. But "Price above Rubies," as the story was titled in 1976, again failed to be published.

John Gray, Ross's champion at Macmillan Company, Canada. They tried unsuccessfully to publish an edition of Ross's stories in the late 1940s.

[UBC Library Special Collections]

From John Gray
Macmillan Company, Toronto, ON
2 May 1949

My dear Jim:
We have had finally and with reluctance to decide against publishing a
collection of your short stories illustrated by Grant Macdonald. There is
really no doubt that from the commercial point of view the indications
could hardly be less favourable. However, we knew that from the first
and still gave the matter serious thought, because we liked the intention of all the work and the quality of much of it.

   We secured several opinions on the manuscript and almost every
one had the feeling that there was rather too much similarity in tone
through more than half the stories in the manuscript. Moreover,
certain characteristics of language, which are striking in individual
cases, tend to recur when the short stories are grouped. The four later
stories—"Cornet at Night," "One's a Heifer," "The Diamonds and the
Mills of God," and "Jug and Bottle"—represent a break in style with the
earlier group and a certain freedom which the other stories lack. On
the whole we all thought that these were more promising, if not actually better, than most of the earlier stories, and one has a sense of you
reaching for newer forms and more varied themes. I hope this means
that there is a great deal more work coming from you one of these
days and that in due course we may be able to be a good deal more
encouraging.

   In case all that seems to add up to a discouraging criticism on the
artistic side, I should like to make it clear that these were factors only.
The commercial argument was almost crushing in the first instance,
and these factors tended to tip the scales conclusively. I think you
know that we do genuinely like your work very much, and I am
confident—perhaps more confident than you are—that one of these
days you will hit your stride.

   For the moment we shall hang on to the manuscript until we
hear from you or Grant what you would like to have done with it, or

until negotiations with the CBC or any other possible purchaser are completed.

All the best to you.

Sincerely yours,
John Gray

To Dr. G.H. Clarke

Editor, *Queen's Quarterly*
Kingston, ON
27 October 1949

Dear Dr. Clarke:

I am very happy that "Jug and Bottle" is going to appear in the *Quarterly*. It has so often seemed an impossible story—the ms has been lying in my desk in an unfinished state for all of two years—and still I have kept coming back at intervals to worry away at it a little more, never, somehow, able to discard and forget about it.

As to "snotty," I yield it readily. It is, indeed, an unpleasant word. I used it, first, because it is good "Army," second because, left to my own taste and ear, I am inclined to be somewhat fastidious and fussy in the choice of words, and I try to remember, when working on a character, that it isn't what is pleasing to me that matters, but what is true to him.

Yes—I feel, too, that while "overbearing" has the right meaning, it hasn't quite the right sound at this place. It might be well to retain it, however; the only alternatives I can suggest are "chesty—upstart—stripe—conscious." May I leave it to you to decide.

Thank you for letting me see the proofs. The few changes I have made—in pencil, so you will see them easily—are intended as suggestions, not corrections, and I defer to your judgment if you disagree with them.

One small point only: in the second paragraph, I wonder is there something to be said for "is" rather than "seem." "Seem" suggests to me a reflective attitude, and inasmuch as these first three paragraphs are a paraphrase of what "most people" have said, I feel that the flat and more emphatic "is" expresses better their callousness and impatience — is more of a piece with the preceding, "Forget him with a clear conscience."

My thanks again for giving a home to this long and unhappy story.

Yours sincerely,
Sinclair Ross

To Dr. G.H. Clarke

Kingston, ON
15 July 1951

Dear Dr. Clarke:

I hope you will be able to find a place in *Queen's* for the enclosed story.[1] It is a featherweight, but Tom at least, I think, emerges sincere and credible.

For all its simplicity — or banality — it was a hard story to write, the problem being to blend the graceless vernacular in which Tom would naturally express himself with the poetic extravagance appropriate to his condition so that the one would not make the other ridiculous. It was broadcast over CBC recently, and the gentleman who read it did a good job on the dialogue, but scrambled through some of the other passages as if he found them downright embarrassing.

If you decide to use it I wish you would be good enough to let me know, before setting it up, of any changes you think advisable. I know I am a terrible old woman about these things, but I have tried it carefully for sound and rhythm, and I think that as it stands there is something like balance between the contrasting parts.

Thank you for the *Quarterly*. There are always many satisfying things in it, and I do appreciate your thoughtfulness in sending it to me.

Yours sincerely,
Sinclair Ross

1.   Ross is referring here to "Saturday Night" published in *Queen's Quarterly* 58 (Autumn 1951), 387–400.

From Robert Weaver

CBC, Toronto, ON

11 February 1952

Dear Mr. Ross,

I am returning the script of "A World of Good," which you sent to us some weeks ago.[1] I am sorry that I wasn't able to comment on the story before; as I remember it came in just before Christmas and our correspondence always gets tangled up at that time of the year. In addition I have been away from the office several times since with bouts of flu.

Three of us read "A World of Good" and, although we are still looking for half-hour stories to broadcast sometime late in the spring or during the summer, we finally decided that we couldn't buy this particular story. I am very sorry to have to return it to you and I hope there is at least some possibility that you will be able to send us something else within the next several months. As for the story itself, all three of us felt quite strongly that you had made a mistake in piling up the sordid realistic details to the extent where it became quite difficult to believe that the husband and wife, who are supposed to be looking forward to the visit of the husband's friend, would ever allow things to get this completely out of control on this special occasion. We felt also that this piling up of detail finally had an effect counter to what you had intended and I felt that before the story ended, much of the sympathy your readers or listeners were presumably intended to feel would have vanished entirely.

The two other people who read the story happened to be both women, and both of them pointed out several things which they felt any woman would feel were psychologically inaccurate in the presentation of the wife. Here is one direct quotation which might interest you. "I don't feel that anyone to whom the surface values are so important would receive a guest in housedress and curlers. She'd be busy putting on the dog, I think, though the 'dog' would have squalid fissures, of course....The best thing, I thought, was the scene where she shows the pictures." Helen James, who produces the *Canadian Short Stories* series,[2] also added that the change into evening dress was out of character with the sort of thing a woman of her type and place would likely do. She felt that the wife would be much more likely to change into an elaborate afternoon dress.

I don't know what you will think of these various comments but I was also disturbed while I was reading the story of what seemed to me some rather shaky bits of characterization. I think it is very well worth your while to continue writing stories with an urban background and I was interested in "A World of Good" as another example of this new tendency in your work.[3] However, I don't really feel that this story came off successfully enough, and we finally decided that we would have to return it to you. As I said earlier, we are still in the market for occasional longer stories, and I hope you won't be discouraged from sending us something else very soon.

With all best wishes.

Yours sincerely,
Robert Weaver

1.   The manuscript for this story is no longer extant.
2.   Helen James of Toronto had a long career with the CBC.
3.   The first piece of urban fiction that Ross wrote was a story titled "Sonny and Mad" set in Montreal. It was turned down by *Queen's Quarterly* in March 1952 and Weaver's reference here to "A World of Good" being "another example" of a new direction in Ross's work suggests that he may have also turned it down for a reading on the CBC. In 1952 he was developing "Sonny and Mad" into a novel, which would eventually be published in 1970 as *Whir of Gold*.

To Robert Weaver

CBC, Toronto, ON

13 February 1952

Dear Mr. Weaver,

Thank you for your letter returning "A World of Good" and again my apologies for pestering you about it so often.

I must admit to being somewhat surprised, not at your returning the story, for it is, I know, a slight one, but at your reasons for doing so, because from beginning to end—curlers, evening gown, photographs, tears—it is a round by round account of an actual experience. The inconsistency in the woman's careless appearance at the beginning and her efforts later on to "put on the dog" is explained by the fact that the poor soul is doing no [such] thing, but is simply seizing the opportunity provided by her guest to convince herself, not him, that "she is still in the running." Her chief concern is re-assurance. The guest scarcely exists for her. Rigging herself up in the vestiges of her pre-marital finery is a gesture of defiance against approaching middle age and the "penalties" of motherhood.

The fault is mine, of course: I should have done a better job of "putting the situation across." It is an illustration, I suppose, of the difficulty of "lifting" from life. The author is so convinced by the experience—its having been experienced making it, for him, indisputable—that he probably takes fewer pains in the presentation than he would if it were something built up from his imagination.

All that, however, by the way. Before long I hope to have another ms to show you.

Yours truly,
Sinclair Ross.

To Roy Daniells
University of British Columbia, Vancouver, BC
10 December 1954

Dear Dr. Daniells,

Thank you for your kind letter, and my apologies for taking so long to reply. Work in the office has been extremely heavy all fall, and as I had a few days coming to me this month I delayed till I had a little more leisure.

The list you sent along is correct, and—unfortunately—up to date, except that "One's a Heifer" is being included in an anthology that the University of Western Ontario are bringing out soon—they said this autumn—and that "Cornet at Night" is to appear in another anthology of Saskatchewan writing that the University of Saskatchewan are publishing next year as part of their program to mark their Golden Jubilee.[1]

I said unfortunately above because I had hoped long before this to have had something substantial to my credit. Sometimes, I must admit, I feel a pretty dismal failure. However, we do what we can, and taking into consideration my beginnings, my equipment and my personal difficulties, I don't see how I could have done differently. At that I still have a certain amount of faith in myself—at times, anyway—and I am working. Part of my trouble has been an unwillingness to go on writing about the West—I felt I was repeating myself, that "The Runaway" for instance, was overworked, a dead-end—and my attempts to handle the urban scene have not been successful. A novel I finished two years ago,[2] concerned with crime and delinquency, made the round of half a dozen New York houses, received a good reader's report from them all and in each case was turned down because of its pessimism and gloom, with the suggestion to do it over and make at least one character worth writing about. Well, as I saw them they were not only worth writing about but also worth doing something about, and my failure I suppose was inability to reveal my intentions. Perhaps, in any case, I am out of my depth in social reform. Now I am working again, about three quarters of the way through the first draft, but it's supposed to be bad luck to talk about work in progress, so I will only ask you to cross your fingers.

I was interested and gratified to hear that you have included me in your New Zealand lectures. My sincere thanks again for your many efforts on my behalf.

As ever,
Sinclair Ross

1. "One's a Heifer" appeared in *Canadian Anthology*, edited by Carl F. Klinck and Reginald Watters, 364–76, and "Cornet at Night" in *Saskatchewan Harvest*, edited by Carlyle King, 189–212.
2. Ross is referring here to the original manuscript for *Whir of Gold*, which was not published until eighteen years later.

To John Gray

Macmillan Company, Toronto, ON
23 June 1955

Dear John:
I think I mentioned to you in a letter some months ago that I was working on a novel, and I have now to report that it is finished except for the final typing, and should be ready to mail out in two or three weeks.[1]

On the chance that you might be interested in reading it I am making a third copy. Of course, as I think I explained a few years ago when I was working on another novel which turned out a rather dismal affair, I am sending it to New York for submission to Harcourt Brace to begin with, anyway—and consequently I cannot offer it to you uncon-ditionally. Added to that there is the likelihood that you wouldn't touch it with a ten-foot pole in any case—it's spiked a little—and so I won't feel in the least hurt or snubbed if I get the thumbs down sign. But if a New York house should be interested and I could tell them that you had read it and were also interested, then we might work out something in the way of a Canadian edition. I think it's readable, though I am so close to it right now that it is difficult to be objective.

I am also wondering if you could do me a favour. There is an agent in New York who has been interested in me for some years, Max Becker of the AFG Agency, 545 Fifth Avenue—he placed *As for Me and My House*—and while he has always been friendly and encouraging, I really don't know anything about him. I feel a little more confident and energetic of late, and think I may manage at least three or four more novels. Therefore—quite apart from the present one—I would like to make a reliable connection. Would it be possible for you to enquire about him from your New York office? Naturally, any opinion would be considered confidential—I would simply not get in touch with him again; I am not bound to him in any way—but of course I will understand if you feel it is the sort of thing you would rather steer clear of.

As ever,
Jimmy Ross

1.   Ross is referring here to the manuscript for *The Well*.

From John Gray
Macmillan Company, Toronto, ON
24 June 1955

My dear Jim,
Thank you for your letter of June 23rd and for the good news that you have finished your novel. I am sure that you are in no doubt that we would like to see it as soon as possible.

I realise that you must submit it to Harcourt Brace—and would wish to anyway. However, if on the first submission it is made clear that we are reading and expect to be interested, there should be no difficulty about our working together. In my experience American publishers only worry about working in Canada with someone other than their own representative if it means they lose all chance of selling their copies to whoever is handling the book in Canada. If it is a case of our buying the American publisher's copies being a condition of our handling the book we should normally be content to do things that way, provided you were agreeable. If we were not content, that is if it seemed patently desirable and feasible to produce the book here, it would be because we saw large popular sales as a possibility. And presumably if we saw things that way the American publisher would be happy enough to publish for the American market alone. I hope that doesn't all sound too complicated.

I am sending off a confidential enquiry about Max Becker and will let you have the result.

Meanwhile the best to you, and you may be sure that I am eager to see the book.

Yours,
John

To John Gray
Macmillan Company, Toronto, ON
25 July 1955

Dear John:
At last I am getting it in the mail—today. Of course it took longer than I expected—and it has been hot. The ms I was working from was such a monkey's puzzle—corrections, deletions, etc., most of them in a weird combination of shorthand-longhand which I have difficulty deciphering myself sometimes—that I couldn't hand it over to anyone else and had to do the typing myself.

It needs to be gone over again, but at the moment I am tired of it and dull—in another two or three weeks I will have a much fresher and keener eye for possible improvements. As it is, however, I think you can decide whether it is the sort of thing you might be interested in. I am so close to it that, quite truthfully I don't know whether it has anything at all or if it is just sordid drivel.

Thank you for enquiring about Becker.[1] I don't think I am committed to him, and in any case I have sent off the first copy to this man Wing whom you recommended.[2] I told him that you had given me his name, and also that I was sending you a copy on the chance you might be interested.

As ever,
Jimmy Ross

1. John Gray consulted about Becker with his counterpart at Macmillan in New York and wrote to Ross on 4 July 1955 that "none of the editorial staff of one of the large publishing houses there has ever met him, and only one or two knew him by name," and accordingly recommended Willis Kingsley Wing, an agent regarded as first rate and "genuinely interested in talent."
2. Willis Kingsley Wing (1899–1985) was considered one of New York's most successful literary agents in the 1950s and 1960s, though regarded by Kenneth McCormick, head of Doubleday, as "a testy, complicated individual, a difficult man to work with." His clientele in the 1950s included such international figures as G.K. Chesterton, J.L. Borges, John Le Carré, and a number of Canadians including W.O. Mitchell, Pierre Berton, and Robertson Davies. In the 1960s he added Peter Newman and Margaret Laurence to his list of clients.

To John Gray
Macmillan Company, Toronto, ON
2 August 1955

Dear John,

I have just had a letter from Wing, and as you are probably interested in knowing his reactions, I quote as follows:

"Thank you very much for your letter of July 20. I greatly appreciate having had the opportunity of reading your novel *The Well*, and first off let me say that I am eager to represent you and am greatly impressed with the writing ability shown in this ms.

"Since you say that you wanted to take another look at it to see about re-working certain sections, I would like to hear from you when you have come to your conclusions about what you would like to do to it. At that time, if you would like, I could give you some comments from my readings, which have been very complimentary, on the whole. You will also probably wish to be guided by what you hear from John Gray. I would be willing to send your ms out now, but I would prefer to have it in the best shape possible in order to make the best impression in the right editorial quarters.

"I see no reason to change your setting from Saskatchewan. You have used this background extremely well...."

As a matter of fact, apart from some polishing, I have no ideas at the moment as to major changes, and I rather wish he had not been so courteously vague. I have just written him to [forward the] criticisms—I may not agree, but again they may set me thinking. I wish that you too would let me know what you or your readers think. Again I may not agree, but the more points of view the better.

It looks as if I am still a considerable distance from an acceptance, but his letter encourages me and gives me a feeling that—and I don't mean only so far as *The Well* is concerned—I have a fighting chance.

As ever
Jimmy Ross

From John Gray
Macmillan Company, Toronto, ON
6 September 1955.

My dear Jim,
Thank you for your letter of September 5th.

I'm shocked at the idea of the first twelve pages of your manuscript having been lost,[1] but for the minute, unless you insist, I don't know that we can help out. Our copy of the script is with *Maclean's* from where we have the news that the first reader was enthusiastic about the book but that the next reader, though equally enthusiastic, was doubtful about the theme in a popular magazine.[2]

So long as there's a chance of this award, I hesitate to recall the manuscript or any part of it. However, it is for you to say. If you think it is important enough to break in on deliberation I will ask them to mail you the first twelve pages. You can wire me about this.

Sorry not to have written sooner but I thought we might have news for you any day.

Yours,
John

P.S. *Since writing this I phoned Ralph Allen[3] on an impulse and found him tremendously excited about the book but puzzled about whether they could handle it. He has promised to decide something by the end of the week — either that they can't or that they can on some basis. Meanwhile, he is reluctant to release the pages unless you are desperate. Keep your fingers crossed!*

---

1. On 5 September 1955 Ross had written to say that the first twelve pages of *The Well* manuscript must have blown off his desk and subsequently been thrown out by his cleaning lady.
2. See letter below from Janice Tyrwhitt dated 9 September 1955.
3. Ralph Allen (1913–1966), a distinguished war correspondent and prominent Canadian journalist, was editor of *Maclean's* magazine from 1950 to 1960. He also wrote fiction. He may have had a special interest in Ross's manuscript because, like Doyle Klyn, he grew up in Oxbow, Saskatchewan.

From Janice Tyrwhitt

Maclean's Magazine, Toronto, ON

9 September 1955

Dear Mr. Ross,

At John Gray's suggestion, we have been considering *The Well* for *Maclean's* novel award. As you perhaps know, this is an award of $5,000 which gives *Maclean's* the right to run the book serially and then returns all subsequent rights to the writer. Although Ralph Allen, the editor, and I agree that *The Well* is an extraordinarily fine book, we aren't sure whether we can ask you to accept a Novel Award at this stage. We foresee great difficulties in arriving at a presentation that would satisfy you, the author, and still give a reasonable amount of weight to the inescapable fact that in presenting a story to a pre-paid audience of more than a million an editor cannot altogether ignore mass tastes and mass prejudices. If we were to publish it in *Maclean's* it would require a good deal of condensation for the foregoing reason. It would also require a good deal of condensation for space alone. We would have difficulty in handling more than 80,000 words and would much prefer sixty or seventy thousand.

We seriously doubt whether it would be possible to make this condensation without emasculating *The Well*. Its structure is so tight and inevitable that it's hard to see how even line cutting would bring it down to a workable length for us, and the tricky sex relationship would of course have to be retained in at least clearly implied form. But we do like the book so much that we'd like to ask whether you would be interested in trying, without commitment, a condensation with these general observations in mind. We certainly don't want you to risk a revision unless you yourself think that it would produce a good book—even though not as good a book as *The Well* is in its present form. It's such a strong piece of work that cutting is certain to weaken it—the question is, how much? How do you feel about this? Perhaps we might talk of a condensation in more detail when you have had a chance to think of it. Incidentally Ralph Allen is going to be in Montreal early next month and if by then we should be agreed that the job has a reasonable chance of succeeding, he'd be glad to discuss any individual points or scenes. We don't, happily or unhappily, have any list of what things are forbidden and what things are permitted in *Maclean's*. We have to proceed according to an unsure and flexible instinct. I'd say, if I were making book on it—and Mr. Allen's guess is about the same—that the odds against our reaching a treatment that would suit both you and us are no better than three to one. So if you are seriously pressed for time our honest advice would have to be: forget this proposal entirely. Naturally we hope you won't.

We have discussed this proposal with John Gray and returned the yellow copy of *The Well* to Macmillan's.

Yours,
Janice Tyrwhitt

To John Gray
Macmillan, Toronto, ON
20 September 1955

Dear John,
Thank you for your letters and the return of the manuscript.

Yes, I'm afraid I did dismiss *Maclean's* letter as the rejection courteous, and now, after thinking it over, I realize I was probably quite wrong. Unfortunately it is typical of me. I always run to meet rejection— and not only where manuscripts are concerned. Perhaps it has become a kind of insurance against disappointment.

As to doing the job, however, I don't know. The money is tempting, and I should like to bring it off in any case, but I see difficulties. As I said in my letter to *Maclean's*, I think it would mean almost a complete recasting of the story. Cutting and patching wouldn't do. But my chief trouble right now is weariness and nerves—it has been a long haul and I am still up to my eyes—so perhaps after a little interval I may have a better approach.

In the meantime I am proceeding with the revision. I thought I had it finished except for the typing, but now I find other things. The last 100 pages especially. Sylvia talked too much; I am convinced now that it weakened her. All in all, I think it will read considerably better, so I wish you would wait for it.

Sincerely,
Jimmy

To John Gray
Macmillan, Toronto, ON
28 September 1955

Dear John:
I have decided to try *Maclean's* revision, and so will not have the revision I promised you for some time. Frankly, I don't see my way yet, but I am trusting that when I get right into it the problems will take care of themselves one at a time. I can cut it all right to the 80,000 words, but as I have already written *Maclean's*, my difficulty right now is knowing how far I may go in handling the relationship between the young man and the wife. However, Ralph Allen is going to see me when he is in Montreal next week, and I am trusting that he will be able to straighten me out.

Keep your fingers crossed for me—I am going to need it.

As ever,
Jimmy Ross

To John Gray
Macmillan, Toronto, ON
5 December 1955

Dear John:
Shortly after receiving your last letter I had to go west to see my
mother, who hasn't been well all summer, and I hope you weren't in
Montreal and trying to get in touch with me while I was away. I should
have written before, but what with the trip and the work involved in
cutting *The Well*, I have been letting other things slide.

I mailed the cut version to *Maclean's* just this morning—75,000
words, or probably a little below. It reads rather tight and thin, I'm
afraid, but perhaps I feel that because I am so close to it. In any case,
I think it will be wise to wait a week or two before starting the next
version. I may hear from them before long, and their comments and
verdict will give me some idea as to whether the tightening has generally helped or detracted from it. I didn't take a third copy, but if you
think it worthwhile I could send you mine to read and return, and you
could let me know if you think I should stay fairly close to this one, or
expand again.

I hope I didn't miss you and that you have still to pay your visit to
Montreal.

As ever,
Jim

To John Gray
Macmillan Company, Toronto, ON
8 April 1956

Dear John:
I see your last letter is dated December 8 and it occurs to me I owe
you a report on *The Well*. Of course you will have heard from *Maclean's*
that they turned it down, and very probably you have heard from
Wing and know that he has done the same. There is no use dwelling
on these things, and it goes without saying that the author is always
wrong, but I do think he treated me very shabbily. I quoted you at
length from his first letter last August—truthfully—so you know that
he had many good things to say about the manuscript, none deroga-
tory whatever, and expressed himself as "eager to represent me." The
revised manuscript I sent him the beginning of March was a great
deal better than the original, polished, the repetitions weeded out, and
reduced by a hundred pages, but his reply was to suggest that I forget
all about it till I mature sufficiently to handle it properly. He also said
it was far too long—after the reduction of a hundred pages; no criticism on this score whatever in the first place—that the plot was banal,
the characters badly done, the castration theme and the episode of
the young girl—"the little innocent"—both pointless. He concluded
that I might show it to John Gray again, but there was no chance for it
"down here." In other words—"Canada may handle tripe, down here
we're more particular." All of which was quite unnecessary and gratu-
itous. A simple "sorry, we don't see any prospect for it," would have
sufficed. As to his criticisms, I don't quarrel with them. Heaven knows
I never made any great claims for the story, or thought I had produced
a masterpiece. But he should have made them last August. His job is to
appraise manuscripts, and his success as an agent would suggest that
he does it well. It is hard to believe that when he wrote his first letter
his critical faculties were on holiday. However that is all past now, and
it really isn't bothering me as much as what I am writing now would
suggest. I don't think about him much—perhaps because when I do

the irresponsible way he treated me makes me so damned mad, and of course there's no point to it.

As to *The Well*, I don't know whether it has any future or not. I passed it on to another agent who thought it worth a try, and it is now with Morrow, who likes it but wants changes. Rather radical ones—they think Chris deserves a better ending and don't want him to commit the murder—so at the moment I'm somewhat up in the air. I'm afraid I'm not even interested any more—I have resigned myself to its being a failure and am willing to let it rest there. However, there was a second letter from Morrow just the day before yesterday, prodding me a little, so I will probably get busy soon on working out an outline.

All this just for the record. If and when anything develops I will keep you posted.

As ever,
Jim

From John Gray
Macmillan Company, Toronto, ON
11 April 1956

My dear Jim:
For some time I have been on the point of writing you about *The Well* though I have not known very long of its fate at *Maclean's*. This was a disappointment for which I felt some responsibility, and I think perhaps on that account I held off writing—not really knowing what to say.

I have heard nothing from Willis Wing and your account of his handling of the book comes as a shock. It is true that from the first he was somewhat less enthusiastic than I but his attitude never prepared me for the letter from which you now quote.

Have you a copy of the revised manuscript which you sent Wing at the beginning of March and which we might now see?

I hesitate to recommend to you publication in Canada alone because you might always feel that this was failure and because, as I indicated to you, our contribution to an American edition might bring about publication there.

I hesitate to comment on Morrow's suggestion of substantial revision but I hate to see you being battered from pillar to post and I don't think you should revise further unless you are convinced. If you are not, then do let us see the script and send it to Ruth May in New York, who has placed several books for us and will at least do a conscientious job.[1]

I hope you can write off this black winter, Jim; I am sure it has been a bad one for you. I do hope that before summer is over we will between us have worked out a promising future for *The Well*.

If you are happy to publish in Canada alone do tell me this frankly and we shall be glad to consider the possibility of doing the revised book for this fall. My warmest to you.

Yours,
John

1. Ruth May (Mrs. Anatole A. Bendukov) was a New York agent who had recently placed two of Ethel Wilson's books with American publishers.

To John Gray
Macmillan Company, Toronto, ON

Apt. 16, 3431 Jeanne Mance Street
Montreal, PQ

23 April 1956

Dear John:

I was very pleased to hear from you, and am taking you up on your
suggestion and sending along the new manuscript—the last one which
I sent to Wing.

Of course it is a disappointment not to make a New York
publisher—or will be, for it is still hanging fire—but I shouldn't look
on Canadian publication alone as failure. You will understand that after
all this chopping and changing I have to some extent lost my bearings, and while I think that as it stands it is right, I see Morrow's point
that as I have drawn Chris he is not altogether a heel, has a lot of good
buried in him, and that it would be just as much in character for him
to stand up to Sylvia when they are ready to murder the old man, as to
submit and go through with it. They have a stranger suggestion that he
should run out, go to town and get drunk, so that Sylvia is able to do the
murder in his absence. I have written arguing against it, and may have
killed it so far as they are concerned. But perhaps it would be better
for me to write more on possible changes after you have read it in its
present form, so that your mind will be clear to judge it as it is, whether
it rings true, is disappointing etc.

But if you aren't convinced, I wouldn't want you to feel that your
earlier enthusiasm put you under an obligation to go ahead with it.
On the contrary, nothing would hurt me more. It may be that it is one
of those manuscripts which seem better at first reading than they
turn out to be at a second—and that would account for Wing's strange
behaviour.

Incidentally, I have just had a friend read it who is sensitive and
discerning—Phyllis Webb[1]—she writes poetry and says she met you

at the Kingston Conference last summer—she has a book coming out this month—and her response is that psychologically it is completely sound and that the present ending is the right one. Her one criticism is that at the beginning the old man talks too much and some of the dream sequences should be pruned a little.

As ever,
Jim

1. Ross and Phyllis Webb (1927–) met in the early 1950s at a party given by F.R. Scott and enjoyed a friendship while both were living in Montreal. Webb's first major collection, *Even Your Right Eye*, was published in 1956 by McClelland & Stewart. They lost contact after Webb left the city in 1960, but read each other's work and followed each other's career. Webb won a Governor General's Award for poetry in 1982.

From John Gray
Macmillan Company, Toronto, ON
30 July 1956

My dear Jim:
Three of us have now read the revised version of *The Well* and we are not a bit less enthusiastic about it than at first reading. I should have written you before about this but half expected to see the alternative ending and thought we might reserve comment until then.

Our present decision is that we would be willing to publish the book as it stands, but of course we might prefer the alternative ending.[1]

As I understand the position now, you will show the book to Morrow again with the new ending, when it is ready. Perhaps you would keep us in touch with developments there and at the same time you can consider whether you would like us to go ahead if Morrow should not be pleased with the change.

Our view of the book leaves aside to some extent the question of its popularity. We would not be altogether prepared to bet on that. But it is a fine piece of work and should certainly not go unpublished. Moreover the sooner you feel free to think about other valuable work the better for all concerned.

My warmest to you,
John

---

1.   On 7 August 1956 Ross reported working at another version of the ending, "something along the lines suggested by Morrow, but it was quite hopeless."

To John Gray
Macmillan Company, Toronto, ON
24 June 1957

Dear John:
I suppose I am impatient, but I can't help wondering about Deutsch's reaction.[1] It is just two months since I sent the manuscript—registered airmail—and so far not even an acknowledgement. No word from New York either. Becker was to give it back to Cady as soon as Viking said no, and after this interval I imagine the verdict is another no and he is trying it somewhere else. It is hardly likely at this late date that you will be able to do it yourself if Deutsch isn't interested, so I suppose we might as well let Becker keep on sending it out—he seems confident of being able to place it although no doubt that is just his agent's "line."

I have two novels pretty well mapped out, but quite frankly I haven't the heart to start. The prospect of a couple of years' drudgery, and at the end of it the dreary business of collecting rejection slips again, makes me falter. By the way, did you know McClelland and Stewart are bringing out *As for Me and My House* in their new series of Canadian paperbacks?[2]

As ever,
Jimmy Ross

1. John Gray wrote to Ross on 24 April 1957 to say André Deutsch, English publisher of Mordecai Richler and Brian Moore, had visited his office and expressed an interest in seeing *The Well* manuscript. He persuaded Ross to send a copy that included the latest revisions.

2. The New Canadian Library was initially conceived of by Malcolm Ross, who was concerned to make available to students some of the best Canadian writing in inexpensive paperback editions. He proposed the idea to Jack McClelland, who could not foresee any company profit in this venture but saw making Canadian literature accessible as "performing a service to the people of Canada." When Malcolm Ross turned to the question of what books to include, *As for Me and My House* came to mind because, though it had attracted no general readership in 1941, it had become something of a classic in the opinion of university teachers and book publishers. This publication would have enormous impact on Ross's future reputation.

To John Gray
Macmillan Company, Toronto, ON
10 December 1957

Dear John,

I daresay that by this time you have heard from Deutsch. The manuscript was returned accompanied by only the briefest of notes: "We regret, etc.......Mr. Deutsch is writing Mr. Gray." (Does it really take a publisher, by the way, over six months to decide he *doesn't* like a manuscript?) I haven't been in touch with the New York agent for some time, but his silence I'm afraid tells the story.

Well, the damned thing has been hanging over me a long time, and I am sure you can understand I would like, one [way] or the other, to get clear of it. To be blunt, are you still interested? From the beginning you have had a good word for it and a little better, but it is to be expected that these rejections may be giving you some second thoughts. Of course I should be grateful and happy if you could see your way to go ahead yourself; on the other hand, if these second thoughts have been piling up, I wouldn't want you to feel committed by anything you said a year or 18 months ago. If you are on the fence and would like to see it again (you have never seen the revised version, which I think tightens and improves the writing) I will send along a copy. But if it is to be No, then please let me know as soon as possible so that, within myself, I can write it off and turn the page.

There are some other things I want to do, but it has been a somewhat muddled year and I have found it hard to settle down to anything. Mother became seriously ill last February, and it was a series of rallyings and relapses until her death in October. Now, after 2 false starts I have a novel lined up and—I think—satisfactorily under way, but I must confess I hesitate at the prospect of two or three years' hard work and for reward just another long drawn out failure.[1] I think I shall probably always scribble away at something—it is my nature—but as the years go on one's enthusiasms—even one's compulsions—become tempered by common sense. There's not much point in knocking myself out if I haven't got what it takes. I'm not a youngster any more.

That is the reason I would like your decision on *The Well*. If you can't do it I think I might be wise to forget the novel, for a while at least, and try my hand at some shorter things which will require a less sustained, all-out effort. I'm afraid this sounds a little as if I were throwing the responsibility of my future as a writer on your shoulders, but of course I don't mean that at all. The problem is one hundred per cent mine.

As ever,
Jimmy Ross

---

1.   There is no hard evidence for which writing project he might be referring to here.

To John Gray
Macmillan Company, Toronto, ON
22 August 1958

Dear John:
Many thanks for your letter and cheque, and also for the copies of *The Well.* I am very pleased, and hope it doesn't let you down too badly. My own hopes for its reception aren't very high, for running through it again I realize how changing the ending has thrown it all out of line and how the cutting has left much of it two-dimensional. But it's too late for laments now. Perhaps in the next one I shall, to some extent at least, be able to redeem myself.

As ever,
Jimmy Ross

To Frank Upjohn[1]
Macmillan Company, Toronto, ON
22 September 1959

Dear Mr. Upjohn:
I received a letter yesterday from Macmillan's enclosing a letter from Mr. Julian Roffman of Meridian Films[2] dated Sept 9 in which he sets forth terms for the purchase of the motion picture rights to *The Well.* Your letter is signed by Miss Isabel Symes,[3] but as Mr. Gray told me that in his absence you would be in touch with Roffman, I am addressing my reply to you.

Miss Symes asks me for my comments on Mr. Roffman's proposal, but I talked twice with Mr. Gray by telephone before he left for the west and told him that I wished to accept Mr. Roffman's offer. Mr. Gray also wired me on the 15th from Saskatoon to the effect that he had talked with Roffman again before leaving and that the contract would be along in a week or ten days. I am sure you know all this, but as we have

Sinclair Ross publicity photo for The Well, *1958.*

[Private collection; Ross private papers]

done nothing so far but talk by telephone, perhaps it is just as well to have my confirmation in writing.

Incidentally I am leaving on October 9th for a month's vacation in Mexico and while away I hope to be footloose and "out of touch." I understand of course that the next move is Mr. Roffman's, but I would appreciate your keeping the date in mind just in case he comes along with the contract at the last minute.

Yours sincerely,
Jimmy Ross

1. Frank Upjohn was vice-president of Macmillan Canada in the 1950s.
2. Julian Roffman was a National Film Board director who cofounded Meridian Films in 1959. He had won the first Oscar awarded for an NFB documentary film, but was eager to make commercially profitable films with his own company. He is remembered as the producer of grade B horror films such as *Bloody Brood* (1959), but his psychological thriller, *The Mask* (1961), enjoys cult classic status.
3. Isabel Symes was John Gray's personal secretary and handled some of his correspondence when he was travelling on business or on vacation.

To Frank Upjohn

Macmillan Company, Toronto, ON
23 November 1959

Dear Mr. Upjohn:

My belated thanks for your letter and for crediting my account with the option money from Mr. Roffman. I arrived home two weeks ago today, but there were a number of things awaiting for me to attend to and I seem to have [been] slow getting re-organized.

I enjoyed Mexico and came back wanting to return, which I suppose is the way it should be. At that I picked up a germ the last week — after not touching water all that time, only beer and coffee — which took the edge off three or four days.

I haven't a television set, but they tell me Roffman has given two interviews and discussed his plans for *The Well* and *Execution*. He seems to have a great deal of confidence and energy—qualities which I envy him—but as it is out of my hands now I find myself not particularly interested. A defensive attitude, perhaps, in anticipation of a film in which not a great deal of my story or people will be left. I only hope it stimulates a little interest and sells a few more copies, for judging by the response so far you have taken a beating on it.[1] Well, perhaps something better next time. I wish I were clever enough to plot out something likely and follow it through, instead of taking an idea as I do and burrowing along underground with it. Unless you are a very good burrower you may come up in the wrong garden.

Again my thanks for your efforts on my behalf.

Sincerely,
Jimmy Ross

1. The majority of reviews for *The Well* were either negative or at best lukewarm and sales accordingly were poor.

To Frank Upjohn

Macmillan Company, Toronto, ON
19 September 1960

Dear Frank:
Since Roffman's option to film *The Well* is about to expire—the 22nd—I should perhaps pass on to you what has developed recently. Roffman was in Montreal the beginning of the month and asked me to sit in on three sessions, which included Roffman, a co-producer from New York called Jean Lenauer, Mrs. Taylor (the "Angel" apparently) and Charles Cohen of Montreal who is to do the script. They didn't exactly tell me but in bits and pieces I gathered that in the first place they went to a

well-known scriptwriter in Hollywood who came up with an unsatisfactory script. Roffman sent it to me—the *third* version—before his visit so I would know their problem and if their man is as important as they say my guess is that he farmed this job out—all the way from Indians to RCMP to a love scene in which the principals discuss Russian scientists and rabbits on the moon. They knew something was wrong and wondered if a repair job could be done. After considerable discussion they apparently came round to my way of thinking and the book itself and decided to have the old man disposed of by a gun instead of a conveniently timed heart attack. But there are difficulties—as a result of the script troubles it is too late to shoot in Western Canada and they are wondering how Oklahoma would do. The story is so closely knit with the west that I don't see how they can drop the one and keep the other. That is their problem, though, and there is no point in concerning myself about it. They listened to my ideas but of course they will use or reject as they feel inclined. As a matter of fact, although they have already made several newspaper announcements—there was another in the Montreal *Gazette* when Roffman was here—no doubt paid a tidy sum to the script writer—I wouldn't be surprised if they don't go ahead. The answer probably depends on what Cohen comes up with: I believe he is in Toronto at the present time working with Roffman. Roffman, of course, made no mention of taking up the option. I don't know what is done in such cases, but I suppose you will be sending him a note to the effect that it has lapsed and we are back where we started. Roffman impresses me as too shrewd a businessman to do anything, or neglect anything that would put him in an exposed position. In other words, if you don't hear from him by the 22nd, the picture is off.

For my part, I think I will be relieved. The money isn't very exciting—we can always use a little extra of course, but after taxes I'll do well to clear $2,000, which isn't enough to make any real difference—and the picture itself would probably only be an irritation. The book is behind me, and the sessions with Roffman made me realize how much I want to leave it there. I am sorry, though, for the trouble you have been put to. *The Well*, I'm afraid, was conceived under an unlucky star. For Macmillans, myself, and now Roffman, it's been headaches all the way.[1]

Otherwise, things are much as usual. I keep busy on two fronts, and right now am looking forward to my vacation, although it's still five weeks away. Mexico again I hope—this time I want to go to Yucatan.

As ever,
Jimmy Ross

1. Roffman in fact arranged in January 1961 to purchase film rights to *The Well* and sent Macmillan a cheque for $3,200. He also tried to arrange for an American paperback of the novel to be issued, but neither the paperback nor the film was ever produced.

THREE

"Modest Hopes" | *Letters 1962–1971*

ONLY TWO OF ROSS'S LETTERS have survived from between
1960 and 1966, part of a twelve-year period (1958–1970) in which
he published nothing new. Letters appear again as he negotiates to
find a publisher for his novel, *Whir of Gold*, trying first Macmillan
and then McClelland & Stewart. His correspondence with Pamela
Fry at McClelland & Stewart, selected here, is the sole instance of
Ross finding an editor who was sympathetic to his artistic goals
and sensitive to the misgivings he harboured about his writing. In
this period he also established a friendship with Margaret Laurence,
who was composing her Manawaka novels and simultaneously
crediting Ross as an inspiration for his work. They corresponded
for nearly fifteen years.

From John Gray

3450 Durocher St., Montreal, PQ

19 October 1962

Dear Jim:

It is too long since any of us have seen you or heard news of you.

Does this mean you have a book on the fire? I certainly hope so.

Yours ever,
John[1]

---

1.   This note reveals that Gray remained a loyal supporter of Sinclair Ross in spite of
      The Well's financial and critical failure. This note and Ross's reply (not printed here)
      saying that he was working on a novel are the only extant items of correspondence
      to or from Ross in the period between 1961 and 1966.

To John Gray

Macmillan Company, Toronto

8 March 1966

Dear John:

I was hoping on Sunday to have a private word with you before I left
but of course it wasn't the occasion for it and what I started to say about
a manuscript was left dangling.

The manuscript[1] is in fact typed out and in readable form. Whether
it is finished, or needs further revision, or is away off the mark, I don't
know. At the moment I am still too close to it. I haven't written about it
before because it seems unlikely that after *The Well* you would be interested in a Ross novel unless it is coming out in England or the U.S.
Furthermore, apart from whether it has any merit, it is an ugly story
and probably a very depressing one. In other words, I don't want to

*Ross at his desk in the advertising office of the Royal Bank of Canada,
Montreal, 1962. [Royal Bank Archives]*

embarrass you with it; but just for the record, in case something should
develop later, I have a copy for you.

As ever,
Jim

1. The reference is to *Whir of Gold*, which Ross submitted to Macmillan in mid-March
    1966.

From Richard B. Wright[1]

To the Editorial Board, Macmillan Company
May 1966

I am against publication of this unambitious and competent novel. I
cannot see its enhancing our reputation as publishers of fiction and I
question whether we'd sell five hundred copies across the country.

What a genuine pity this is, for Sinclair Ross is a fine writer. Even
in this terribly trite story restricted by the often-tedious observations
of his narrator, Ross manages to charge his prose with a rich and vivid
imagery that seldom seems forced or misplaced.

But for all that I can't see that this novel will do at all. It's really too
quaint. It's not great enough or profound enough to transcend its own
familiar weariness as a story of a gawky young farm boy's struggle
to distinguish between goodness and evil and his growth from that
experience. Ross is either making a genuine effort to revive a played-
out genre or he is more hopelessly out of touch with reality than I can
believe. This has a strong whiff of the urban novel of the thirties about
it. Its uncomplicated innocence and serious tone by way of James
Farrell;[2] its theatricality most evident in the characters of Charley and
Mad by way of the gangster movies, its excessive naturalism ("we had
pork chops and chocolate pie"); and its sentimental ending; all this is
reminiscent of another time.

Indeed for me, reading this novel was like sitting in a dusty abandoned theatre watching three people perform a play by Clifford Odets.[3]
With regret then, I vote against publication.

Dick Wright

1. The future award-winning novelist worked at Macmillan in the 1960s. This is his
    reader's report on the manuscript for *Whir of Gold* sent to John Gray.
2. James T. Farrell (1904–1979) was a novelist and short story writer in the naturalist
    mode. He is most often cited for three novels set in the streets of Chicago that were
    published in 1935 as *Studs Lonigan: A Trilogy*.
3. Clifford Odets (1906–1963) achieved celebrity with such early naturalistic plays as
    Waiting for Lefty (1935) and *Golden Boy* (1937). All his stage works had socialist themes.

From John Gray
Macmillan Company, Toronto, ON
20 September 1966

My dear Jim:
We have delayed much too long in writing, out of a reluctance to give
you disappointing news about your book. The fact is we all admire your
writing as much as ever, but the central problem of this novel never
really convinces. The result is a book about which it is hard to be enthusiastic. If you found a publisher in New York, we would be glad to take
part of an edition from him; but to publish on our own without more
enthusiasm than we feel would, I think, be a mistake. There seems to
be a failure at the heart of the book, and consequently the main characters are not real most of the time.

In spite of this there are some fine things in the book: the flight
from the scene of the crime, of course; and all the flashbacks to
boyhood and the beautiful black horse.

This latter sequence made us wonder whether there wasn't something struggling to be written about the horse. I know you have done

some of this before and done it well, but have you something more? If a book along these lines appeals at all, I wish you would write it. You would do it superbly and enjoy doing it.

Jim, what has happened so far to the novel in the United States? Is it close to publication, subject perhaps to revision? And what about the boy and his horse? Does the idea interest you?

Yours ever,
John

To John Gray
Macmillan Company, Toronto, ON
27 September 1966

Dear John:
Thank you for your letter and the return of the manuscript. I am sorry to have bothered you with it. You may recall that when I first wrote about it I expressed doubts, and I should have put it away for a while and then read it again with a fresh eye before sending it out. But it is difficult sometimes to judge your own work.

In May your Miss Perry wrote that someone outside the house was reading it. In June Mr. Bacque[1] said you were getting further readings. Perhaps then during the time you had the ms you accumulated a little sheaf of reports, and if you have not thrown them out I am wondering if you would pass them on to me. It may be that this is something that is "just not done," a request I shouldn't make, but if you have no objections they might be useful in deciding what the ms needs in the way of revision or whether it might be wiser to write it off as a mistake. There's no sense throwing good effort after bad. I daresay some of the reports are not very flattering but don't hesitate on that account.[2]

No—I don't "see" a book about a boy and a horse right now but I appreciate your making the suggestion.

Yours truly,
J.S. Ross

---

1.   Author James Watson Bacque (1929–) was an editor at Macmillan from 1961 to 1968.

2.   In a letter dated 7 October 1966, Gray said he would send along "the relevant parts of three or four reports," but added apologetically that they "don't add up very clearly." Ross acknowledged receipt of the excerpts on 1 November 1966, but made no further reference to them.

To Margaret Laurence[1]

Elm Cottage, Penn, England
4 December 1966

Dear Margaret:

I finished *A Jest of God* a few days ago and it is good to be able to write, honestly, without polite hedging, that it is a fine, deeply-felt novel and—most important of all—that it has made me feel and understand a human problem, or predicament, to which I had never before given much thought. That is, it has extended me a little.

Poor Rachel—I didn't *like* her and I wouldn't particularly want to know her, but as I read I became aware of, and at least to some extent experienced, her little hell of loneliness and frustration. What I think might be called the "cage" chapter—in which, when she thought herself pregnant, she kept *pacing*, looking for a way out—that was superb. It was so good, in fact, I felt the outcome—tumour instead of pregnancy—was just a bit too easy, and the critic in me reared up and said no, she should have gone through with it. But it was also so good, drew me in so deeply, that I was *relieved* it was only a tumour, and if you can involve your readers in the fate of your characters to that extent then the way you did it was the right way.

Another of the first enthusiastic readers of As for Me and My House: *Margaret Laurence, student at United College.* [McClelland & Stewart Archives]

The town—and having lived so long in small towns I feel myself something of an authority—was first-rate. The feeling of being watched and discussed until, despite yourself, in self-defense, you draw in, become pettily careful—it all came back to me. And Rachel's mother—real enough to make me itch to put a good swift boot up her selfish, sanctimonious old behind.

And now, having made my acquaintance with the lady, I want to see what kind of job she did with this book called *The Stone Angel*. Alvin Goldman[2] also recommends a book of short stories. I see one in *Modern Canadian Stories*, which has just arrived, but I haven't had a chance yet to settle down to it.

My sincere thanks for the kind things you have been saying about me. Jack Sword[3] sent me a clipping from the *Winnipeg Free Press* and in Saturday's *Star* (Montreal) I see you have acknowledged me very generously. I hope I deserve it. I have just been reading in the Introduction to *Modern Canadian Stories* that my trouble is probably "devotion" to my job in the Royal Bank.[4] Well well! Of all the reasons critics and biographers trot out to account for an artist's failure to mature—drink, drugs, sex, neglect, ill-health—this one is surely unique. A first for Can. Lit. It is so incredibly inept, in fact—appearing as it does in a piece of writing which presumably is intended as serious criticism—that I can't help wondering if the fellow is taking a swipe at me. Instead of starving in a garret he played it safe and worked from 9 to 5...But I shouldn't be burdening you with this and I'm sorry. It's just that right now I'm *so damned mad*. At least when the time comes to leave Canada my bags won't be overburdened with regrets.

On the subject of publishers, Macmillans finally turned down my novel. It failed to convince them. Six months to the day; 270 pages of typescript that a reader could run through in a few hours. To explain the six months John Gray wrote they were reluctant to give me bad news. Another first?

I had a good month in Mexico, returned satisfied I could make my home there should Europe not work out. As it was my third visit I didn't spend much time exploring ruins or climbing pyramids but I rode, ate well, dawdled in some delightful towns—Oaxaca, San

Cristobal, Guanajuato, San Miguel—and to cap it all picked up a bug which—fortunately not until I got home—knocked me out for 10 days. Not serious, but I'm still dragging my feet and looking ahead glumly to a long cold winter. Already it is cold: down to zero last night with a mean wind. It's old age and thin blood, I suppose—I just can't take it any more. A disgrace to Saskatchewan.

I hope you are now comfortably "at home" again with your family and that the new novel is progressing. My warm good wishes—I know what a long, lonely journey it is.

I will drop you a line again—a report—when I read *The Stone Angel*.[5]

Sincerely,
Jim

N.B. Please excuse the typewritten letter. My handwriting is an impossible scrawl.

1. Ross did not meet Margaret Laurence in person until May 1967, but this letter makes clear that a correspondence had begun well in advance of that meeting. It was almost certainly initiated by Laurence, who often attributed her success to writers like Sinclair Ross and Ethel Wilson. They made her realize "the simple fact that novels could be written *here* out of one's own background" (Margaret Laurence to Hugh MacLennan, 16 February 1970, QUA).

2. Alvin Goldman (1927–) was born in Winnipeg and graduated from University of Manitoba. He made his living as both a writer and filmmaker with the National Film Board, living in Ottawa and Montreal. Ross came to know him through Doug Tunstell, a former student of Roy Daniells in Winnipeg and also an employee with the National Film Board. Goldman would remain a loyal friend for the rest of Ross's life.

3. John "Jack" Sword (1915–2001), born in Saskatoon and raised in Winnipeg, joined the Royal Canadian Air Force in 1942. He and Ross met during the war and though Sword went on to a career in academic administration, twice serving as acting president at University of Toronto, the two men remained friends. The clipping he sent from the *Winnipeg Free Press* and the piece Ross refers to from the *Montreal Star* apparently both contain testimonies about Ross's importance to Laurence as a writer.

4. *Modern Canadian Stories*, which reprinted "The Lamp at Noon" and "The Painted Door," was edited by Giose Rimanelli and Roberto Roburto. Rimanelli, described by

Earle Birney in a foreword as "one of Italy's important men-of-letters," describes Ross as "suspended mid-way" between early success and an uncertain future, "a silent writer, and perhaps a bit too shy, entirely devoted as he is to his work as an employee of the Royal Bank of Canada" (xxiii–iv). The story by Laurence in this collection is "To Set Our House in Order," which would become part of *A Bird in the House*.

5.   If Ross wrote a letter about *The Stone Angel*, Laurence seems not to have kept it because it is not part of her archive at York University Library.

To Adele Wiseman[1]

Montreal, PQ

From Margaret Laurence

Elm Cottage, Penn, England

11 September 1967

Dear Adele,

I have just finished writing [an] Introduction to Sinclair Ross's short stories, for New Canadian Library. The stories all hang together so much—and in the end they reveal a prairie ethic that is positively frightening—the man has to prove absolutely strong in his own eyes; the woman has to endure all, silently. Impossible standards, and so people break down. Reading the stories, I felt such a sense of connection with the characters, even though they were in an era slightly before my adulthood. But I know them pretty well. The men who can't turn to their wives for comfort, in time of disaster, and so turn—I joke not—to their horses. The stories are all of a piece, and thank goodness they are coming out as a collection at last. Don't suppose Jim intended it that way, but within the era and that idiom, he has portrayed an entire people, their spiritual goals, their vulnerabilities. He really doesn't have to worry about whether he ever does anything more. He's done it. Not possible to communicate this to him, though....[2]

Margaret

1.   The novelist Adele Wiseman (1928–1992), best known for the 1956 novel *The Sacrifice*, was living and working in Montreal in the 1960s and during that time interviewed Sinclair Ross, although Ross and Wiseman remembered the occasion differently. Wiseman said it was for CBC radio, whereas Ross remembered it as an interview for students in a high school auditorium. A friendship developed between the two writers.

2.   The rest of this letter does not concern Ross. This section has been quoted by James King in *The Life of Margaret Laurence*, 428.

From Jack McClelland

McClelland & Stewart, Toronto, ON

15 October 1967

Dear Sinclair Ross:

Delighted to have your letter. I am glad that you have made the changes and I am sure that it will strengthen the book,[1] although I must confess that we were very much of the opinion that the stories didn't need any further work. I have passed on your comments to our editor as well as to Bob Weaver. I think the points you make will be useful to them at their end of things.[2]

Yes, we can certainly send galleys to you. We don't normally do so on the New Canadian Library it's true, but then most of the books are straight reprints and the situation doesn't normally arise. We will, as you suggest, have to ask you to deal with the galleys quickly, but if you can promise that, we will be delighted to send them along.

I don't think you should have any real doubts about the success of the book in the series. Short stories will never sell as well as novels I don't suppose, but *As for Me and My House* is one of the most successful of all the NCL titles. It is going to go on selling for many years and I am sure the short stories will do the same. I should probably admit to you that I had never read *As for Me and My House* (although I knew it by reputation of course) until Malcolm Ross recommended it for inclusion when we embarked on the New Canadian Library project. I have great faith in Malcolm's judgment and as it turned out, I didn't read the novel until several years after it appeared in the NCL. I can now write you a belated fan letter. It is a superb novel and certainly one of the finest that has ever been written in this country. I may say that I am delighted to hear that you are retiring and that this will give you the opportunity to do a few more books. The psychedelic world has changed a lot of things, but it hasn't much altered the market for good writing whether the background is Saskatchewan or Nova Scotia. If I may, I would like to give you a call next time I am in Montreal and perhaps we can arrange to have dinner and discuss the changing pattern in Canadian reading.

With all good wishes
Sincerely,
J.G. McClelland

1.   McClelland is referring to his company's forthcoming edition of *The Lamp at Noon and Other Stories* in the New Canadian Library series.
2.   In his letter to McClelland dated 10 October 1967, Ross refers to making small editorial changes to some of the stories and to making "Not by Rain Alone" and "September Snow" one story in two parts.

To Margaret Laurence
Elm Cottage, Penn, England
9 December 1967

Dear Margaret:
I'm a bit slow saying so, but your Introduction does please me.[1] As I wrote to Bob Weaver, it's flattering so of course I like it. Do I deserve such generous treatment? Well, that's another matter. I'm not putting up a fight, just summing it up as generous and *discerning*. I was particularly pleased at the very end when you speak of these people coming through with dignity, for to me they have always been more than clods. Roy Daniells says somewhere they aren't peasants[2] which in a way is right—I know what he means—but peasants aren't necessarily lacking

in dignity. If I had thought Bob might pass on my remarks about the death of the husband in the "Painted Door" I would have kept my big mouth shut—or rather my fingers off the typewriter—for while it is true that I had never thought of it as suicide you have every right to your interpretation. A friend I discussed it with the other evening says at a deeper level it is *suicide*. I may not have thought of it that way, any more than the man who would have had self-destruction in mind, but his despair and shame, the way he retreated and relinquished himself to the storm and let it carry him—it amounts to the same thing.[3] All I can say now is that I am sorry for the trouble I caused you.

McClelland was down about 2 weeks ago and took me for lunch. He says he is enthusiastic about the book but that of course has to be discounted considerably. (It's terrible, isn't it, learning the hard way that things have to be discounted? By nature I'm the world's prize ninny—I *want* so badly to believe people and even at my age, incredible as it sounds, I *do*—at least till I start thinking things over.) I'm doubtful myself—I'm afraid that grouped together the stories are going to seem terribly monotonous and repetitive. However, if my plans work out, by the time the book appears I'll be away from Canada, and how flat it falls, or what they say about it, doesn't concern me too much.

As you know, my plans were for Greece, but the country is bristling with question marks and I don't know. I may try it for a few months, just as a tourist, and decide in the fall about settling in. As second choices there are Italy and Spain and some of the Mediterranean islands, to say nothing of Mexico—again I don't know. My neck and shoulder keep yammering Go *somewhere* out of the damp and cold.

I have had a self-centred summer—my neck again, for it was a chilly, humid summer—and I have seen few people. A few evenings ago I went for dinner with Koula (is that how you spell it?) and Alec Lucas;[4] this Wednesday I see Alvin Goldman[5]—and of the ones you know that's it. Alec told me—to my surprise, for I didn't have a suspicion the wind was blowing that way—that Adele is married[6]...I'll probably learn more from Alvin.

And I will just mention that I lent The Stone Angel to a friend on the faculty at McGill[7]—from Winnipeg, with a good ear and eye—and she is enthusiastic—went down at once and bought *A Jest of God*...I was delighted, incidentally, to see they are making a movie of *Jest*...[8] I hope the result will be a credit to the story and that they have paid you *pots* of money for it...Incidentally again—how's the new one coming along?

Sorry for the way this letter is typed. It's a borrowed machine—my own has to be repaired or discarded—and I can't find the damned thing to set the margin.

Sincerely,
Jim

1. Laurence wrote the introduction to Ross's *The Lamp at Noon and Other Stories*, which was published in the New Canadian Library in 1968.
2. In a talk he gave on CBC Radio, 2 December 1941, Roy Daniells put it this way: "The farmer and his wife who appear in so many of the stories of Mr. Ross are not peasants or share croppers. Yet they can scarcely be called independent; the ceaseless fight against the elements, the bondage exacted by the soil leave them scarcely any margin of wealth or even of leisure." Roy Daniells Papers, UBCL, box 14, folder 5.
3. To Robert Weaver on 26 October 1967, Ross wrote about the husband's death in "A Painted Door": "It wasn't intended to be [suicide]. He was simply dazed and hurt at discovering her infidelity, withdrew, unable to face her, and wandered off, drifting with the storm, not really caring. And, having already fought his way through the storm for several hours, we can assume he was pretty well exhausted."
4. Alec Lucas was a professor of English at McGill; he taught Canadian literature and edited *Great Canadian Short Stories* published in 1971. Koula was the first name of his Greek-born wife.
5. Alvin Goldman (see letter to Margaret Laurence dated 4 December 1966) was at this time adapting "The Painted Door" for a CBC Television production in 1968.
6. Adele Wiseman married Dmitry Stone in 1966 and they lived in Montreal until 1969.
7. Ross is referring here to long-time friend Doris Saunders, who was a visiting professor at McGill for a year.
8. *A Jest of God*, retitled *Rachel, Rachel*, was made into a motion picture directed by Paul Newman and featuring his wife, Joanne Woodward, in the leading role. The film was released to popular and critical acclaim in 1968. See Ross's letter to Laurence dated 10 December 1968.

To Pamela Fry[1]
McClelland & Stewart, Toronto, ON
10 March 1968

Dear Miss Fry:

My apologies for not getting in touch with you before but I have not
been well and my plans haven't worked out very well. I have disc
trouble—you usually hear it called a slipped disc but my doctor tells
me such a thing is impossible; it's a *deteriorated* disc, worn down on one
side so it pinches—it's one of the reasons I am getting away from this
climate—and not only has it been cutting up but I have had a severe
attack of sciatica—wicked—plus a couple of old-man ailments, the
less said about which the better. So I have just existed this last month,
in a filthy humour, and now find myself with a great many things not
done and a great many urgent last-minute things to do. I might make
Toronto next weekend but it's not likely. Frankly, I just don't feel up to
meeting people. My sixty years are showing.

However, it seems almost certain now I shall be back in Canada for a
few weeks in 1969 and Toronto will be one of my destinations. There is
a novel about Saskatchewan I want to do—no, *set* in Saskatchewan—
and some brushing up will be necessary. This sounds idiotic, I
know—why not do the brushing up before I go?—but I won't know
what I don't know—what I've forgotten—until I get started. There is a
murder and a trial and again I won't know until I am into it how much
I will have to learn about court proceedings, legal technicalities etc.[2]
Besides, this is not the time of the year to wander about Saskatchewan
and into the bargain I am irritable and jumpy and I *want* to get away.

Long before then, however, I hope to send you the ms of the novel
I told you about.[3] I took it out a few weeks ago and dipped into it and
while it's not important by any means I think the writing is not bad
and the characters very much alive. It needs tightening—the woman
talks too much and some of her speeches will have to be telescoped into
brief summaries without quotation marks—but I have the feeling now
it's worth a little more work.

I am sorry not to have met you but as I say next year is coming. And my warmest thanks for your interest and the trouble you have taken to speed *The Lamp at Noon* on its way.

Sincerely,
Jim Ross

P.S. I will have to stay at a hotel for a few weeks while looking for an apartment but as soon as I have a permanent address I will drop you a line.

1. Pamela Fry, English-born, was an editor at McClelland & Stewart in the 1960s and 1970s. Of all the editors Ross worked with over the years he felt the closest association with Fry, although they only met once in person during a short trip he made to Toronto in 1970. She was very enthusiastic about his writing and repeatedly invited him to visit the publishing house offices.
2. The writing project he refers to here would eventually be known as "Price above Rubies," written as a sequel to *Sawbones Memorial* but never published.
3. The reference here is to the *Whir of Gold* manuscript.

To Margaret Laurence
Elm Cottage, Penn, England

20 Spetson St., Athens, Greece

10 December 1968

Dear Margaret:
Sorry—but at least it hasn't been discrimination. I haven't written to anyone this summer. And I think I can put the blame fairly on the weather—the Greek seven-day-a-week sun. Every morning, reacting like a one-day-a-week Montrealer, I say to myself a day like this is not to be wasted indoors and away I go gallivanting. Result: sea, sun, retsina and no letters...*Next year* I'll try to be my age.

Greece so far has worked out fairly well. Problems, irritations by the score of course, but as yet I can't regret the move. Nor have I intentions — as yet — to return. Whether I'll stay in *Greece* is something else again. One of my *big* problems is the language. It's tough, and while I don't have too much trouble making myself understood I have trouble understanding them. I'll be fair with myself and try a while longer, at least through the winter, and then if there's no improvement I'll probably start thinking Italy or Mexico. I'm what Marshall McLuhan would call a victim of the printed page: I have developed my eyes at the expense of my ears. I started lessons last week and my teacher, a very intelligent woman, says it's always the same with adults, especially if they're readers, and of course *the older the worser*. I know a number of Athenians who speak English and French so I don't exactly feel isolated; still, I'm an outsider. (But what the hell — haven't I always been?)

I have an apartment which I don't like *too* well — I was in too big a hurry. There are things a newcomer doesn't know: that it's fine on top, for instance, on the top floor with a little terrace in the summer (forgive my redundancies) but cold and windy in the winter. In fact some days the wind howls the way it used to in Saskatchewan. The weather is good — for me at least: the Greeks say the winter is early and severe: yesterday 63, today 55 — but heating is another matter. I know Europe is not like America or Canada in that respect and probably "my blood will thicken up" as they say — the Greeks just put on sweaters and apparently don't mind — but at the present time I find it chilly. I bought an electric heater a while ago but the damned thing burns your knees while the shivers keep running up your back...However, in the spring I'll probably move and next winter plan some travel to warmer places, Egypt and Morocco, where I've always wanted to go.

But the summer was fine — almost to the end of September in fact. Most of the time I spent out of Athens — Samos, Lesbos, Rhodes, Skiathos — and as you have been in Greece there is no point in my boring you with superlatives. Next summer, starting I think in April, I hope to see many more of the islands and also to pay another visit to Italy — and and and. Well, I suppose it's better than being bored and wondering how to kill the time. Some day I would like to write a book about Greece, but there is so much to see, and in my 6 months I have revised my opinions so many times, that I think it would be wise not to rush it.

And now guess what I saw the other evening? That's right—*Rachel, Rachel*. I daresay the people jarred on you a little, or at least didn't match the pictures you had of them, but for me they were "just right" and Woodward of course was superb. I was vaguely disappointed because it wasn't Manitoba—I don't mean the 4th of July signs, but the "feel" of it, the atmosphere—but as a westerner I am a special case and I don't really mean to criticize. The drama came through beautifully—to the Greeks as well as to me. All the way through the house was silent and intent. In fact, because they were your people and your story, I was so proud I felt like shouting.

I hope your new novel is finished and ready to burst into the light of print. I assume it isn't out yet because, while I am of course a bit behind the times here, I read *Time* regularly and frequently the *New Statesman*...I am also curious about Adele's novel—I didn't see her before I left but Alvin Goldman told me she was just finishing it[1]...I have heard nothing about *The Lamp at Noon* except a note from Pamela Fry of McClelland's that it had received some favorable notices, but as she sent no clippings I assume they weren't *too* favorable.[2] I ran into a Canadian tourist this summer who said he had seen one "review," he didn't remember which paper, but the book was used just as a spring-board for a little essay on the sorry lot of the Canadian writer. Which is nonsense, of course. *Your* lot is not sorry. It's just that for anyone who wants to write, working in a bank is hazardous.

After my long silence I haven't the brass to ask for a reply to this. But of course, if ever you are in a charitable mood, or feel expansive and loquacious after a bottle of good wine—

As ever,
Jim

1. The reference here may be to Wiseman's second novel, *Crackpot*, which however was not published until 1974.
2. There were very few reviews of *The Lamp at Noon and Other Stories*. The only one of note was by Gordon Roper in the annual "Letters in Canada" issue of *University of Toronto Quarterly* (Summer 1969): 363 in which he wrote that Ross's stories had "the same concentration in form and emotion that [made] *As for Me and My House* one of the classics of Canadian fiction in English."

To Pamela Fry

McClelland & Stewart, Toronto, ON
26 March 1969

Dear Miss Fry:

At long last: I have been re-working a manuscript and should have it typed for the last time within ten days or two weeks.

You probably remember that in a telephone conversation before leaving Canada I promised to let you see it; but that, of course, was a long time ago and before I put it in the mail it seems only sensible to check with you. I am sure McClelland's receive a great many novels and your "in" basket at this time may be piled high. I think I should also warn you it has been seen and rejected by another Canadian house, although I do feel it is in much better shape now—cut and tightened for one thing, and the writing considerably improved.[1] Myself, I have a "soft spot" for it—which explains the re-working—but I appreciate that that in itself is of no concern to you. One virtue, it's short—probably 60,000 words—and I think a reader will run through it quickly—no involved or "difficult" passages. On the contrary, it's probably too obvious and transparent, with too many why's and wherefore's. (I suppose it's age setting in, but often when reading a modern novel I just don't "get" it. Others do, however, so there's no point raising *my* voice in defence of "connective material.") Similarly the sex is awfully square. There's a fair amount of it, but after *Portnoy's Complaint*[2]— which I have just finished—it seems rather maidenly and bashful. All in all, I don't think McClelland's run the least risk of passing up a contribution to Can. Lit. if you tell me to go and peddle it elsewhere. On the other hand, if you are interested and have time to give it a reading, I shall be delighted to send it along.

Sincerely,
Sinclair Ross

1. Ross is referring here to the manuscript for *Whir of Gold* and its rejection by Macmillan.
2. Philip Roth's *Portnoy's Complaint* both shocked and delighted readers in 1969 with its graphic and comic sex scenes, particularly of male masturbation.

To Pamela Fry

McClelland & Stewart, Toronto, ON
10 April 1969

Dear Miss Fry:
I have your letter of April 1st and in response enclose the manuscript entitled "A Whir of Gold."

I appreciate your letter and its "welcome" ring, for after a final reading of the manuscript I feel anything but happy about it. A bit guilty and ashamed, in fact, to be taking up your time with it. Spotty, slack, dull, pointless—a big *So What?* on every page—I can only wonder why I have persisted, failed so dismally to *see* it. However—as we have been corresponding, and as I have two titles in the New Canadian Library, I appreciate that you may feel uncomfortable about saying, "This is a hell of a novel—why don't you take up photography?" However, I would be grateful if you would be blunt. I am well on in years and used to obscurity—even comfortable in it—and a firm NO will not be a surprise or a big disappointment. I would much rather, in fact, have it firm so that I can forget these unhappy people and—perhaps—put my mind to something else.

Sincerely,
Jim Ross

From Robert Weaver
To the Editorial Board of McClelland & Stewart
May 1969

I have mixed feelings about Sinclair Ross's new novel "A Whir of Gold." To begin with, I'm pleased that he has written another book after a literary career that includes one novel (*As for Me and My House*) and a half dozen or more short stories that have a permanent place in Canadian writing but which have never given him, either in terms of money or a public, the status as a writer that I'm sure he once hoped to achieve. His influence on some younger writers (Margaret Laurence is the primary example) has been very significant, and no critic concerned with the development of Canadian literature is likely to ignore him, but he has suffered many frustrations. So it is a pleasure to see a new novel—and one that breaks away from the Prairies and is set in Montreal where Mr. Ross lived the latter half of his life.

Having said this, I must now say that I think the novel presents some problems. It is a modest book in almost every respect, and I feel that this is not a favorable time for modesty in Canadian fiction. I suspect that many critics—and readers—will feel that while Montreal today is the setting of "A Whir of Gold" the feel of the novel is not particularly contemporary. It has for me in fact much of the feeling of *As for Me and My House*; both novels have essentially three real characters, both are inward turning and almost suffocating, both make relatively little use of the communities in which they're set (in one case the Prairie town, and now Montreal). I can see the possibility that reviewers will discuss "A Whir of Gold" as minor and rather old-fashioned, and I can't foresee any large sale for the book.

Despite these practical difficulties and some personal disappointment with the scope of the book, I think that it should be published. For one thing Sinclair Ross is obviously doing his own thing here, and we cannot really ask him to write a larger, more dramatic and more socially involved novel if that is not the kind of fiction that his temperament and his career would lead him to write. I think it's a novel that should be published in a modest edition with modest hopes for it, and that it is the kind of manuscript (and Ross the kind of writer) to make this book a good candidate for some publication assistance from the Canada Council.

A footnote for literary historians: the horse Isabel that makes her appearance in the flashback in this novel is possibly also the horse Isabel who is the subject of a short story, "The Outlaw," written about 1950 and published in *Canadian Short Stories*, an anthology of stories broadcast by the CBC and edited by Robert Weaver and Helen James.

From Pamela Fry
To the Editorial Board of McClelland & Stewart
5 June 1969

I have been corresponding with Sinclair Ross ever since he moved to Greece. ["A Whir of Gold"] is a revision of the one originally rejected by Macmillans, although I gather the "rejection" was some sort of mistake....[1]

This is a love story, gentle and rather sad in mood, but with an underlying toughness of characterization and motivation. Essentially it is concerned with how people destroy love because they are afraid of it. The locale is Montreal. The central character is Sonny, a young out-of-work jazz clarinettist from Western Canada. He is living in a rooming house, and his neighbour across the hall is a seedy, sinister little man called Charlie, who is obviously some kind of small-time racketeer. Sonny picks up a bouncy little waitress called Madeleine, and she comes to live with him. A struggle begins between Madeleine and Charlie for possession of Sonny. There is an unsuccessful robbery in which Sonny is wounded. Mad nurses Sonny back to health, and finally his big chance as a musician arrives, but it finishes his relationship with her.

I think Ross does exceptionally well in capturing the quality of two country kids in the big city (Madeleine is originally from Nova Scotia), and there is a genuine warmth and reality in the relationship between these two. There are also some very evocative sketches of Sonny's childhood on the prairies.

The book is a kind of vintage Ross, beautifully written and constructed, with all his remembered economy and simplicity of style. It is not likely to become a best seller, but it is something we could certainly take pride in publishing. I agree wholeheartedly with what Hugh and Bob[2] have to say on the subject, particularly because I am certain that another rejection would kill Ross dead as a writer. But an acceptance might prove a sufficient shot in the arm to ginger him into writing another book.

1.   Fry's reference here is not fully explained by her correspondence with Ross. In a letter to Fry (see 26 March 1969) he explains that another publisher had turned the manuscript down but does not refer to a mistake made.

2.   Hugh Kane and Robert Weaver were the other two readers to submit reports.

From Pamela Fry
McClelland & Stewart, Toronto, ON
12 June 1969

Dear Mr. Ross:

I hope you got my night letter safely—I was so pleased when I heard we were going to publish "A Whir of Gold" that I felt I must let you know immediately.

I myself enjoyed the book immensely. The love story has great warmth and gentleness and Sonny and Mad haunted me for days after I had finished it. I kept worrying about them. I also thought you brought off very well the contrast between their essential innocence and country simplicity and the brash cruelty of city life. And I liked Sonny's nostalgic reminiscences of his childhood. I have only read the book once, but I do not think it will need much, if any, further work. There is a possibility some of the dialogue could be slightly tightened, but I would have to read it again to be sure of this. Let me know your own feelings on the subject.

We are thinking in terms of a probable Fall 1970 publication date. I gather, since Macmillans rejected the first draft of this manuscript, you have no further commitment to them. However, could you let me know exactly what the position is? I think I should close this letter with Jack McClelland's comment after he had seen the manuscript: "The day we can't publish Sinclair Ross is the day we shouldn't be in publishing."

Again, with many congratulations, looking forward to hearing from you,

All the best,
Pamela Fry

To Pamela Fry

McClelland & Stewart, Toronto, ON

8 July 1969

Dear Pamela:

I hope you don't mind the familiarity. But it does look as if you're going to be "stuck" with me for a while, so perhaps we can relax. My name, incidentally, is Jim.

Yes, I think I can do something with Mad's dialogue, and your suggestion for breaking it up and putting bits into the third person are good. Something more in the way of background for her—at this moment I don't know. Perhaps a few asides about her family, but I don't want to clutter her. Something sharp and "revealing" if I can hit on it.

The same with Charlie. I agree he probably impresses the reader as two-dimensional but to round him out—well, as you know, the problem is that it's a first-person story. Sonny is talking and Sonny knows only what Charlie tells him; and Charlie, sharp and wily, isn't going to tell very much. A slip, perhaps—again if I could hit on something "revealing"—Sonny, I suppose, could run into someone who knows Charlie and his family—but that, I'm afraid, would seem contrived.

We'll see....As to his interest in Sonny—Sonny, of course, can only speculate, and he does, in fact, speculate at some length—pages 104/106. (Don't pay too much attention to this: I'm really just talking to myself, trying to *see*.) I don't think of Charlie as a "villain" but rather as someone who is sick and frightened. And *that*, of course, is why he wants Sonny. As Sonny describes himself, he is, relatively, at least, healthy, normal, uncomplicated; and Charlie instinctively reaches for him—someone to lean on. This need, of course, is the last thing Charlie would admit. He twists it, convinces himself he wants to help Sonny.

Rebel without a Cause[1] approaching middle age. And scared. His family, the safe little world of job and respectability—he has thumbed his nose at that, turned his back. And no return—his pride would never let him. But the world of the criminal is tough, cruel—and he's not really up to it. He could face it, though, could go on, with someone like Sonny as a partner.

The psychological "structure" I think is sound. The problem is that Charlie doesn't know what's going on inside him; and I don't want Sonny to blossom into too sharp and discerning a psychologist. Can I bring him into the open a little more? No promises, but I'll try. I need a little time and your letter of only yesterday. I'm leaving tomorrow for two weeks in northern Greece — Athens is a furnace — and will take the ms with me. I have one of those unfortunate minds which won't be pushed. No taps — it comes or it doesn't. Perhaps while contemplating a mountain...In any case, keep your fingers crossed for me.

Needless to say, I'm keeping mine crossed: you say you have hopes of arranging something in England or U.S. I absolutely refuse to believe it — *but*...

Still enjoying Greece and still having one hell of a time with language; although I get along well enough and have no real problems. I am seeing as much of it as I can this year — have just returned in fact from the south, and in September hope to go to Turkey — because I'm not sure about next year. The sun is still shining but there are a few faint rumbles over the horizon. No plans, however, to return to Canada, except for a visit sometime. Feeling fine — I forget I have a damaged disc, weeks at a time without a twinge — so if not Greece, I'll try another place with the same kind of climate.

I know you're busy so don't take time for a letter — just a note, if you would, to let me know when you would like, or will need, the revisions.

Sincerely,
Jim Ross

---

1. Ross is referring here to the popular motion picture about adolescence directed by Nicholas Ray and featuring James Dean in the lead role.

To Doris Saunders
University of Manitoba, Winnipeg, MB
30 September 1969

Dear Doris:

It's very gratifying—"heart-warming" is the word—that you should want me in your Manitoba *Mosaic*,[1] but of course I don't belong there; and I couldn't write three hundred words on the influence of Manitoba on my work, much less three thousand, for the simple reason that it had no influence whatsoever.

If I have any claim to be considered a "writer" it must be based on the stories in *The Lamp at Noon* and *As for Me and My House*; and they are, as you know, one hundred percent Saskatchewan. True, I wrote them while in Winnipeg, but I was looking back, and drew on Manitoba not at all. If I had written them in London or Timbuktu they would have come out exactly the same.

I know—there were you and Daniells and a few others—but it was after the publication of *As for Me...* that I met you. I was happy, of course, to hear from people of discernment that I had not been wasting my time, but as you would be the first to agree, there was no influence.

So what could I say? With the others represented in your book, it is entirely different. Margaret and Adele, for instance; they not only spent their childhood in Manitoba—their roots; they also went to school and university there and had any number of influences, yourself, I dare say, among them.

I am not brushing off your suggestion, or wiggling out, or being sticky. In fact, I have delayed writing a few days in order to sleep on it; but the more I think about it the more convinced I am that if I did write an article it would be contrived, padded, insincere—phony—and you wouldn't want that any more than I would.

However, if despite all this you would still like to have me in the "Anthology" part of the book—well, fine, I should be delighted. But in that case, I think, only a brief editorial note would be required, in which I am recognized and labelled as an outsider but welcomed, let us say, as an old neighbour whose work will ring a few bells for

Manitobans too. I hope you won't think this an impertinent suggestion; I certainly don't mean it that way.

Incidentally, I have a new novel coming out next year—not until the fall, by the sound of things—but again, rat that I am, I have jumped Manitoba. A down-and-out musician from Saskatchewan, a lady of buxom charms and dubious virtue from Nova Scotia, and they do their thing in Montreal. And now, having heard that much, aren't you glad I jumped? McClellands are bringing it out. The title: *A Whir of Gold*.

Yes, I have read *The Fire-Dwellers*. I found myself resisting it at first, then I liked it and became absorbed. As I wrote Margaret just a week or so ago, what I think especially good is the way she makes everyday, suburban lives compelling—a real achievement today when so many novels depend on far-out situations and revved-up sex.

Speaking of Margaret, I saw *Rachel, Rachel* in Athens. Excellent, I thought, and Woodward was just right. And speaking of films, when I go to one here—they all come, including the "cowboys"—I am tremendously busy keeping up with the titles, so much so that frequently I forget I understand English and could, if I wanted to, just relax and listen. The titles are usually fairly brief and simple and my Greek—my reading Greek, that is—is at the stage where I get about 90% *if I hurry*—no time to dawdle over "assassinate" or "explode" and "figure out" is it passive imperfect or conditional. An outrageous language—I seem to be standing still. They understand me but half the time I don't understand them. I suppose if I persist—say for another two years—but that's an awfully long time to keep saying, "Sorry, again please"—and Italian is such a temptation.

I am going to Italy next week—just Rome and Naples, I think, although if the weather keeps good I may wander. (Right now, here, it's wonderful—sunny and not too warm; yesterday it was 82 and will probably be the same today. In the evening, eating outside, you need a jacket.) I want to see Salvatore in Naples[2]—I think I told you about him—he's nearly 14 now and I think, from his letters, fairly bright—and as to my other reasons for going to Italy, well, perhaps you can guess. Things are a bit uncertain—although, one can't help asking, where aren't they? I'll have to decide this winter.

Your trip to the Far East gives me itchy feet. Japan especially I would like to see, but of course I would have to suppress my insane insistence on travelling on my own. In fact, it's getting more difficult every year—at least in this part of the world, the Aegean and the Mediterranean. The Germans and Scandinavians are prosperous and they come for the sea and sun in hordes, like the Goths under Attila. They take entire hotels for the season, one group following another, and it's getting difficult to reserve even weeks ahead. Last June, the Italian Tourist Office here told me Italy was booked solid till the last week in September—so I'm waiting.

I was in Istanbul for two weeks during September—and had to change my hotel three times—"a group coming in, everything taken so you can stay only two nights"—but despite the irritations enjoyed it thoroughly and hope to go back sometime to travel further. In the main an ugly, drab city, with many beautiful things in it. Good food—better than in Greece, although I don't dare say it here—you know how they love each other—and the Turks themselves seem kind and friendly—not at all the American-hating xenophobes I expected. I "fell" for the mosques—my Scotch-Presbyterian Waspish makeup notwithstanding—even though they have loudspeakers instead of muezzins to call the Faithful to prayers. Wonderful to take off your shoes and pad around on your tired, tourist feet on the thick carpets.

When I shall get around to a return visit to Canada I don't know. I have a novel I would like to do sometime about a small town in Saskatchewan, but things have changed so much since my time I need a refresher course; but it's an expensive trip and the old Scotchman hesitates. In 25 years *As for Me and My House* has earned me, all told, including two radio performances, less than $1,500; so even if I were to do the book and get it published, I would likely end up in the hole.

Sorry I haven't written before. I mean well—so well, that's the trouble, that I keep saying No, not today, I'll wait till I have time for a *long* letter....And again my warmest thanks for inviting me into Manitoba *Mosaic*.

As ever,
Jim

1. *Mosaic* (University of Manitoba) began publishing in 1967. Doris Saunders, who had retired from the English Department, was asked to guest edit an issue of the journal devoted to Manitoba writing and authors.

2. Salvatore was a boy Ross was sponsoring through the Save the Children Fund.

To Pamela Fry

McClelland & Stewart, Toronto, ON

31 October, 1969

Dear Pamela:

I'm taking you up on your offer to look over and comment on what I've done to Charlie, the villain in the piece.

These few pages seem out of all proportion to the chopping and changing I've been doing, but as I said before, because Sonny knows only what Charlie tells him, it's been hard to build him up within the limits imposed by the first person narrative.

What I have done, or tried to do, is:

Emphasize that he is sick and scared. I let Mad put in her oar a few times—she's nobody's fool.

Given him a family and, along with it, an explanation—or at least a suggestion—of how he came to be what he is. It doesn't attempt to go to the roots of course; obviously he "began" long before.

Given him a homosexual tilt. I didn't want to do it, and while writing the story never "saw" him that way, but it does probably make sense, explains his interest in Sonny. As I've done it, I don't think it's very obvious—it might easily, I am sure, be missed—but for the sharper reader, the armchair psychologist, it should help tie things together. Sonny, of course, doesn't suspect anything: important, for if he did, being still basically a simple, country boy, it would be an instant "Good-bye Charlie" and then where would my villain be? At the same time, the bit at the very end of the new chapter, the dream where the girls refuse his ticket, suggests that he knows subconsciously the way the wind is blowing.

As to tightening the dialogue — and the writing generally — I find some slack spots — I can't send that along since there probably won't be a page without changes: a few words in or out, paragraphs broken, etc. However, the enclosed pages show fairly well what I'm doing. For example: page 58 of the first ms, the paragraph beginning "Mouth and eyes followed the memory —" and then see the enclosed revision, page 58 again but at the bottom of the page, now two paragraphs beginning "Her mouth drooped, hardened —." I find, in fact, there's not a great deal to *cut*, but along with breaking it up I can put some bits into the third person.

And now a favour, if you have a moment to read it again: her *big* speech, at the very end of the story, when she tells Sonny about going to church, etc. — do you feel that this is one of the places where she should be cut or put into the third person? Myself, I feel right now that, except perhaps for a little tightening and some word-out word-in polishing, it should be left as it is, all of it in her own words. Otherwise — recapped, without the rhythm she gives it — I think it might lose something. But I would like your reaction — whether or not the lady's too long-winded.

You mentioned in your letter that I might also give some thought to Mad's background, rounding her out a bit. Well, I've given it a great deal of thought and so far haven't come up with much. For one thing, in so much Canadian and American writing the "small town" is a cliché — just say Main Street and the reader's got the picture — and I suspect, doesn't want to hear about it again. No, I'm not being mulish, but I just wonder if what is there already isn't enough. I have a few little things — the problem is to find a place for them — the book is tight — but I'm not sure they will make much difference.

Incidentally, regarding the new chapter for Charlie, it turned out there was a very good place for it, and in addition to its purpose of saying something about Charlie, it helps — I hope — to *articulate* — that's a fine word—Sonny's consent to play along with Charlie. It bothered me before as being a bit abrupt.

Sorry to break in on you with this—I'm afraid I'm as long-winded as Mad is. But if you can manage to put all those *other* mss. out of your mind for a little while and give me your opinion, I shall be very grateful.

Sincerely,
Jim

To Doris Saunders
University of Manitoba, Winnipeg, MB
2 November, 1969

Dear Doris:
Having fun getting settled in your new home? It must have been something of a wrench after 17 years, and humans being what they are, such acquisitive creatures, I'll bet you had one *hell* of a time sorting and culling your possessions in order to leave yourselves breathing space. It alarms me, I know, the way I'm starting already to accumulate here. Such useless things—in Lesbos, for instance, I bought some goat bells—Heaven knows why. Also in Lesbos, I saw a potter at his wheel and couldn't resist an ouzo pitcher and the little cups that go with it. [excerpt][1]

I enjoyed my trip to Italy—weather and food good—an understatement— and except for breakfast and one meal at Salvatore's place ate outdoors for the entire three weeks. Many temptations—but the country itself doesn't seem to be in very good shape—strikes, rioting, the government gasping for breath, to say nothing of inflation—the pensioner's bugbear. Salvatore is 15 now and a gangling six-footer—still at school and planning next year to go to a trade school. To be a "machinist"—I suppose he'll work in a garage. I visited the family—friendly and likeable, although the signora speaks only the Neapolitan dialect and the father lapses into it frequently so that at times there was a communication problem. An enormous amount of food and wine—their own—and they sent me back to the hotel laden with apples, pears, grapes, walnuts—plus about a gallon of the wine—all of which, of course, I promptly turned over to one of the porters in the hotel. Attractive children—Lorenzo, Giuseppe, Eugenio, Sophia, Claudio, Irene—well fed, well dressed, but parents and children all sleeping in one bedroom. It's distressing, of course—Salvatore is almost a young man—but I can't afford to put them into an apartment. (No—I didn't adopt Salvatore—just got in touch with him through the Save-The-Children Fund.) And this I know has no bearing on the plight of the children, but you can't help becoming impatient (that's a mild word) with that old so-and-so who is so determined on the birth control issue. Salvatore's parents are probably 40/45—good, I'm sure, for at least another two.

As to *Mosaic*—I'm sorry I must say No again. For one thing, truthfully, I'm busy. Since there was time, I started picking at the ms of the novel—"textual" changes, one word in, two out, etc., plus a new chapter to strengthen one of the characters—with the result that the ms is so messed up it has to be completely re-typed. And apart from that, I just don't feel up to what you suggest.[2]

When it's a Proust or a James or a Kafka exploring the sensibility and creative processes the result is *interesting*—but for someone like me—not just a minor writer, but *minorissimo*—well, I think it would be somewhat pretentious. In other words, I haven't the voice, the authority, for that sort of thing. Moreover, I'm not altogether "with" you. Writers and artists aren't all the same—on the contrary—so I think it's not wise to generalize. Even a Proust or James—his findings would be *interesting*, of course, but not necessarily valid for anyone else.

Another moreover—artists themselves as well as psychologists seem pretty well agreed that the "creative sources" are in the subconscious, and they are also agreed that self-analysis can seldom do more than scrape the surface. So that unless it's someone capable of rare insights, there's a chance he'll come up with the wrong answers. (Woolly, I'm afraid—I'm trying to think as I type.)

Myself now—while in Manitoba I wasn't, as you say, "living in another world." Not at all—I was very much aware of Manitoba and Manitobans and I don't suppose I averaged an hour a day at my novel. It was just that *As for Me* and the stories in *The Lamp at Noon* happened to be about Saskatchewan. Naturally, while writing, I was looking back. Later, while in London, I worked on a novel (discarded after about 200 pages) about a young soldier from Manitoba, and *then* I was looking back to Winnipeg. You see what I mean? *I* don't understand myself—my "creative processes" if you like, why I did this and not that—so how could I write about them? For all I know, Manitoba did have an effect on my writing, did work its way into *As for Me*—but if it did, so what? It's the result that counts.

But having mumbled my way through all that, I think your suggestion would be a good subject for a *critic*. Yourself, for instance—using me as a springboard. Years and years in Manitoba and now he up and says he wasn't influenced—what gives? Then away you go with comparisons, speculations, conclusions. But it's far beyond me. I always say that when I write I like to "feel" Saskatchewan under my feet. I do—I feel "safer"—but I couldn't for the life of me say *more* than that. Pressed, I would probably come up with something brilliant like, "Well, I suppose it's just that when you're a child you're more impressionable." But does it hold for others? Gabrielle Roy, to stay in Canada—she grew up in Manitoba but she wrote very well about Montreal in *The Tin Flute*. So did Hugh MacLennan, and he's from Nova Scotia.

So I repeat, it's beyond me. I couldn't begin to gather up the pieces and arrange them coherently, so they "go" somewhere. I haven't the training for it. But no—of course I don't think you're importunate. On the contrary, it's gratifying you should take me so seriously. And I do wish you—unnecessarily, I'm sure—the best of luck with *Mosaic*.

Yes, I suppose I'm lucky to be away from Canadian weather. Today was sunny, windless, not quite hot—what the Greeks call "a joy of Gold." I had lunch with a Greek friend and for coffee we moved to a sidewalk café—and after a few minutes moved again into the shade. But still there's another side to the coin. It gets chilly at night, dropping to 50/55, and there's no heat yet. Not till we "need" it—which last year was the first week in December. Sometimes, frankly, it's a bit miserable. I have an electric heater but of course the damned thing just burns your knees, and the other areas continue to shiver. They tell me I'll get used to it—at the moment I'm just getting sweaters. I wouldn't mind one of those English long-handled warming pans ...

When you see Chester say hello for me.[3] I often think of him and the way he used to go after inflated egos. I'm sure he's responsible for the sorry shape I'm in today. There's influence for you![4]

Sincerely,
Jim

1.   At this point Ross gives a lengthy account of some of the books he saw for sale in the shops in Athens.
2.   See letter to Doris Saunders dated 30 September 1969.
3.   Chester Duncan was Saunders's colleague at the University of Manitoba. See letter to Saunders dated 23 October 1942.
4.   Ross's observations in this letter were edited by Saunders and published with Ross's permission as a short piece titled "On Looking Back" in *Mosaic* 3 (Spring 1970): 93–94.

To Keath Fraser[1]

London, England
28 November 1969

Dear Mr. Fraser:
I am sorry for the delay in answering your letter. I was out of Athens for a while and when I returned some Greek friends from Canada were in Athens[2]—with the result I was somewhat disorganized. Although in strict honesty, that's pretty close to my permanent condition.

Of course, I shall be delighted to meet Mrs. Fraser and yourself when you come to Athens. We'll go to the Plaka for dinner and bouziki[3]—much more fun that Can. Lit. and the stories in *The Lamp at Noon*.

Still, I'm very pleased to hear you have reviewed them for *Queen's* and look forward to seeing the magazine.[4] In fact, I have seen nothing in the way of criticism since the collection came out. McClellands wrote that a number of papers had commented favorably, but as they didn't send any clippings I concluded that the favorable comments were probably the faint praise that damns.[5]

You say *February* and I think that will be fine. I expect to be out of Athens for two or three weeks this winter, and while I don't know the exact dates—it depends on someone who is coming from New York—I should be back not later than the first week in February.

Yours sincerely,
Sinclair Ross

1. British Columbia fiction writer Keath Fraser (1945–) was working on a PHD at the University of London in the late 1960s and early 1970s.
2. Ross is probably referring to a visit from Koula and Alec Lucas. See letter to Margaret Laurence dated 9 December 1967.
3. The Plaka is an old section of Athens with many restaurants where characteristically the bouziki, a mandolin-like instrument, provides music for Greek dancing.
4. Fraser's "review" was actually a full-length article titled "Futility at the Pump: The Short Stories of Sinclair Ross," *Queen's Quarterly* 77 (Spring 1970): 72–80.
5. See letter to Margaret Laurence dated 10 December 1968, note 2.

To Pamela Fry

McClelland & Stewart, Toronto, ON

P.O. Box 1490, Omonia Square
Athens, Greece

10 May 1970

Dear Pamela:

Thank you for your letter telling me to expect the galleys the 15th of May. It was waiting for me when I returned to Athens—I had gone gallivanting while waiting to hear from you—and I sent a night letter just in case you might hold up mailing them until you heard from me.

I'm sorry you haven't been feeling well and I know what you mean about the urge—desperate sometimes, at least it used to be with me—to pack it all up and break free. I was 43 years a bank clerk and it was even worse probably; for you, I imagine, are interested in your work and I, frankly, wasn't. Sometimes I wonder how I stood it—and sometimes I wonder how the Bank stood me. I'm afraid I wasn't exactly what you'd call an asset.

I spent a little over a week in southern Greece—as I say, I have just returned—and surprisingly the weather wasn't particularly good. Windy and chilly part of the time, with a little rain thrown in. But very beautiful: Pylos—"sandy Pylos" of Homer where King Nestor has his palace—or at least just ten miles away—but it's a pretty dull ruin, just a few "stumps" of walls protected by a hideous zinc shed; then on to a place called Kalamata and two good excursions. Very proud of myself—climbed a mountain, steep and stony, just a goat path, and was rewarded with a view that took in snow-covered mountains, the sea and a vast panorama of other mountains, valleys and plain. I have a considerable amount of travel in Greece planned for the summer, Crete, Northern Greece, some islands, but I may bog down. It's getting difficult...you go to a hotel and the clerk says disdainfully, "Well, just for tonight—then we have a tour coming in." Or "Yes, if you could wait two days." It's only the beginning of May and the first night in Pylos I had to sleep in a private house, then found a very "Spartan" room with a cold-water tap and nothing else. Kalamata I was lucky—the last room in a good hotel. The thing to do, of course, is to join a tour, but myself I loathe them...I *want* to see as much of Greece as I can this summer, because it may be my last year. I've said that before, and before next spring I may change my mind—but probably 3 years is enough.

Thank you again for hurrying the galleys. It shouldn't take me long to go through them—I'll lock myself in—and you should have them back within not much more than a week.[1]

Sincerely,
Jim

---

1. Ross hurried through the galleys and returned them in May, but the project was plagued with a series of production problems that resulted in a text with numerous errors and in numerous delays such that the book was not ready for the Christmas trade. Ross was thoroughly discouraged and on 3 January 1971 he wrote to Fry acerbically: "I have gone through Whir hurriedly, but even skimming I spotted a number of errors. Such as 'laying low' for 'lying low,' 'dead path' for 'dead patch'—'ignominiously' with an 'i' missing and 'sense' with a 'c' etc.—I just can't understand how a proof reader could miss them."

From Pamela Fry
McClelland & Stewart, Toronto, ON
13 July 1970

Dear Jim,
I am very sorry indeed that it has been so long since I wrote to you—but I have been away from work for nearly a month. "Total fatigue from overwork," my doctor said firmly—"and you're going to have to stay home until you are back to normal again." Which I am and, indeed, only returned to work today.

I am also extremely sorry for the incredible MESS regarding your galleys. Some idiotic new method was tried, which was supposed to be cheaper, but which finally resulted in causing us all more, in money and strain, than if it had gone to a *real* printer in the first place. You will be relieved to know that it is now in the hands of a proper printer. It was supposed to go off today, but I have checked with our production department and find that the proofs are now due tomorrow. I will see that they are rushed off to you Air Express the moment they arrive. To be honest, I am really furious about this whole business. The ms was so clean, and had so few changes that it should have been in press weeks ago—and I hate to think that we have also succeeded in messing up your summer plans.

On the positive side, you will be pleased to know that your suggestion for the title—WHIR OF GOLD—has been approved. I am also delighted to hear that you will be coming to Canada this fall—it will be good for the promotion of the book and will, I hope, finally give me a chance to meet you.[1]

By the way, do you want any kind of dedication? If so, will you let me know immediately?

Again with apologies for all the ridiculous confusions and delays—

All the best, as ever
Pamela

1.   Ross was in Toronto in November 1970 where he was interviewed by Earle Toppings for the series titled *Canadian Writers on Tape*, which was distributed in 1971 by the Ontario Institute for Studies in Education. See the appendix to this volume for a print version of the interview, the only formal discussion of its kind that Ross ever agreed to give.

To Alvin Goldman[1]

Montreal, PQ

12 January 1971

Dear Alvin:

Sorry for the delay in replying. I've been under the weather—the old bag of bones has been ganging up on me....[2]

I was sorry to hear you had lost your mother. These things are always painful, even when it's someone with whom we've lost close contact. I suppose it's the memories and also perhaps—it was in my case, at least, upsetting even though completely irrational—a certain sense of guilt. We're all such strange creatures, and there are so many "why's" and "wherefore's."

I am very pleased that you liked Sonny and Mad and found them convincing. They had both become real to me and, silly as it sounds, I had grown rather fond of them. I have seen only one review—a friend sent the clipping from Winnipeg, but clipped close, so I don't know the paper—by Chester Duncan.[3] Surprisingly kind; he thought it didn't quite come off but said he was very moved at the end. Criticized Mad as being incredibly good, with which I don't agree. She was devoted to Sonny, which is not the same thing at all. Apart from Sonny she was fairly tough and unscrupulous. Even going to church—it was all she could think of, a drowning man clutching at a straw. She didn't go in search of grace or forgiveness. There was nothing transcendental about her goodness. By nature a warm, big-hearted girl but not, as he calls her, "an angel of mercy."

Now The Well—I appreciate your offer to take an option on it but I'm hedging.[4] First of all, you see a film but I see a novel—by that I mean a much better novel than the one published. Since seeing you I've gone through it and there are some things in it that aren't bad—the woman's scheme to get rid of the old man—perhaps I flatter myself but, through all the things I didn't like, I felt it worked, built up a considerable amount of suspense. With the new ending I told you about, with the writing tightened and sloppy bits eliminated or straightened out, I feel it just might "come off."[5] Something else which I suppose is a bit petty-minded: it was published with a very bad ending, contrived, forced, unconvincing; and if the film is done with the new—and, I think, greatly improved—ending, it will look as if someone had to doctor up the story for me—in other words, that I was too dim-witted to do it myself. I know, only a handful of people read the book in any case, so what the hell? Who cares? Well, I do, and at the moment I can't see around it....[excerpt][6]

I'm still planning to move to Spain, but as yet I haven't done anything. Except learn there's a boat March 14, so if all goes well it will be then. A lot of work: packing books, disposing of the furniture and odds and ends I've accumulated—you don't realize until you do it how many things have to be attended to. And then of course all the new problems when I arrive—but I'm not looking ahead that far.

"Hello" to Dorothy—I wish she were here so I could invite myself for a good dinner. You're lucky!

Best wishes for 1971
As ever,
Jim

1.   See note 2 of letter to Margaret Laurence dated 4 December 1966. Alvin Goldman and his wife Dorothy were loyal friends for more than thirty years.
2.   Ross continues here with a lengthy account of illnesses including a cold, sinus infection, and prostatitis.
3.   See Chester Duncan, "Not All Is Gold," *Winnipeg Free Press*, 19 December 1970, 14NL.
4.   Alvin Goldman wanted to write a screenplay based on *The Well* and was trying to secure Ross's permission before starting on the project.
5.   For any future versions of *The Well* Ross wanted to restore his original ending where Chris remorselessly carries out Sylvia's plan to be rid of her husband, but then leaves her without feeling either guilt or regret.
6.   Ross continues at length to weigh the pros and cons of a film version of *The Well* without coming to a decision.

To Margaret Laurence

Elm Cottage, Penn, England

29 January 1971

Dear Margaret:

My warmest thanks for the kind things you had to say about *Whir of Gold*. Yes, so far as I am concerned, Sonny is the boy in "Cornet at Night" grown up, and I was very pleased that you "get" it. But my God, woman, you're as bad as Mad: it's a *clarinet*, not a horn.

No, McClelland's haven't sent any reviews, but a friend in Winnipeg clipped out one by Chester Duncan.[1] He was surprisingly generous in his praise, although in some places he misread it. Mad, he felt, was incredibly good—an angel of mercy—but in fact, except where Sonny was concerned, she was fairly tough and unscrupulous. Even though, as I knew her, she was by nature a warm, big-hearted girl. But doing things and making sacrifices for someone you are devoted to is not particularly virtuous. Even the Bible has a comment—"the Pharisees do as much"—something like that. And she went to church for *Sonny*—a drowning man clutching at a straw—not for grace and forgiveness. Someone in Toronto clipped out another for me from the U of T *Varsity*—Stephen Chesley[2]—and his review was also very favorable although he felt Mad wasn't full and believable enough, as her role is "crucial to my ideas"—damned if I knew I had any. But both had read the book, taken it seriously, and I was—am—pleased.

On the other hand, I am not at all happy about McClelland's. It was a solicited novel: I was diffident about sending it to them and even wrote Miss Fry, "Are you *sure* you want to bothered with it—it's already been rejected by Macmillan's"—and later, when forwarding the ms. "Whatever you do, don't hesitate to say bluntly it won't do"—in other words, far from twisting their arm, I gave them an easy way out; so why then *did* they accept it when they had so little faith in it as to give me nothing at all in the way of an advance—they held up the contract till the last minute, and why, if it was worth publishing, was it not worth proof-reading? There's no point in going off at a tangent about it, but after all—at least at the moment—I have two titles in their New

Canadian Library; surely I deserve routine courtesy and consideration. Their excuse that they set it up by computer is pure you-know-what. However they set it, computer, steam-engine, donkeys, the responsibility is theirs—they have proofreaders. It raises some unpleasant doubts, and I'm left wondering why, or who.

However, right now I have other things on my mind, and as it's almost February I must get down to packing books, cleaning out drawers, sorting out clothes and all the rest of it—to say nothing of trying to find someone to buy furniture. Maybe I'm crazy—now that the time draws near I'm getting terribly sentimental about Greece—and in fact they have been three good years and I leave with good, warm memories—but it's the old story, I just can't learn their damned language (and am spending too much time trying). They understand me, but I don't understand them. It isolates me, makes it difficult to know people, and moreover makes me feel terribly stupid. There's been so much to see I haven't minded, but now I begin to feel I would like a place where I can settle in and say "This is it," and Greece is not the answer. Heaven knows how Spain will work out but at least the language won't be such a problem—I already get along fairly well. I was there for a month last fall and liked it. It may be a bit more expensive—it's hard to tell when you're a tourist—but not a great deal. The expense is the moving and buying new furniture—unless I can find a furnished apartment which will take my books. I can't afford to do it too often—certainly not on my handsome royalty cheques.

So when I shall be able to visit England and take advantage of your hospitality is a bit uncertain—perhaps towards fall. I want very much to see England again and explore a bit. My memories are all wartime and I daresay I shall not find much that is familiar. In the meantime, another good boot on (in, up?) your Manitoba fanny to speed you along with your new novel. And another very big thank-you for your sympathetic reading of Sonny and Mad.

As ever,
Jim

1. See note 3 of letter to Alvin Goldman dated 12 January 1971.
2. See Stephen Chesley, "*Whir of Gold* Builds on Past for Modern Tale," *The Varsity* [University of Toronto], 27 January 1971, 12.

Succès d'estime | *Letters 1972–1974*

THE LETTERS IN THIS SECTION, drawn from several sources, reflect a growing interest in Sinclair Ross's writing, especially among members of the academic community. Part of this interest was generated by Margaret Atwood who, in *Survival*, identified *As for Me and My House* as essential Canadian reading. This in turn created the optimum condition Ross needed for continuing to work. The largest number of letters here record the writing and publishing of *Sawbones Memorial* and its reception by critics, including Atwood herself.

To David Stouck

Simon Fraser University, Burnaby, BC
10 January 1972

Apartado 5362, Barcelona, Spain

Dear Mr. Stouck:

My sincere thanks for "Notes on the Canadian Imagination."[1] Of course
I was pleased—a weak word, in fact, for my response—that you should
have such good things to say about *As for Me...*, but apart from that, it
impresses me as a first-rate piece of critical writing. I liked particularly
sections 1 and 2, where you describe and assess the Canadian imagination in more or less general terms, before getting down to cases and
illustrations. It hadn't occurred to me before that the Canadian landscape might be considered—or should I say, might be—an objective
correlative of the artist's "isolation...his experience of fear, sadness
and the challenge to endure." And as all artists, not just those in
Canada, suffer from a sense of alienation, you have set me off on a little
journey of exploration, trying to discover the objective correlative for
the Americans and English and French who don't, at least not always,
have an appropriately grim and lonely landscape to "take it out on."
Faulkner I can see, the decadence of the old South and the intrusion of
the lethal Snopeses; James, no; Whitman, no; Eliot and his wasteland,
yes; Flaubert, yes, although I only know *Madame Bovary*; Balzac, no;
Stendhal, no—and so far into the night.

I am interested that several times you speak of the Canadian artist's
sense of nature's "indifference," because that feeling, very strong,
has always been behind anything I have written. There is, in fact, one
place where I come into the open and point it up—in *As for Me...* when
Paul and Mrs. Bentley are sitting on the riverbank. I even used to be
defiant about it—say from 20 to 30. All by myself I had come to the
momentous conclusion that there was no hostility, only this indifference. It seems somewhat ridiculous now, and I wonder why I did feel
so strongly about it. I suppose because, in my reading, I had absorbed

a strong dose of what I think is called the *anthropomorphic* feeling or attitude towards nature—a hell of a word, it should be outlawed. "The storm struck in all its fury," "the sun beat down implacably"—that sort of thing. (Although at the same time, when you're out say in a bad blizzard, it's hard not to feel that you're "battling" it, that it is disapprovingly aware of you.) It's a parallel to something I say about Philip and religion, which most youngsters today, I daresay, in this faithless age, with all the battles far in the past, would find meaningless: his doubts were his own, were "achieved" doubts.

One thing that surprises me: you say my other writing is considerably less effective than *As for Me...* and myself I have always felt that the short stories are the best I have done. No, I'm not disputing your judgment—I'm a very poor critic of my own writing and I appreciate, furthermore, that an outsider can often see better what is going on, especially if the unconscious is involved, than one can oneself. It's just that to me *As for Me...* is a dreary book—sincere, yes, but naive. Some things—beginner's luck—I did better than I knew. Keeping Philip off-stage, for instance—it gives him a power, makes him a presence looming in the background more impressive for the reader, I think, than when they see and hear him. Which is why it can't be—or is unlikely to be—dramatized. A Canadian film company, after a couple of tries at a script has, apparently, given up.[2] As soon as he emerges from his study he's a stick. And Paul, the ridiculous schoolteacher—I didn't bring him in with that in mind, but as it worked out he was a useful chorus. A bit of a nut, he could say things for me, quoted by Mrs. Bentley in her diary, which she couldn't say. For of course that is the problem, the limitation, with a first-person novel, keeping within the narrator's intellectual and imaginative range, keeping to his vocabulary, denying him flights, excesses or even humour which the author would like to indulge in. In *Whir of Gold* I had to go back and up-grade the narrator. I had started him out a big, simple country lunk and then woke up to the fact that that was what I—and the reader, supposing I ever had one—would be "stuck" with. As it is, I have probably slipped in places, although I think all the imagery is true to Saskatchewan. My own verdict, incidentally—I don't know whether you have read it—is a shaky novel with some fairly good things in it. And I think the writing holds its own, although somebody reviewing it in the *Windsor Star*, a bit viciously, said "Ross is reluctant to write a sentence..."[3] Well, I suppose it's all part of the game or business or what somebody has called "the lamentable trade of letters." Stamps or butterflies would have been more fun.

Again my warmest thanks—and yes, I should indeed appreciate a copy when it appears.

Yours sincerely,
Sinclair Ross

1. This general essay was published in *Canadian Literature* 54 (Autumn 1972).
2. Over the years, several filmmakers have taken out an option on this novel, but none have succeeded in bringing it to the screen. The most ambitious project of this kind was undertaken by Peter Pearson in the early 1970s and this may be the reference here, though as of January 1972 the project was far from being abandoned. Later that year Ross would meet Sheila Kieran, who was connected to the project (see letters to and from Kieran).
3. Bob Ivanochko, "Ross Novel Whirs around Montreal," *Windsor Star*, 30 January 1971, 12.

To Keath Fraser
London, England
6 May 1972

Dear Keath:
Yes, I know—I'm getting worse. But just wait until you're 64 and suffering with prostatitis. In fact I have been really under the weather, a dreary business involving a few days in hospital. I had the operation about ten years ago but still get the infections every so often and this was the worst yet. Still taking antibiotics. I hope though for just 2 or 3 more days when I go back for another laboratory test. That was March and then for three weeks in April I went south—Alicante, Granada,

Málaga, Cadiz and Cordoba, dutifully taking my pills all the way. Enjoyed it, although room hunting took off the edge a bit—and it's just the beginning of the season. They expect 40 million this year and don't know where they're going to put them. I was in Granada 4 nights, for instance, and in 3 hotels. "Tonight only—a group coming in." I went to look things over—I may move. Living, it seems, is a bit cheaper, especially apartments, and the weather is much better. On the other hand I like Barcelona—if I could find a satisfactory apartment within my price range. Buying an apartment might be a solution—they have very easy terms, $2,000 down and the rest at the rate of a low rent—but of course I would prefer not to be tied down. And the catch is that if I sold it in a few years I couldn't take the money out of Spain...life is all catches. Some of us, it seems, get caught before we're started.

Was delighted to have *Ginger Coffey* and your travel pieces. I like your writing here—and in the introduction to *Coffey*—much better than in your review of my stories in *Queen's*.[1] Probably more relaxed. And you're young to be writing introductions to the New Canadian Library—congratulations. Thank you for filling me in on Aldington.[2] I daresay your study of him has involved a tremendous amount of work but it must have been interesting and I suspect you have enjoyed it....I don't wonder a bit at your being "secretly pleased" that you will probably not be returning to Canada for a while. Now is the time, when you are young, to travel—and to absorb as much as you can of other places and people to carry with you when eventually you do return. Canada, I am sure, especially the west, is changing at a fast clip but probably needs stimulus, that is to say people who can see beyond Canadian horizons. And by the way, when you *can* tell me about your project which will take you back to India, remember I am all ears.... No, my French is by no means impeccable—nor my Spanish. In fact, I'm a damned poor linguist. I thought after a year in Spain I would be getting along famously and at top speed but I still stumble and stutter and make a mess of the verbs and I still have to keep saying *despacio, por favor*.[3] Especially in Andalucia, where they "eat" their words. But wait—*another* year.

I'm afraid I never thanked you for *Saturday Night*. The December issue came and frankly I was waiting for their bill because while you had mentioned a special newsletter—at least I think that was what you said—you didn't say you had subscribed for me. Then January didn't come, and then February and March came in the same mail. I suppose in winter there aren't many boats. So now, thanks and apologies together. It is good for me, if only to be reminded that life and problems go on in the land of the Maple Leaf. Some of the articles I find don't interest me, others do. At the moment a *Saturday Night* writer—Myrna Kostash[4]—is in Barcelona to do an article on me (why oh *why*?). When I received Fulford's[5] cable—on my return from Andalucia, it had been waiting 2 weeks—I replied yes thinking it would be too late and that his writer would have gone back to Canada. I assumed somebody must be here on holiday or perhaps doing a job in London—but no, the lady came specially all the way from Toronto, which strikes me as the last word in reckless, foolish spending. We met for a long talk and dinner yesterday, are having dinner again tonight, and I think she wants to get down to brass tacks tomorrow afternoon. Can't you just hear me scintillating? That's what worries me—what I say will be so flat and dull she will be forced to dress me up a bit. After all, she was sent here to do a *story* on me....I don't get it—she says *Saturday Night* are doing a special issue on Canadian writers—well good heavens, if they give only 6 or 7 the treatment they are giving me, she says about 4,000 words, what kind of volume will it be? And if I get 4,000 why shouldn't Callaghan and MacLennan and Margaret get 8,000—to say nothing of the new writers, such as the one you mention in your letter, Dave Godfrey.[6] No indeed, a light has not yet dawned....[7]

You sound as if you are enjoying life in London. I keep thinking of indulging myself but I don't know when. I would dearly like to take a month to poke around but from some conversations I have had with English tourists it's expensive. Perhaps in September—although at the moment apartment problems are blocking the view.

Hello to Lorraine—I hope she's having a high old time since she left her job—and I don't just mean French.

Again my thanks for *Ginger Coffey* and the articles. I read—and enjoyed—*Coffey* years ago, and am looking forward to dipping into it again.

As ever,
Jim

1.   Ross is referring here to Brian Moore's novel, *The Luck of Ginger Coffey*, and to Fraser's article, "Futility at the Pump: The Short Stories of Sinclair Ross."
2.   Fraser was writing a doctoral dissertation on English poet and critic Richard Aldington, at the University of London.
3.   Slowly, please.
4.   Myrna Kostash, freelance journalist and later the author of several books, interviewed Ross in April 1972 and her article titled "Discovering Sinclair Ross: It's Rather Late" appeared in *Saturday Night* 87 (July 1972): 33–37.
5.   Robert Fulford (1932–), journalist and radio host, was editor of *Saturday Night* from 1968 until 1987.
6.   Dave Godfrey (1938–) was co-founder of Anansi Press with Dennis Lee. He won the Governor General's Award for his 1970 novel, *New Ancestors*.
7.   Ross was aware of the considerable quickening of interest in Canadian writing in the early 1970s, but could not see a public role for himself in this national literary renaissance. Although the interview with Kostash proved to be both pleasant and rewarding in terms of the publicity Ross received, he remained reluctant to accept further invitations: "CBC have suggested an interview—they would come here—but I think I will duck out. I'm just not the right material for it, I would be miserable and unhappy about it—literally in dread—for weeks—and the result would be of little or no practical use to me and would mean just a dull half-hour for the watchers" (Ross to Stouck; 20 October 1972).

To Myrna Kostash
Toronto, ON

Apartado 591, Málaga, Spain

22 October 1972

Dear Myrna:

Sorry—your letter in front of me is dated August 12, which makes me several weeks late in replying—but the new address tells at least part of the story. I hunted apartments in Barcelona this summer till I was up to the ears—everybody owns his apartment, at least in the fairly good areas, and the few that are available are expensive, so I finally, and reluctantly, made the decision to move here. Barcelona is an interesting city, and I had come to feel at home in it, but apart from the apartment problem there are other things: the weather, for instance, tending to be damp and chilly and not good at all for my ruptured disc; and the prices—it is, at least is reputed to be, the most expensive place in Spain. In any case, here I am, not yet a thorough Malagueño but, I hope, on the way.

I have an apartment right beside the sea—12th floor, the top—with a view, sea, mountains, port, which I haven't got used to yet, just can't believe. I stare and stare and go on staring. What it's going to be like in winter when there's a strong wind—and in July and August when the sun hits his stride—is something else again, but they keep putting up these buildings on the sea shore, facing south—some of them very expensive, *de lujo*[1]—so it must be what they call a "desirable location." The apartment itself is fairly satisfactory, three small rooms which seem poky (or should that be pokey) after my big room in Barcelona, with a balcony just big enough for a small table and a couple of chairs. The owner consented to take out some of his things, the worst, but I'm still campaigning for the removal of others. He's been renting it to tourists for a month or two at a time—that's what goes on in all these buildings—but he thinks a steady tenant may be a change for the better. In any case, the lease is only for a year, and by then I may want to stay or at least will know if I can do better. Incidentally, it's about $25 a month cheaper. In fact — though I sincerely hope not — finances may bring me back to Canada in a year or two. The government now takes off a straight 15% tax on non-resident incomes and in another year it's going to be 25%. And while you can live cheaply in Spain, you wouldn't want to. It's alright for a few months perhaps on a tight budget, camping out, roughing it a bit, but I'm at the age when I don't want to rough it and I want to settle in not for a just a few months but for life. There is a very narrow "middle ground" in Spain — that is, for people like me. The jump is fairly abrupt from low income to high income — and prices are going up at a fairly fast clip. Well, we'll see. In the meantime I have that view, good plumbing and hot water.

Málaga itself, after Barcelona, seems a very cluttered — pokey — little city. An impressive facade, the park and the palm-lined boulevards, and then an endless warren of rather mean streets and small shops. Restaurants not very good, at least compared with Barcelona. A few expensive ones — for tourists — and then that abrupt drop I mentioned. Not, of course, that I'm going hungry; and I'm in the habit of going a couple of times a week to Torremolinas for a meal. The round trip, including waiting for the bus, is less than an hour and costs about 33 cents, and the restaurants are countless, good — at least those I have tried — and reasonable. Competition is keen, which makes for good service. Torremolinas itself — well, it's fun to watch — and, while I haven't had time yet to browse, they seem to have good book stores. And despite its reputation, nobody has tried to persuade me to do — or buy — anything I shouldn't do or buy. Getting old is really hell! In Málaga, however, Raphael has befriended me: he shines shoes, is 34, a widower with 3 children — that, at least is his story — and he tells me confidentially he knows Málaga inside out and anything I want he can get it for me — *bueno* or *malo*,[2] just name it.

Speaking of apartments, I hope yours is working out according to expectations. I think I know what you mean about a "Mediterranean" way of living — rather unbuttoned and uninhibited. We are — I'm thinking of a typically Anglo-Saxon setting — indeed, in many things, a pack of hypocrites. And yet the Latins and Greeks — at least the

Spanish, I have been in Italy only as a tourist, up to my eyes in galleries, churches, etc.—are very, very conscious of their neighbours too. The impulse to *far buona figura*[3]—or better, perhaps, the fear that they might not *far* it—is extremely strong and to a considerable extent controls their lives. You see few in Greece under the influence of drink—in my three years I think I saw three—I don't of course mean feeling good, a bit high—a few more but not many in Spain—and yet they drink a good deal—but that fear of cutting an absurd or disgusting figure takes them home to do it. You seldom see on the streets a far-out, fairy type of homosexual, mincing and fluttering—in comparison, say, with Greenwich Village—yet they say there is a great deal of homosexuality, that it is increasing, or at least recognizing itself. But they certainly do have a greater range of gesture and voice—seem so much more alive and exuberant than ourselves. But things are changing. You can see it on any Málaga street, even the ones frequented by tourists: the older housewives out shopping, shouting, gesticulating, bunting everybody out of their way, big, ungirdled, everything hanging and shaking just as the good Lord made it; and the younger, much more self-conscious ones, carefully dressed for the outing, determined too but in a restrained, tight-lipped way. And the windowfuls of furniture, smart bathroom fixtures, cutlery, chinaware, casseroles and gadgets etc. for the kitchen, suggest that advertising has successfully introduced the demon of pride in household possessions. Too bad....My God, how I chatter when I start.

By the time this reaches you the Election will be on top of you. I read in the *Herald Tribune* that Trudeau will probably win with a small majority and that there's hell to pay about statements leaked to the papers to the effect that the program of bilingualism is a failure. Surprise! Surprise! In the midst of it all I hope the spirit of Canadian nationalism keeps going and also keeps its head. Writing, for instance—it will be a pity if Canadians start tub-thumping for Canadian books just because they are Canadian and not because they are worthy of it. On the subject of books, my warmest thanks again for your good efforts to boost me on CBC. I haven't received the September issue of *Saturday Night* and I'm bursting with curiosity to see if there were any letters about "us," but it may catch up to me yet. Barcelona has been very good forwarding things. Interested to hear you have been interviewing western farmers and have found they, too, lack a public face. Best wishes for the book on the West you are undertaking[4]—there is a great deal to be told. Just don't keep too busy with other things.

Write—at least a few lines—when you have a moment. Hello to Bill.[5]

Sincerely,
Jim

P.S. If you're interested, and are near a library, my story "The Flowers That Killed Him" is in the latest issue of the Journal of Canadian Fiction. *The journal is $2.50 a copy so I can't send it to my friends.*

1. Luxury (apartments).
2. Good or bad.
3. To cut a good figure.
4. Possibly a reference to Kostash's work on *All of Baba's Children*, a popular and highly regarded history of Ukrainian Canadians published in 1977. In her introduction to that book, however, Kostash writes that she did not begin working on her history until 1975.
5. Kostash at this time was married to news broadcaster Bill Cameron.

To Peter Pearson[1]
Toronto, ON

From Sheila Kieran[2]
Hotel Palacio, Málaga, Spain

30 November 1972

Dearest Peter,

This is a straightway attempt to get down on paper some Rossian things.

Physically, he is exactly as I thought he would be: very neatly put together, suit, not especially tanned.

We sat in the airport over Dubonnets (it seems to be my favorite airport drink) and his first questions were about you. He had met Milne,[3] had seen—and been enormously impressed with *Best Damn Fiddler* (but had, perhaps, been led to believe that it was more of a joint effort than it in fact was)—and was terribly suspicious of me. He said several times how uninterested in *As for Me and My House* he now was (a statement which turned out to be less than true as the evening progressed). He had thought I might be a journalist wanting a story and having used your name simply to see him.

We drove in the pouring rain from the airport to Málaga and Mr. Ross tried to get me a room at a smaller hotel but it was filled and we walked over here. The room is *muy grand:*[4] you come down a corridor with the w.c. (and bidet) on your right, then the bathroom, leading onto the bedroom with bed, etc. and bar! About $9 per night. My room looks over the air-conditioning unit, some ugly offices and the tower of a very old building (church, I think—will investigate later).

Mr. Ross (I know him only well enough to call him Mr. Ross) agreed that we would meet at nine, said he would be prompt (I never for a moment doubted it) and I came up here. I changed into my dress and went down to the lobby where Mr. Ross appeared—promptly at nine. It was beginning to spit rain so we agreed to eat in the hotel dining room. It's funny here—so different from Paris. There is no Spanish food on the menu, so one gets poor imitations of American or French food—on chipped plates served by a waiter whose condescending manner marks him as a maître d' of the future. Ross was terribly disappointed, but it really was fine—as we got into the wine we got chummier and, in fact, quite personal.

He looked after his mother until she died [15] years ago at the age of 82 (I've got one million pesos bet that she's the key to Mrs. Bentley); his sister died three years ago and he has a brother from whom he gets a Christmas card (he's a retired Ford plant foreman in the States). He has two nieces. He left Greece because he despaired of learning the language, speaks Spanish with a very decided accent but can make himself clearly understood and is somewhat offended if waiters address him in English. He moved from Barcelona because the weather was so bad (he has a ruptured disc in his neck), although he quite liked the city. He knows no one here but is content to read, to write, to go about.

His pension has dropped about $100 a month in the past year because of Canadian tax regulations and some decline in the Canadian dollar. He is delighted to learn that As for Me and My House has sold 40,000 in that New Canadian Library edition, though he gets only 4.5 cents per copy.

He is very fond of Whir of Gold and thinks that it would make a splendid movie ("please tell Peter"); he is working on a novel he is sure will never be published ("not at all about the prairies—it's about the thoughts of a man as he lies in a hospital, having been shot by his wife"—!).[5]

He asks, concerned not to embarrass me, whether I have ever read As for Me and My House and implores me to tell him—"not just because I'm sitting here with you but what you honestly think"—and is amazed that anyone not Protestant brought up in Prairie Saskatchewan might find anything in his book. He turns over in his mind, several times, the notion that there is a universality to his work. His lack of insight on this point is not stupid—it is clear that, as I said to him, he wrote as a man in his 30s at one level, unaware that he was touching within himself, themes of wider and more enduring significance. Therefore, his new understanding of the book's importance may, for him, be a journey inward, to discover in himself a sense of uniqueness that blends with human experience, rather than being isolated from it. (His sense of isolation must be the result of his Prairie background and is a part of the thing that Margaret Atwood is talking about, surely. I plan, incidentally, to leave *Survival* here—I know he will want it.)

He tells me something he says he hasn't told anyone else—the origin of Philip Bentley. "I was working in the bank and was quite active in a Young People's Group—I don't think I *believed* exactly, but I thought religion was a good thing—and next door lived a minister I didn't especially like. He took me aside one day and suggested that I would make a fine minister. But I never saw the church as a way out. The minister had one of those samplers in his house—it said 'As for me and my house, we will serve the Lord,' and that was how it got started. I meant the story to be from Philip's point of view—of a man who was a hypocrite, but who had the strength to understand that he was a hypocrite but not the strength to break out. But the woman kept getting in the way. People ask me how I knew so much about a woman—I just [say] 'well this is what I think she would do now'." (What follows is actually from conversation): "I don't see how you can portray Philip—in the book he isn't a character, he's a presence behind the closed study door; but how can you put that in a movie?"

Yes, sometimes he wishes he were married, though he sees himself as a man who needs to get away from people, and he enjoys his travels and is amused that others may wonder whether he wouldn't have preferred a companion. But he says, quite wistfully, that he thinks now that he would really like a son.

He doesn't smoke, doesn't drink hard liquor, but loves wine, and rations himself to a half-bottle daily. He says that he is surprisingly uninterested in what is happening in Canada—he isn't bitter and certainly doesn't feel, he says, that he had to leave because he was unappreciated ("I've never taken myself seriously enough as a writer to believe that"). But he says, at another time, that he follows all the *Herald Tribune* stories about Canada with great interest.

Every once in a while, the writer-observer peeps through his mild exterior: in the taxi from the airport, passing a church—"The people here now just ignore the Church; they say 'Yes, I believe in God, but I'm not interested in the church or in priests.' They're Protestants and just don't know it," he says with a smile.

At supper a quite hilarious description of getting mixed up with a Turkish basketball team in the Athens airport. ("They had been playing in the Bulgarian league and had just lost and so were going home.") Descriptions of "one tall, dark, curly-haired young man" after another. "Pretty soon," he says, "they surrounded me like a teepee."

1 December, 1972

Mr. Ross came at eleven and we went to a sidewalk cafe on one of the squares near the hotel. There was an awning but the sun came down, and was quite warm. In front of the poles separating the cafe from the street were orange trees with oranges on them. Mr. Ross said they were bitter, were never eaten but simply swept away when they ripened and fell, in about three weeks.

Afterward, we walked along a lovely avenue of plane trees and palms, with gardens and poinsettia trees to our right. I took some pictures and wanted one of Mr. Ross, but he has a horror of being photographed and I didn't press. Then we walked over and caught a bus to Torremolinas, about 10 miles away....[letter abridged at this point]

[In the evening] we went off to La Algeria, a pleasant little restaurant....Our first toast, in excellent Spanish wine—*Sangre des Torros*—, was "to our absent host" and we got slightly and pleasantly smashed together again. He asked me to call him by his first name, which is Jim (he thought Sinclair, his middle name, was distinctive for writing, but it's not a name he especially likes and he never uses it in personal contacts).

...He has all kinds of story ideas floating around: the man who is in hospital after being shot by his wife is in the psycho ward. "He's a nut; he has these dreams—they don't mean anything. They're not about his mother; they're about his father and his brother, but he won't tell them to the psychiatrist because they're out to get him and he knows that it's better to lie. He's an artist; his brother is a big lawyer married

to a woman with a million and the artist's pictures are causing a
scandal and the brother wants him shut up. They're a series of pictures
called '[Disasters] of Peace'—you know, El Greco did '[Disasters] of
War.'...I wonder if you can get across the idea of someone who feels
that everyone is against him? It's really about the artist, about how he
is shut out of society and of how society tries to get rid of him. I don't
imagine it will ever be published.

"I would like to write Philip's diary. I'd like to write the story of
a marriage—his diary on one page and hers on another. I think my
next project will be the story of a doctor.[6] He's 75 years old and they're
opening a new hospital and it's the opening ceremony; it's his thoughts
and the thoughts of the people who come, as well as what they say. He's
a good man and he came to this town 50 years ago because he believed
that he could do some good. He knows that sometimes he's been bitter
or spiteful; the difficult thing is that there wouldn't be any suspense; at
the end, the evening would just be over.

"I have another idea; a young doctor comes to take this man's place
and he falls in love with a woman, an English war bride who's now in
her forties.[7] She gets worried that people will find out and she murders
him. I have some very good ideas for it. That woman and her husband
would be among the people in the book about the old doctor.

"I'm tired of naturalistic writing" (from an earlier conversation;
"I didn't finish *Five Legs*,[8] I couldn't understand it"). "I'd like to try and
do the kind of thing Graeme Gibson has done, though maybe not so
complicated. I feel that a book should be accessible to people."

We got into politics, and he knows Mitchell Sharp[9]—interesting
because he looks like a slightly greyer carbon of Mr. Sharp. "How is his
wife—I always thought she was such a dull woman, nice but not exciting,
and I wondered how she got along with all that's involved in his job."

...By eleven Jim and I were solemnly assuring each other that we
didn't seem tight "though you seem a little," he said. "You're sort of
holding yourself in." At eleven-thirty we went back to my hotel for final
farewells. (I knew that he would want to sleep late and that it would be
burdensome for him to have to haul me out to the airport, etc. Besides,
if I were having passport trouble, it was urgent that he not be around.

Back we went; he admired my room. He had mentioned earlier in the day that he admired Jungian psychiatry. I took three books with me to Spain—*Survival* to give him and the two Davies books. I don't suppose I have ever given a gift away before, but I thought you would be pleased and I knew that he would enjoy them, *The Manticore* especially, so I gave him all three books.

I want to send him my extra copy of *Shrug*;[10] he would also be interested in Mr. Pearson's biography. He likes impressionist paintings; his mother's name was Catherine (sometimes called Katie) and he will be 65 on January 22.

"May I tell you the story of my birth? there were times, you know, when my mother didn't see another woman for two months; my father sometimes had to take produce to an Indian reserve 70 miles to the north and he would be gone a week.[11] Anyway, my father went to get the midwife, a half-breed named Mary Bell.[12] My parents were teetotallers, though they kept some brandy for 'medicinal purposes.' Anyway, when Mary Bell arrived, my mother asked would she like a hot toddy. My father went out to feed the animals and when he got back, Mary Bell was out stiff on the floor. So I came into the world unassisted."

He left me a copy of a magazine called *The Journal of Canadian Fiction*, published in NB, which recently carried a story of his called "The Flowers That Killed Him." I read it last night; it's the story of a boy at his father's funeral, reflecting on the fact that his two closest friends have recently been sexually assaulted and murdered. (You see there is a very dark side to the man.) I know you didn't care for *Whir of Gold* ("I would say," he said, "that it's not good, but it's got some good things in it")—though I didn't tell Jim that. It may be that this man—everyone's bank clerk uncle—had one good story in him, and that one a masterpiece. Who knows? It certainly is more than most of us have. I just can't tell; I'll have to read *Whir of Gold* when I get back.

I saw very little of Málaga, as you can tell. I went, after all, to see the man, not the place.

Sheila

1. Filmmaker and television producer Peter Pearson took out an option on *As for Me and My House* in 1970 and hired novelist Graeme Gibson to prepare a screenplay from the novel. Kate Reid was tentatively signed to play Mrs. Bentley. Pearson's National Film Board feature, *The Best Damn Fiddler from Calabogie to Kaladar*, won numerous national and international awards in 1969–1970, as would a second feature, *Paperback Hero*, in 1973. In 1972 he was in the gruelling process of trying to raise money for the filming of *As for Me and My House*.

2. Writer Sheila Kieran, a writer and divorced mother of seven, was a close friend of Peter Pearson and broke from a trip to Paris to see if she could locate and interview the reclusive author of *As for Me and My House*. Her ten-page account of her visit to Málaga is abridged here, omitting her account of shopping in nearby Torremolinos and further travel plans.

3. Gilbert Milne was a co-producer of the film project.

4. Very big.

5. A reference to an unpublished ms titled "The Disasters of Peace," referred to in more detail later in this letter.

6. Ross outlines here the main idea for *Sawbones Memorial*.

7. This is the plot for "Price above Rubies," a sequel to *Sawbones Memorial* that was never published.

8. Graeme Gibson's *Five Legs* was published in 1969 by Anansi Press and was regarded as an experimental novel.

9. Mitchell Sharp (1911–2004) was a cabinet minister in successive Liberal governments from 1963 to 1976. He was married to Daisy Boyd, his first wife, from 1938 to 1975.

10. Kieran here refers to Walter Stewart's 1971 political study titled *Shrug: Trudeau in Power*. Ross was favourably impressed by Trudeau, chiefly for his insistence that government should have no jurisdiction in the bedroom.

11. Peter Ross would take bags of oats and other food supplies to the reserve at Lac La Ronge and bring back furs.

12. Her full name was Mary Belle Clifford.

Ross in retirement, Málaga, Spain, c. 1973. [Private collection; Ross private papers]

To Sheila Kieran

Toronto, ON

11 January 1973

Dear Sheila:

I have your interesting and generously long letter of December 31 — it
puts me to shame — and first of all let me say I did acknowledge *Mike*.[1]
Just a card, but I sent it the same day or the next. I gather you haven't
received it as you say you would like to know what was my response to
Fifth Business and *The Manticore* and in the card I mentioned them, briefly
but with enthusiasm.[2] In fact I found them brilliant and engrossing and,
as I think I also said in the card, I can't wait for the third.

I am amazed that Robertson Davies should remember me. I met
him only once at a luncheon with half a dozen or so U of T professors
when *As for Me...* was first published, almost 32 years ago. E.J. Pratt,
Northrop Frye, Earle Birney, a Dr. Brown (I think E.K.) — their names
meant absolutely nothing to me, I just munched and mumbled. So
raw, hickish, tongue-tied and generally impossible a guest of honour
perhaps made the occasion memorable. How it came about, Dr. Roy
Daniells (Intro to *As for Me...*) knew I was coming to Toronto and said
you must look up Dr. Brown, Victoria College, and gave me a letter of
introduction. Dr. Brown was very interested in Canadian writing, etc.
etc. Fine, except for one funny little hitch at the beginning: someone
directed me to the office of the wrong Dr. Brown, who turned out to
be a Doctor of Divinity, United Church. But he was geniality itself, and
rising to the moment told his secretary to order a copy of the book at
once, then called the right Dr. Brown who arranged the luncheon.[3] I
often wondered if he, the wrong Dr. Brown, read the book, and if so
what he thought of the hypocritical and adulterous Philip...If you see
Robertson Davies again say Hello for me, Saskatchewan style, and tell
him I read his books with unbounded pleasure and admiration. How I
wish I could do it!

Yes, I can understand what the death of Lester Pearson must have
meant to you. Even to me, who never saw the man except on TV, it
was a jar and a wrench, especially as I was reading *Mike* and he was

emerging from the book so warm and alive. A pleasant, easy style, completely lacking pretentiousness.

As to the film of *As for Me*—it's disappointing of course.[4] And just when I was beginning to think the cat must be in the bag! A few days ago I had a letter from a friend in Toronto congratulating me: he had seen in the *Star* that the money was available and that they were going ahead. You say the Govt. of Sask. may be interested—again I can only hope and cross my fingers. It's all out of my hands. Some time, I suppose, I shall hear from Oro films.[5]

Thank you again for your staunch interest in my contract problems.[6] Yes, I need and want a lawyer's opinion, but I am letting it lie for the present, as it looks now as if I may be coming to New York before long, perhaps March, and I will fly up to Toronto for 2 or 3 days.[7]

What an unpleasant experience to lose your passport—or to think you had lost it. It hasn't happened to me yet—touch wood—but I am always relieved when I get it back. Once, after I had mine, someone else's was handed to me along with my key. They put them in the wrong pigeonhole—that's probably what happened with yours.

Your job as a TV producer sounds interesting but 65–80 hours a week is too much, especially when you have a family to look after. But of course you like it, and that's more than half the battle. Wonderful weather the last 2 weeks—65 & 70F—they're sunbathing and swimming. From my balcony I survey the scene sometimes with binoculars, but seldom discover anything to cause a tumult in the glands (sour grapes!).

Sincerely,
Jim

---

1. Ross is referring here to *Mike: The Memoirs of the Right Honourable Lester B. Pearson*, the first volume of which was published in 1972, the year of the former prime minister's death.

2. In that undated Christmas card note, he also wrote: "In poise and elegance and acumen [Davies] seems to me to be head and shoulders above any other Canadian novelist."

3. The lunch took place the next day at Hart House.

4. Wood Gundy had withdrawn its financial backing for Peter Pearson's projected film of *As for Me and My House*.

5. Oro Films was the name of Peter Pearson's company that made both industrial and commercial films.

6. In a letter to Kieran dated 30 November 1972, Ross complained bitterly (as he had done during their meeting in Málaga) of the treatment he had received from McClelland & Stewart over the publication of *Whir of Gold*. He resented the fact that the Toronto publishers had world rights to the novel and had written themselves in as exclusive agents, while giving the novel a poor production and ignoring a "movie bite" for more than four months. He wanted a new contract for *Whir of Gold* and considered withdrawing *As for Me and My House*, to which he retained copyright, if McClelland & Stewart was not willing to co-operate.

7. There is no evidence that Ross ever made this proposed trip to North America in 1973.

To Margaret Atwood[1]

Alliston, ON

15 January 1973

Dear Margaret Atwood:

Survival—to say nothing of the inscription—is not just flattering, it's out and out rejuvenating. I feel I have shed at least ten of my sixty-five years. As the effects may not be permanent, couldn't you do it again?

On the subject of age, Mrs. Bentley made her first dowdy and somewhat wind-blown bow almost 32 years ago—February 14, 1941, to be exact—an ironic date, considering her barren and frustrated years with Philip. How right you are in *Survival* when, speaking of the baby, you say, "If they think *that's* going to save their marriage they're crazy." It surprises me she holds her own this well. There seems to be a little clock ticking away on her table—or is it in Philip's study—and gratifyingly every so often someone comes along to wind it up again.

I must confess I don't know "Margaret Atwood." But then, *Survival* and Fulford's *Read Canadian*[2] bring home to me how few I know; I'm nothing short of a disgrace to the maple leaf. This morning, however, as one small step in the right direction, I am ordering *Surfacing* from a Toronto bookstore. It had better be good!

My warmest thanks for your gesture.

Sincerely,
Sinclair Ross

1.   In the fall of 1972 Margaret Atwood sent Ross a copy of *Survival: A Thematic Guide to Canadian Literature* in which his work is praised for its incisive portrayal of Canadian themes and values. This letter to Atwood is the first of at least seven Ross wrote to her in the mid-1970s.

2.   *Read Canadian: A Book about Canadian Books* was edited by Robert Fulford, David Godfrey, and Abraham Rotstein. Although the selections have not stood the test of time especially well, *Read Canadian* is notable as one of the publications that marked the ascendance of Canadian nationalism in the early 1970s.

From Sheila Kieran

Toronto, ON
1 March 1973

Dear Jim:

By now you will have received a mysterious parcel of books from the Book Cellar. If you have divined the identity of the sender, you will know that your mother was right—that you should never have taken the first step on the road of accepting gifts from strange ladies. What happened is that I simply cannot enter that bookstore without thinking "Jim would enjoy that," or "Jim probably won't enjoy that but he should at least see it." In any event I hope that the selection gave you some amusing moments.

Without wishing to gush, I can only term the news that you might visit here electrifying. Please let me know as soon as possible when or if you are coming. I do not wish to impinge on your sense of privacy, and I am painfully aware that mine is not the most serene of households.

However, I have several unoccupied bedrooms and you know that you are most welcome to use them at any time. I assure you that this would not embroil you in the horrors of houseguestery which, I know, would be painful and awkward for us both. I do not wish to make you the centrepiece of a cocktail party, I have no desire to exhibit you on the hoof to my neighbours, relations, friends or creditors—though I think you know that I consider you a most dashing fellow. I simply wish to be as helpful as I can; you would, perhaps, allow me the pleasure of making a quiet supper one night for you, Peter, and perhaps Graeme Gibson, if you are in the mood. I look forward to hearing your plans.

I have decided to return to France and assignments from *Chatelaine* have made it possible for me to go ahead with definite plans. I arrive Paris May 7th and, if Madame Vanier will see me, so that I can do a story about a village she and her son run for the disturbed and retarded,[1] I will go to that village, some 60 kilometres from Paris on May 10th. On May 16th I go to Lyons to eat in the restaurants there, about which I have heard so much. Since my return I have become friendly with a very fine lady who is a native of St. Jen de Luz where she still owns a house. She has invited me to use the house and I expect to be in St. Jen de Luz from about the 16th to the 21st of May. I will then go back to Paris and I leave May 29th. I am wondering if there is any chance that you might find your way northward in May. As you know, St. Jen is just about a block and a half from Spain.

Peter's new movie will not be released until the late spring, but those who have seen it—I have seen two or three reels—have raved about it.[2] The Americans in it are singing Peter's praises O.T. in the big bad movie world. In the meantime he wanders through our lives as always—cranky, ineffably kind and dear.

I did an interview with Robertson Davies and he was genuinely moved at your generous appraisal of his work. You will be delighted to know that your sense of his two recent books is nothing less than prescient—although *Fifth Business* was written to stand alone and *The Manticore* was meant to be the end, Davies has a work in progress, to be published in 1975 which will complete what has become a trilogy.[3] Last Sunday there was a review of some books on Jung written by Davies and it is good to know that he is established among the literary mafia in New York.

I bought another dozen copies of *As for Me and My House* and have given them to various friends. One young woman of 30, veteran of a maimed marriage, returned her copy saying the book was so true and so painful that she could not finish it. I think about our dinner at the hotel and wonder again if you know the power, after all these years, of your own mind and creativity.

I look forward most affectionately to hearing from you and with mounting excitement to seeing you, either here this month or in Europe in May.

Sheila

1. Jean Vanier (1928–), son of Pauline Vanier and Georges Vanier (Governor General of Canada, 1959–1967), is a philosopher and theologian who established a series of homes for handicapped men in France and in other parts of the world.
2. Pearson's *Paperback Hero* is the film referred to here.
3. The third book in the Deptford trilogy is *World of Wonders*.

To David Stouck
Simon Fraser University, Burnaby, BC
19 March 1973

Dear David Stouck:
The date on your letter embarrasses me: December 21. Good intentions but something always gets in the way. This winter, for one thing, I haven't been very well—a severe and prolonged attack of the 'flu which I couldn't throw off. The old machine is gradually wearing out—one of the signs is the time it takes to recover from an illness or for a cut to heal. Still not much energy or ambition, but next week hoping it will rouse me a little, I'm going to Morocco. Two or three weeks, depending

on how I like it and how I feel. Perhaps the mosques and camels and snake charmers will have a rejuvenating effect—one can at least hope.

You write with enthusiasm of Willa Cather and I must confess I don't know her—only *Death Comes for the Archbishop*, many years ago, and the much anthologized "Paul's Case." But I am putting her on my list—a long one—for I find that the way a book is written is for me as important—often more so—as the story or material. It's bad form to talk of other writers when one is trying to write oneself—especially other Canadian writers—but between ourselves I have never been able to appreciate Morley Callaghan because of his style.[1] I suppose he knows exactly what he is doing, what effects he wants, but to me he is "flat." I must be wrong, so many good critics praise him; it's just that to me there's something lacking...However, on the subject of Willa Cather, just let me wish you luck in finding a publisher for your essays. I hope some day to read them.

As to my story "The Flowers That Killed Him," I hung my head and stood two hours in the corner when your letter came. For yes—horrible confession—I meant it to be taken seriously. I was trying to put across the ambivalence of the boy's feelings towards his father—a dislike of his father which went a long way back, reinforced by a sense of something wrong, unhealthy, together with a kind of pity and loyalty. The way he brought off the "execution" was a form of loyalty, so no one would know—although you might contend it was to spare himself and his mother as well. It is salutary to know how far one can be out: I meant the boy's "flat," unemotional way of telling the story to suggest a tremendous amount of repressed emotion. There are bits scattered here and there which I thought would serve as chinks through which the light would shine—but it adds up to what I feared when I began: patricide needs a Dostoevsky.[2]

On the subject of my morbid streak, I received a letter recently from a student in an Ontario university which was both interesting and alarming. The story "One's a Heifer"—what was in the stall? His instructor had ridiculed him in class for his small-boy body-in-the-barn interpretation, and into the bargain told the class that anyone giving that interpretation on an examination paper she was setting would receive zero...What *was* in the stall?

Speaking of writers and appearances, lectures, etc., I suppose to a considerable extent it depends on one's personality and gifts, but I am sure that I am better out of the public eye. I also feel you are right when you say it must use up a great deal of energy—it must at least take the edge off the "urgency" to speak your piece. *Saturday Night* sent a writer last spring to interview me and I found it a rather upsetting experience, even though the poor girl was very easy with me. At sixty-five it's much too late to try blossoming into a public personality. Since then I have had four invitations to be interviewed and turned them down—it's awkward, for I suppose they want to give me a boost. But I can't help saying at my age why make what's left of life miserable?

In a quiet, small way I keep working, although what I'm embarked on now is something in the nature of an experiment—at least for me—and I'm not sure what it will amount to—if anything. I'm using very plain material—I'm sure you could call it pure prairie corn—but it's the method of presenting it which interests me. Dialogue and some stream-of-consciousness musings—not a word of connective tissue, not a single "he said" or "she looked out the window"—nobody introduced, situations and characters established by the dialogue. Fairly short—no suspense, of course. I don't know, but I see possibilities for exploring a number of situations if I could develop the method. Yes, I know—I keep telling myself—sixty-five is not the age for experiment—but absurd as it must sound, there are things I would like to say and as yet I haven't found the way to say them...Well, at least it keeps me from spending too much time seated with a glass in a sidewalk cafe. Which is where I have just come from—a glorious day, the sun strong but not yet with a sting—the Mediterranean as blue as it's supposed to be.

I was very pleased to have your letter, and look forward to another when you have a little spare time. And I keep my fingers crossed for the book of Cather essays.

Sincerely
Jim Ross

P.S. Regarding your article "The Canadian Imagination," I didn't mean to criticize your referring to my short stories as "less effective." Heavens no—but none the less I appreciate your troubling to make the change.

1. In conversation Ross made the same observations about Hugh MacLennan's writing. Callaghan and MacLennan were the pre-eminent writers in his time, enjoying both critical and popular success.

2. Ross is most likely thinking here about *The Brothers Karamazov* by Fyodor Dostoevsky (1821–1881), which he admired and read at least twice.

To Margaret Atwood

Alliston, ON

7 May 1973

Dear Margaret Atwood:

I took *The Edible Woman*[1] with me on a recent trip to Morocco and read it in Marrakech. Unfair, I know—all the distracting local colour, snake charmers, camels, couscous—but the lady took the competition in her stride and came home fit and hungry—ravening, in fact, for a thick, juicy, underdone steak.

Alerted by the Introduction to what an important book I had in my hands, its subtleties, different levels of meaning etc., I began somewhat apprehensively—would I be up to it?—but after a few pages, Klinck-Dawe to the winds,[2] I was just turning the pages and having a whale of a time. The only time I wasn't having a whale of a time was when I was biting my nails with envy. Brilliant, witty, devastating—it's hard to avoid the reviewers' adjectives. There are so many "good bits" that will stay with me—such as "Peter never shed or shone in the wrong places," and the poor businessmen who hurried through their lunch in order to hurry through their work, etc. I admire—the word is "envy"—the deft ease with which you handle surface. Surface alone, of course, is only surface, but when you have control of so many other things it gives you enormous range. You can practically take on anything.

My only complaint, a small one, is that while Marian's behaviour is extreme, her circumstances are not. In fact, even by North American standards, she is a fortunate, well-equipped young woman. Attractive (otherwise Peter wouldn't have been interested), intelligent, a university education (granted that I, who had to struggle like hell to get through Grade XI,[3] am perhaps inclined to give too much importance to a BA, but even though it may not open social and economic doors—is that the only reason young people go after [degrees]?—it should open a few windows), emancipated (no religious or moral scruples, for instance, about sex), on her own, no responsibilities, no family peering over her shoulder—in other words, at least it seems to me, she does have alternatives. She is not trapped in her job with S.S. She doesn't have to ricochet from Peter to Duncan. She could have sent Ainsley packing and not taken so long to clean the Frigidaire. Peter and Seymour and their kind do indeed cast long menacing shadows across today's wasteland, but Marian, because of her assets and equipment, is one of the fortunate few with a fair chance of holding her own with them. (All right, tell me to go jump in a bullring. You recognize, no doubt, the inner directed, pre-Depression voice of an old man: Don't just stand there, *do* something!) Valid or not, however—and I am more than ready to believe I may not be completely or properly tuned in on the modern predicament; it's just that it seems to me a severely limited range of choice has always been part of the human predicament—it doesn't matter, for while reading I was "with" Marian, sharing her horror, running from Peter; it was only after I had closed the book I began to think maybe a good swift boot or two wouldn't do the young lady any harm. ("These young people today don't know they're born—if they'd had to go through" etc. etc.)

One of the things about *Surfacing*[4] that impressed me—not the most important—is your feeling for nature, or better, your sympathy with nature. From a reading of *EW* I could believe the author was city born and bred, who would think of nature in terms of a weekend at a resort, with perhaps ten or fifteen minutes for a sunset and appropriate stirrings of the soul, but you present nature, instead, in its raw, cold, sometimes voracious reality. And of course it matches the drama wonderfully; it's just there, just revealed, just right, not arranged for effect.

As to the drama itself—frankly, I haven't altogether sorted out my responses: I will just say I accepted her descent—went down with her, in fact—better than I did her surfacing. The descent, it seems to me, is a stripping away of everything right down to primitive essentials; I found it frightening and couldn't shake it off...A remarkable novel; a little later I intend to read it again. Both of them for that matter. You write very well indeed, with authority and power. I look forward to the next one.

Sincerely,
Sinclair Ross

P.S. I intend to move on to Margaret Atwood's poetry. I have been reading the few poems in the recent Oxford Anthology—see what you've done to me. Ordering today.

1. *The Edible Woman* was Atwood's first novel, published in 1969.
2. Carl F. Klinck (1908–1990) was a leading critic of Canadian literature in the early years of the discipline. Alan Dawe of Vancouver wrote the introduction to the 1973 New Canadian Library edition of *The Edible Woman*, praising it as a "rare dish" and describing it as a book about keeping one's "sanity and humanity in the plastic and over-packaged world" of the mid-twentieth century. Ross liked *The Edible Woman* best of all the Atwood novels he read, particularly its range of humour from the slapstick to the satirical.
3. Ross was at the top of his high school class in Indian Head, Saskatchewan, so this modest statement is not exactly true. Perhaps more accurately he is recalling the struggle to make ends meet that year, specifically the expense of room and board in town while his mother was working as a housekeeper on a farm in Abbey.
4. Ross ordered a copy of Atwood's 1972 novel *Surfacing* from a Canadian bookstore in January 1973, but was sent another copy of *Survival* instead. He wrote to Atwood 13 March 1973: "In their note apologizing for the error they write 'Survival, Survival, Survival—these days it seems to be nothing but Survival'."

To John Moss[1]

University of New Brunswick, Fredericton, NB

15 May 1973

Dear John:

I am sorry—I should have acknowledged your article long ago but as usual I have been letting things get in the way. For one thing (remember you said I should go, you're responsible) I went to Morocco for 18 days, Tanger, Rabat, Marrakech, Fez, and then, just a day or two after returning, I suffered a fairly severe spasm in my damned neck which kept me busy for another couple of weeks exercising and feeling sorry for myself; then an English couple here with their car suggested a few days in Seville[2]—and I'm just back.

And now your essay:[3] I have been through it twice, the second time slowly and carefully, doubling back sometimes—agreeing and disagreeing. I am of course fascinated that you should think of it developing in the way a musical composition develops. I had never thought of that, and can only say I didn't plan its structure: it's a long time ago but it seems to me it just grew. I did my best to get inside Mrs. B. and just let her carry on—does that sound stupid? I do remember, very distinctly, thinking "I'm writing this blind," just as a pilot sometimes flies blind, for I was trying to *be* Mrs. B, to enter emotionally into a situation in which I had never been. However, there are contradictions: I say I let her carry on but of course I did select, to some extent I did exercise control—I must have, although I don't remember how much—and certainly I knew where I was going. In any case, to attempt at this time to capture my state of mind—or mindlessness—while writing would not be very helpful. In fact the seriousness with which you and others take the book might tempt me into deluding myself that I did write with artistic intentions etc, knew exactly what I was doing, and I think it better that I do not put on my best clothes and "rise" to being the author of a book about which some good things are being said. Much better to keep in the background.

I will say, however, that I felt, and still feel, much more sympathy for Mrs. B. than you do. You accuse her of being mean, petty, bitchy, possessive, vicious, waspish—her whimsy acid—and I feel inclined to rear up and say yes, but you, the reader, know these things about her only because *she* tells you. E.g. page 178[4]—"because it had been such a humiliating afternoon I played brilliantly, vindictively—to let Philip see how easily I could take Steve away from him." It seems to me that after a humiliating afternoon it is not surprising she would have an impulse to retaliate—she is very human, neither she nor I pretend she is a saint—and she is honest and big enough to admit her vindictiveness—which, human nature being what it is, human propensity for self-deception being what it is, is surely a mark in her favour. Moreover, is the confession itself not to some extent cleansing? And page 180, last sentence: she is not *spying* on Philip and Judith in the morbid sense of wanting to watch them. She wants desperately to reassure herself that he is not with her—something entirely different—and myself I do not lose sympathy for her in the least that she should be "driven" to this rather than sit at home in a "state of righteous dignity." You say "the wretched demeanour of a creature lost in the world." I cannot agree with that. I would say a primitive creature, ready to brush aside conventional behaviour when it is in her way—behaviour and thinking. "Righteous dignity" is the last thing for her. She discusses it in another place: she is wronged, she has her rights, but what good would it do her to insist on them? Page 176, at the bottom you speak of her cynical arrogance—well, not to me. Relief, yes, and certainly we don't admire her here—it is one place where indeed she is not a saint—but remember she loves Philip, however much you may deplore her way of loving him, and Judith is the "other woman." Here she is a *terrible* woman—terrible in the real meaning of the word. She is naked—honestly, ruthlessly, terribly naked, but she is not cynical. Arrogant, perhaps: but is not every woman fighting or scheming for the man she loves arrogant in the sense that she believes she and only she is the right woman for him? Tears at this time for the poor sweet girl—oh, what a shame—would they not be suspect? How many women in such circumstances would be able to rise to genuine magnanimity? Perhaps I have a poor opinion of humanity but it seems to me that—with exceptions, of course—people just aren't made that way.

I suppose it is unfair of me to say these things for as the author I cannot help speaking with some authority and I may cause you some concern. Just let me say that while I disagree in these places I am more than willing to concede that your interpretation may be valid and that writing as I no doubt did from the unconscious I may have said, or let slip, more than I knew. And of course, on page 182 you say your purpose has not been to reveal the whole of her character...but only those characteristics which create ironic tension etc.

And in many places I do agree, for instance, how alone she is, and that her possessiveness has helped embitter their relationship. What amazes—and gratifies—me is that after all these years you and others should be still interested in and concerned about her. Whatever kind of woman she is, I suppose I can conclude that at least she is very much alive. As to the larger significance of the book—you use such terms as cosmic dimensions—and I can only withdraw, somewhat puzzled, almost with a guilt feeling that I have slipped something over on you, since to me it is just a small, quiet, ordinary story, about two unhappy people. It is not for me to comment on the cosmic irony implicit in the book or Ross's vision. In fact, the last few years I have had the feeling the book has slipped away from me and gone its own way.

These are rather mixed-up, incoherent remarks, I'm afraid—an attempt to be honest plus the recognition that you may see better than I do. I don't like to use the word grateful, although I suppose it is approximately the right one.

Sometime let me know if you have plans for or hopes of publication. It is an impressive piece of writing and I would like to read the whole of it—I gather I am one of five authors discussed.[5] I assume Sir George Williams is, academically speaking, a step in the right direction and I offer my congratulations and good wishes.[6]

Sincerely,
Jim

P.S. As I read this over, it occurs to me that over the past 32 years I have very seldom felt impelled to speak up on behalf of Mrs. B. It's usually "That terrible

Philip—what a life for the poor woman," and my reply, even though not spoken is "Think of the poor man with her always waiting outside the study door, fixed on him." In other words, my basic sympathies are with him.[7] It was intended to be his story, filtered through her, and of course possessive so-and-so that she is, she took over. But I am not contradicting myself: I still have a great deal of sympathy for her too. She, in a way, is trapped as much as he is.

1. John Moss (1940–) was a graduate student completing a PHD in Canadian literature at the University of New Brunswick. He would eventually become a professor of English at the University of Ottawa, where he organized the Sinclair Ross Symposium held in April 1990. A correspondence with Ross was initiated when Moss wrote on 12 October 1971 inviting him to contribute a story to the *Journal of Canadian Fiction*, a new mix of fiction and criticism edited by Moss, David Arnason, and John R. Sorfleet. Ross's "The Flowers That Killed Him" appeared in the first issue.

2. The identity of this couple has not been determined, although they were likely friends that Ross made in London during the war.

3. Moss's essay on *As for Me and My House* formed part of his popular study, *Patterns of Isolation in English-Canadian Fiction*, 149–65.

4. The page numbers Ross cites refer to Moss's essay, which at this stage was a PHD dissertation chapter.

5. *Patterns of Isolation* is actually divided into three parts and the second part, "The Geophysical Imagination," in which the essay on *As for Me and My House* appears, includes discussion of Thomas Raddall's *The Nymph and the Lamp*, Ethel Wilson's *Swamp Angel*, Sheila Watson's *The Double Hook*, and Charles Bruce's *The Channel Shore*.

6. Moss began his teaching career at Sir George Williams University (now Concordia) in September 1973.

7. This view is perhaps best expressed in a letter from Ross to Mrs. Irene Fowlie, a graduate student at University of Calgary, where he writes: "I have a fairly good opinion of Philip. So far as I am concerned it is *his* story. I thought it might be effective having her tell it, only she took over. But to me it is his basic decency and honesty which makes him so aloof and sour and difficult. He hates himself because he has worked himself into a false position—and self-contempt and a feeling of guilt in turn...." The letter breaks off at this point. Only page 1 of this letter has survived with Ross's papers.

To Keath Fraser
University of Calgary, AB
28 June 1973

Dear Keath:

As you know by this time, procrastination is my middle name. I put off answering your first letter from India—you gave me an address—until it was too late, and your card about three weeks ago brought me up with a jolt to how the time flies. What a wonderful trip it must have been, and how envious I am. I hope you are writing it up for publication. It is a part of the world I would dearly like to see myself, but taking into consideration my years and infirmities, it is hardly likely I will ever make it. I was in Morocco this spring for three weeks—all very tame, good trains, comfortable hotels—and even that pretty well exhausted me. It was all fascinating, incidentally, but I felt terribly "excluded"—they are such "professional" beggars for one thing; they don't leave you the slightest illusion that they are interested in anything but your money—and I suppose the fact that they are Mohammedan also has something to do with it. I sometimes had the feeling that while it made no difference to me it did to them. However, despite the frustrations—it's hard to get around on your own and I don't like groups—I may try again next year if I'm here. I came away with feeling that if I could penetrate their world it would be wonderful.[1]

And Richard Aldington? Satisfactorily disposed of once and for all? Writing about your travels will certainly be a change and I daresay something of a relief—you can relax a bit. It must be terrible writing a dissertation and weighing every word and phrase with the Board of Examiners or whatever they are called in mind. India is not overdone in the travel magazines and I am curious to know if you are thinking of using your material commercially—I mean not a university publication. A magazine such as *Holiday*, for instance—but then, you don't need me to make suggestions, and in any case I wish you success with it.

On the subject of writing, I am at work myself on a short novel which I hope to have ready to submit to the publishers this fall. Something of an experiment—at least for me—in technique—and in places, style too—and I rather think it will be booted back to me fast. But I've enjoyed doing it and it's gone fairly fast—again I add "for me." I woke up with something of a surprised and pleased start not so long ago to realize that publishers are bringing out very short novels—100 pages—these days, and I rather think that is "my" length. A number of critics and reviewers have said I am really a short story writer and I think they are *partly* right—I have the wind for a novella. The difference between 250 pages and 125 pages is not 125—it's getting over the hump and then flogging myself for the rest of the way. We'll see—I have several ideas which I think would work out at about 125 pages.

This spring I read Margaret Atwood's two novels *The Edible Woman* and *Surfacing*—an enormous talent, I would say, especially when you consider her poetry as well. At the moment I have *The Journals of Susanna Moodie*² and I am so impressed I intend ordering some of the others...I am also reading right now *Booze* by Gray—a very different kind of Canadian author but first rate. This one and *The Winter Years* have shown me how much I don't know about Canada—how many Canadian novels *haven't* been written.³

Perhaps I'll be in London this fall—the pressure—within me—keeps mounting. Although a recent two week trip to Madrid, Burgos and Salamanca—I am just back—makes me realize how little of Spain I know—even though I'd been in some of the places before...The number of tourists this year seems down a bit—monetary problems, I suppose. Just the other day I read an article in a Spanish paper which cautiously admitted not that the number was down but that it was less than anticipated—so there's no harm hoping that within the year the government will devalue the peseta.

Let me say again how much I enjoyed your "Indian" letters—I've read and re-read them, always, as I say with envy. Return good for evil and drop me a few lines about yourselves before long, and have a good summer...Hi, Lorraine, how do you like being in purdah?

As *ever*,
Jim

1. Ross gave Myrna Kostash a similar but slightly more detailed account of his trip in a letter dated 27 June 1973. There he writes: "I was in Morocco this spring, Tangiers, Rabat, Marrakech, and Fez, and found it both fascinating and frustrating....The things you want to see are nearly all in the *medinas* or old quarters where you are hopelessly lost after twenty paces—not only the maze of streets and lanes but the pushing, pulling crowd. They warn you it's dangerous and it probably is. Myself, all I encountered—everywhere—were beggars; literally by the hundred, who don't just put out their hand but encircle you, pull at your clothes, and *follow*—there's no escape. Your coins are soon gone...it's just a struggle to make your way out.... Many of the children very beautiful—fine bone structure—I suppose it's typically Arabic—and big black 'liquid' eyes."

2. This book of poems by Atwood published in 1970 recreates the life of the Ontario pioneer from a specifically twentieth-century perspective. It has remained one of Atwood's most highly praised books.

3. James Gray (1906–1998) was a journalist and historian who wrote several popular books about western Canadian history including *The Winter Years* (1966) about the Great Depression, *Red Light on the Prairies* (1971) about prostitution, and *Booze* (1972), focussing on the whiskey trade. Ross was reading these books, he explains in his 27 June 1973 letter to Kostash, as background for the novella he was writing (*Sawbones Memorial*). To Kostash he writes "I have been working myself the last six months on a short novel...which slips back and forth over a town and district in Saskatchewan for fifty years and a great many times questions came up which I couldn't answer to my own satisfaction—hence the prodigious outlay of $7.95 for *Booze* to be sure they were making home-brew when I said they were."

To Anna Porter[1]
McClelland & Stewart, Toronto, ON
23 November 1973

Dear Mrs. Porter:
Three years ago McClelland's published my novel *Whir of Gold*—all the correspondence was with Pamela Fry—and now, in accordance with the terms of my contract, I enclose my next "work," a novel entitled "Sawbones Memorial."

The material I'm afraid is pure prairie corn, but the "way" it is done may have possibilities. (You may have to read 10 pages or so before you see what I'm doing.) I have in mind a number of situations which might lend themselves—and lend themselves better than this one—to the same treatment. The drawback as I see it now after this, my first experiment, is that it calls for awfully *good* dialogue. Working on it I discovered how useful are all those little "He frowned and stubbed his cigarette," "A strange light shone in her eyes, part fear, part passion," how they ease the burden for the writer and help him around the corners. And for that reason, because my dialogue hasn't the bite and brilliance, you may not want to read further than those first 10 pages. Although I sincerely hope you do push on and reach the "soliloquies" of Sarah and the old doctor—I suppose you would call them stream of consciousness. I find myself rather liking them, and while I daresay they're pretty old hat compared with much that is being written today, for me they're out and out *avant-garde*. I amaze myself.

In any case the ms is short, 40/42,000 words. In fact, I woke up only a year or 18 months ago to the number of 100/150 page novels—I suppose one should say novellas—which publishers are bringing out these days. It has been suggested several times that I am a short story writer rather than a novelist, and while I was never able to agree—the short story has always seemed too confining—I now wonder if the suggestions aren't half right. As I wrote not long ago to a friend, it's a matter of "wind." The difference between 125 and 250 pages is not just 125 pages, it's reaching page 125 and then flogging myself the rest of the way. This one I did quickly—at least for me, who usually progresses like a snail. I had got bogged down in a novel—about an artist,[2] and artists, like writers, are as hard to write about as they are to live with—and thinking an interval on something completely different would be a good way to come back and see it with fresh eyes, I started last January, more or less for fun, not taking it very seriously, and then kept going. Eight months at the most, allowing for some travel I worked in; and some parts, the "soliloquies," I must have run through the typewriter 10 or 12 times.

When you read it you will probably say it only proves that an old man shouldn't try experimenting and that if he risks the sudden leap from Copp-Clark's *High School Composition*[3] to stream of consciousness he can expect to come down with a hard bump. Well, I'll be disappointed of course—even when it's a bad book, a writer puts a lot of himself into it—but at least, something unusual for me, I enjoyed doing it. And maybe a few what-not-to-do's which will be useful in the next one.

What's in my mind, however, is the possibility that your response might be, "Well, it just might do. The 'manner' makes it something of an oddity and the material so far as it goes is no doubt authentic Saskatchewan; some westerners might be interested,"—and on the chance that your thinking should run along those lines I will say this, in the hope that it will help you in your decision:

I would not agree to a contract which did not differ in a number of respects from the one you gave me for *Whir of Gold*. Clause No. 20 of that contract gives you the option to publish my next two works on fair and reasonable terms, and as we both signed the contract we both have something to say about what is fair and reasonable.

(1) Elementary—though not by any means the most important—I would want an advance of at least $500. For *Whir of Gold* you gave me no advance whatever.

(2) I would want both a hardback and paperback edition. I see that you often do this, and as I pointed out to Mr. Laurence Ritchie[4] in my letter of July 17, my name must be known to at least 200,000 Canadians—sales of *As for Me and My House* in the NCL are now 50,000, it has been read in Canadian universities for years, my short stories have been used over and over in anthologies for high school use, and I gather from letters that interest has quickened to some extent as a result of the little boosts given me by Robert Fulford and Margaret Atwood.

(3) I would not agree to McClellands being written into the contract as agents. (At this time, since there's a good chance you won't be interested in the ms in any case, I hesitate to elaborate on my reasons. If necessary, I can do so later.) However, in the event of acceptance, I should be delighted to have you *act* as agents, at least for the time being; but I would want to be free

to turn to another agent at some time in the future if I decided it would be to my advantage to do so. It's in my mind that I might later try to find someone to "handle" me—but of course I don't know, considering my small output, if anyone would be interested.

(4) Because of the "soliloquies" I would not agree to having clause 3 (c) included, which gives you the right to change the ms to bring it into line with your house standards of punctuation, syntax etc. Should you be interested I am sure I should want to go over the ms again very carefully—and probably retype it—but the changes would be to improve rhythm, substitute a sharper word for a dull one, that sort of thing, not to whip it into standard high school English. The way it is written may be a very bad way, but it is the way I intend it—it is the "work"—and apart from textural changes which I myself might make, it is not for re-writing. Of course if you had some suggestions—I daresay you've had a lot of experience with this sort of thing—I should be only too pleased to give them careful consideration.

(5) I would agree to giving you an option on only *one* more work—i.e. Work No, 2 referred to in the contract for *Whir of Gold*, the present ms, *Sawbones Memorial*, being Work No. 1. And to rush ahead a little, in the event of your wanting to publish Work No. 2 when it comes along, I would give you no option whatever on my future work, that is Works 3 and 4 etc., supposing I can stave off senility long enough to get that far. (Not long ago I read an article on Old Age in *Time* or *Newsweek* which said that the human brain, at about 60 or 65, starts losing grey cells at the alarming rate of 10,000 a day. Talk about a Sword of Damocles!)

However, the foregoing does not necessarily mean that I would not offer you Work No. 3 et al.—not at all. I know there are a number of new, smaller houses now in Canada, but I don't suppose any of them could do more for me than you—although having fewer writers in their stable, and fewer big names, they might have more time for me. In other words, I suppose it would be six of one and half a dozen of the other; and I would not change just for the sake of changing. But it depends on you. That is to say, whether you see Work No. 3 et al. will depend on what happens with Nos. 1 and 2. Blunt, no-strings attached rejections, incidentally, will have my whole-hearted respect.

And the same for Work No. 3 et al. should, all hazards circumvented, we ever get there: no options on the future. I am getting old, and for the few years left I don't like the idea of being tied down. It seems unlikely you should care one way or the other in any case. I daresay you have me appraised well enough to know that the probabilities at this late date of my blossoming into a best-selling Arthur Haley are slight. At least, since *Whir*, you haven't asked me what new [work] I had coming along.

The above list, of course, of what I will and what I will not agree to, may not impress you. And I appreciate that if you make difficulties, hold things up etc. there's not a great deal I can do. You have infinitely more working for you than I have. If you do make difficulties, however, it won't be too important. I plan a sequel to *Sawbones*—having to do with Caroline and Nick—and anything that I feel is worth salvaging, I can, with a few changes, work into the new story. And in the meantime it will just be a matter of picking up my few belongings and departing, not to bother you again except, in due course, to send along another typescript, Work No. 2.

I say this to keep things clear, so there will be [no] misunderstandings, but I sincerely hope it doesn't work out like that at all and that when the time to send Work No. 2 [comes] I will do so with enthusiasm and crossed fingers. At the moment, I don't know what Work No. 2 will be. Not the sequel to *Sawbones*: I haven't made up my mind how to tell it, spread it around among several characters or give it to Caroline as a straight first-person narrative—and as it involves a murder and trial I should come to Canada and have some sessions with at least one criminal lawyer and if possible sit in on a few court hearings to get the hang of things and soak up a little of the atmosphere. There are also the fragments of two novels I have dropped and now I'm going back to see what I've got. One especially I like—about an artist who has been shot and is now in hospital, out of physical danger but struggling for his sanity—I have been trying for a mixture of zaniness and terror which I think is all right—but whether I have the range and deftness to bring it off is something else again.[5] Then I have 2 other novels, fairly well thought out, in the manner of *Sawbones*, one about the effects of crime on a town; and then a couple of travel books; and then...

However, back to "Sawbones"—it is short, and I think fairly easy to read. You or your readers will probably skim through it in a couple of hours and have a verdict for me in a few weeks. In any case I will wait 3 months, and if I haven't heard by then will conclude you are not interested. I enclose my cheque in blank to cover return postage, *airmail*.

Yours sincerely,
Sinclair Ross

1.   Anna Porter, who became publisher of Key Porter Books in 1982, was editor-in-chief and later vice-president at McClelland & Stewart between 1970 and 1979.

2.   This is likely a reference to a manuscript Ross was working on titled "The Disasters of Peace," the title alluding to Goya's famous etchings, "The Disasters of War." (See letter from Sheila Kieran to Peter Pearson dated 30 November 1972.)

3.   Copp Clark, a Toronto firm in business from 1841 to 1998, published a series of monographs on the teaching of English. These were used throughout Canada in the first half of the twentieth century.

4.   Laurence Ritchie was employed at McClelland & Stewart in the 1970s and 1980s.

5.   Another reference to "Disasters of Peace" (see note 2).

From Jack McClelland

McClelland & Stewart, Toronto, ON

2 January 1974

Dear Sinclair Ross:

This is just an interim note to let you know that we would very much like to publish *Sawbones Memorial*. Normally you would hear directly from Anna Porter on this but she is away on vacation and won't be back for another 10 days and I thought we should let you know as soon as possible that the reaction here has been extremely enthusiastic and we do want to publish.[1] Anna has already told you I know that there is no problem with the conditions that you establish in your letter. On her return I'll let her pick it up from there, work out the contractual details with you, appoint an editor, etc. so for the moment let me congratulate you on a major accomplishment. You have charted new territory in terms of form and have done so with great skill and accomplishment.

Best personal regards.
Sincerely,
Jack McClelland

---

1.   Not all readers were enthusiastic. Lily Miller and Greg Gatenby submitted positive reports on the manuscript, the latter "greatly impressed" with the novel, praising the sharpness of characterization and the innovative technique; but John Newlove describes himself as "disappointed in the extreme" with what he calls a "tired theme" and dull writing. The undated reports are part of the McClelland & Stewart archive at McMaster University Library, CC54.

To Jack McClelland
McClelland & Stewart, Toronto, ON
12 January 1974

Dear Mr. McClelland:
I am very happy of course to have your letter and know you are
prepared to bring out *Sawbones Memorial*. Also somewhat surprised,
for while I like it myself, and am on a friendly footing with several
of the characters, Caroline and Duncan, Sarah, Nellie, the old doctor,
I wondered when I read it over for the last time if I didn't have just a
collection of anecdotes and small town gossip.

Once under way, with what I wanted to do clear in my mind, I
had little or no trouble with the "way" it is done — it seemed to take
care of itself. What concerned me was giving depth to the people, for
jumping from one person or pair of persons to another — and for brief
visits — makes for shallowness; and I was also afraid of coming up with
a sentimental, nostalgic picture of an old country doctor.

At the moment I see or "feel" at least three more books in the same
manner, but it has its serious limitations of course, and I wouldn't
want to be confined to it. (Presumptuous of me, I know. I say this as
if I had twenty-five or thirty years in front of me, instead of — to be
optimistic — five or ten.)

In any case, we'll hope old Doc has enough of what it takes to win
a worthwhile number of nods from the reading public as well...It was
kind of you to write personally to tell me the good news; I appreciate it.

Sincerely,
Sinclair Ross

To Anna Porter
McClelland & Stewart, Toronto, ON
15 January 1974

Dear Mrs. Porter:

I probably should be writing this to Mr. Jack McClelland but I am reluctant to bother him with it, and if it is of any importance I daresay the discussion will involve you as well in any case. I replied a few days ago to his letter of the 2nd telling me he would like to publish *Sawbones* and I was so pleased by the news, by the gist of it, that it wasn't until after I had written that I began to think about one of his sentences: "You have charted new territory in terms of form."

Well, probably it doesn't matter and I'm more than likely splitting ethical hairs, but a French writer, Claude Mauriac, son of the famous François,[1] did something roughly like it some 15 years ago: 2 books at least, *Dîner en ville* and *La Marquise sortit à cinq heures*. In case you haven't encountered them *Dîner* is 8 or 10 guests for dinner, with a sort of seating chart for an introduction. They talk and think and remember and the reader watches for clues. Somebody is addressed, say, as Madame X, so you consult the chart and deduce that the person addressing her is either Monsieur A or B. No indication a few lines farther on that B — or A — is now not talking to X but thinking about something that happened years ago between him and Madame Y, on the other side of the table. On and on — that is roughly the idea. Clever, sophisticated, fascinating — if you are up to it. *La Marquise* is probably even more confusing. It is a street intersection in Paris and he seems to be trying to reproduce what he would catch if he placed a tape recorder in the street, a special recorder that captures both voices and thoughts. Snippets of talk, of thought; people cross and recross; a couple talk and make love in a hotel bedroom; an old scholar is writing a book about the street, a homosexual dresses up to step out for the evening — you deduce all this, nothing is stated, and for a while you are flipping back desperately to see if you may have missed a clue. I lost interest and decided, both times, it wasn't worth the effort, but still I said to myself,

"Perhaps not a bad way to write a book, only why so difficult, why turn it into a puzzle?"

It was about the time the new Royal Bank building in Montreal was completed, and watching people as they walked through, commenting, admiring, visitors, guided tours, staff from other branches, I thought maybe you could do something with a new building—not necessarily a bank. Conversations and reminiscences that would reveal ambitions, successes, rivalries, etc. one era passing and a new one coming in—but I didn't take it very seriously. It would be hard to do, and lacking suspense would likely have little or no appeal. The idea was there, however, and years later I found myself thinking about a new school in a small town—easier to handle than a modern skyscraper—and then, I don't know exactly when or how, the school became a hospital. As I told you in my previous letter I had got bogged down in a novel and I thought this might be a good time to see if it would work. But simple, accessible: the people the important thing, not the form.

Sawbones is so different from Mauriac—straightforward, flat-footed, easy—that it seems doubtful a comparison would ever be made. Since starting to think about Mr. McClelland's "You have charted new territory" I have had myself in the dock and I think what it boils down to is that I have dropped all introductions and connective material too. I suppose you could say I took a tip from him. Unethical? I don't think so. That it might be had never occurred to me before. No more unethical, for instance, than for film-makers to make use of techniques developed by Godard and Truffaut and Fellini. What concerns me is that it may have been because of the form rather than the content, what you believed to be the book's originality, that decided you in its favour; and as I do owe the idea to Mauriac it is best to speak up now, before anything has been done or any announcements made.

Yours sincerely,
Sinclair Ross

1. Claude Mauriac (1914–1996) was one of the practitioners of the French "new novel" in the 1950s and 1960s. His formless works of fiction spurned the tense, dramatically constructed novels of his father. François Mauriac (1885–1970) was a major French Catholic novelist and playwright whose writings turn repeatedly on the questions of sin, grace, and salvation. He was awarded the Nobel Prize for Literature in 1952.

From Anna Porter

McClelland & Stewart, Toronto, ON
29 January 1974

Dear Mr. Ross:

I have just received your letter of January 15 and am amazed. I keep thinking of the Greek philosopher (I can't remember his name, but I'm sure you will) who wandered all over the streets of Athens with a torch in the hopes that he might be able to say "behold, there is an honest man."[1] No, it wasn't because of the form rather than the content that we have accepted the book for publication. It's an excellent book, and it's original even if Claude Mauriac has already written *Dîner en ville*.

I look forward to your reply to my letter of January 16 about the contract and our proposed editor for the book.[2]

Best wishes,
Anna Porter

1. Porter is thinking here of Diogenes (d. c. 320 BC), one of the Cynics, who, on the basis of an austere honesty, sought to expose the false conventions and practices by which most people lived. His advocacy of simplicity and self-sufficiency also resonates in Porter's connection of Diogenes to Ross.
2. Lily Miller had succeeded Pamela Fry as senior fiction editor at McClelland & Stewart; her enthusiasm for the novel in manuscript made her the obvious choice as the book's editor.

To Anna Porter

McClelland & Stewart, Toronto, ON

4 March 1974

Dear Mrs. Porter:

Sawbones Memorial: herewith the new version, with a summary of revisions attached.

All the revisions I think are improvements, although at the moment I'm so fed up with *Sawbones* that I ask myself if they aren't a bit cracked at McClelland to be remotely interested in it. Some of the characters, however, have shaped up and become real to me and I feel a certain enthusiasm for the sequel which I hope to do some day. (Tentative title: *Price above Rubies*.) Perhaps I shall be ready to start in about a year—as I said before I could do with a small-town refresher course, which means a trip to Saskatchewan. Nor have I decided how to do it. A straightforward "linear" narration would be the easier way—Caroline as I now know her is articulate, sensitive and alert, and would make a good narrator; but I think it might be better, certainly more modern, broken up with the pieces laid around the reader. Probably 20/22 years later; the occasion, Sarah's death. Robbie, now a medical student and, to his father's chagrin, something of a hippy, not really interested in medicine, comes home for the funeral—just at the Easter break—and insensitively brings a friend—which would serve me, however, as a good way to recapitulate. He tells his friend the old stories as they filtered down to him as a child, his mother, Nick, the murder—and they both speculate. Someone at the funeral watches Caroline, poised and still beautiful, and remembers the day she saw her running up the street, screaming and spattered with blood, her dress half torn off. While Caroline recalls what really happened and the role old Sarah played in the subsequent years; while Duncan in his honest, not very bright way, tries again to understand; while Nellie, still sharp and shrewd, ponders the pieces and tries to arrange them; while Stanley—married now and a farmer (Duncan hurried up the marriage at the same time he "banished" Benny)—wonders what part he and Benny may have played etc. etc. This way Nick, the most important character, would never appear on stage—throwing drama away probably; on the other hand, hovering in the background, he might be more of a "presence." I'm still not sure.

All of which, of course, is an irrelevant leap ahead. Right now it's *Sawbones*—very much on stage—and as yet we haven't settled the contract. I thought it was all settled—in your letter Nov 28 you say "I see no reason why I should not comply with all your conditions" (confirmed by Mr. Jack McClelland in his letter) but your letter of January 16 raises some questions.[1] Well, I don't want to be hard to get along with—I have no illusions about the value of anything I have written as a "property"—and at least on some points I am willing to be flexible—but at the same time I know you have a great many authors, all claiming time and attention, and if I don't speak up in an effort to make sure I'm not swamped and forgotten, who's going to do it for me? Since *Whir of Gold*, in fact, I have been asking myself what's the point of publication if it only means a few indifferent or worse reviews and a thousand copies sold.

What's the point—and yet I keep on scribbling. I'm just comfortably into the next one, ten typewritten pages of the first draft—I broke off to revise *Sawbones*—but it's firm in my mind and I think I see my way. Another small town but not necessarily Saskatchewan—and the effects of a crime committed seven years before. The occasion: the release from prison of the culprit. At this stage of course I'm not sure, but I think it will be about the length of *Sawbones*, probably a little longer, and if all goes well and I don't gad around too much this summer I should have it ready to show you in 10 or 12 months.[2]

But right now to hell with it—the sun is shining gloriously—yesterday it touched 80—and I'm going *out*.

Sincerely,
Sinclair Ross

1. It is difficult to determine what "questions" remained for Ross at this point because in her letter of 16 January 1974 Porter agrees to all the terms he had set forth in his letter of 23 November 1973.

2. There is no evidence that Ross ever completed this manuscript and submitted it for publication, nor is there a title attached to any of the references to this story.

To Lily Poritz Miller[1]

McClelland & Stewart, Toronto, ON

4 October 1974

Dear Miss Miller:

It was kind of you to write again about *Sawbones*; I am sure that as one book leaves your desk it is promptly replaced by another and that the pile is always high.

In your letter you say the official publication date has been set for October 26, so yesterday when the 2 copies I had ordered over and above my allotment arrived I was pleasantly dumbfounded—alright, pleasantly surprised.

Yes, I do like it, very much—it pleases both eye and hand. Obviously a great deal of care has gone into its preparation and I am grateful. I'm also delighted you didn't use my picture. The quotes on the back cover are gratifying, only the one about *As for Me and My House* being "as timeless as *Genesis*"—of course, I know you didn't invent it, but I keep wanting to exclaim, My God, did somebody really say that! Well, I cross my fingers and hope that poor old Sawbones isn't expelled to oblivion and Outer Darkness—I'll be satisfied with that.

As yet I have just read it through very quickly and, every page of the way, it seems exactly in accordance with the second set of proofs and my few remarks in the accompanying letter. Again, my warmest thanks for taking such good care of all my changes.

Now that's all over and behind me, I find myself liking the soliloquies best. I'm an old man to be talking about development, but they are the direction, I think, in which I would like to go. Although at the moment there's one looming up which I'm afraid of: a woman whose son is just finishing 7 years in prison. It's the sort of thing that easily turns sticky; I may duck it.

There's no problem at the moment, but if and when one turns up I shall certainly take advantage of your invitation to write you.

Sincerely,
Sinclair Ross

1.   Lily Miller, senior trade editor at McClelland & Stewart, was put in charge of *Sawbones Memorial* in March 1974. She assisted with editorial changes required, and the correction of galley and page proofs.

From Margaret Atwood
Alliston, ON
27 November 1974

Dear Sinclair Ross:
Many thanks for your letter and the kind words...and also for the autographed copy of *Sawbones Memorial* that arrived the same day. I had in fact, acquired *two* copies...my own, and one I got from the CBC to review...as you can see by the enclosed hastily written and very badly typed review, I liked it very much indeed (luckily bad typing doesn't matter with the CBC because it's voice anyway!)...in fact my review copy has its margins sprinkled with words like WOW and ZAP and RIGHT!, which is what I do to review copies when overly excited. I read it all at one sitting and was entranced. The Ladies Auxiliary lady should be required for all Ladies Auxiliaries, though it might ruin them for future novelists. The petty spite and seedy nastiness really come through, but so does the humour...poor Nick is going to have one hell of a time when he finally gets back. (What *about* Maisie Bell? My guess is that there was nothing in it...) the ending is brilliant. (But so are lots of other things.)

Meanwhile it has already snowed, a little, and my pond is almost frozen over, with the ducks and geese sitting in the 6-foot clear spot in the middle, looking dismayed. I am holed up finally after traipsing around the countryside doing poetry readings for about a month... working on 4 short stories and edging up to a novel.[1] Some of the stories are rather frivolous, I feel; I don't think I'm by nature much of a story writer. I'd think of retiring and becoming a Sheep Farmer, if I didn't already have some stupid and obnoxious sheep. Have finally outflanked the mice though.

I would love to have you come and visit when you finally make your trip...if you wouldn't find a farm depressing.[2] It isn't flat, and the house dates from 1840 or so, complete with ghost (all he does is walk up the stairs and along the hall, and I myself have never heard him). We have a tractor and fixings, and took the hay off ourselves this summer, which was hard work. My biggest farming insights have been into prices and the squeeze in the middle (the farmer caught between escalating costs and falling or static prices). They develop enormous patience and a kind of fatalism which I haven't yet. (But don't come to Canada unless compelled, inwardly or outwardly; in some ways it's just a great big Upward, but then I guess so is everywhere else.)

Best as always — Margaret A.

1.   The writing Atwood refers to here likely includes the novel *Lady Oracle*, 1976, and the collection of short stories *Dancing Girls*, 1977.

2.   Ross thought that to write a sequel to *Sawbones Memorial*, one set in the 1960s, he would have to make a trip to Saskatchewan, which he had not visited since his mother's death in 1957.

To Anna Porter

McClelland & Stewart, Toronto, ON

29 November 1974

Dear Mrs. Porter:

Thank you for your letter of November 20th replying so promptly at length to mine of the 11th.

Yes, I suppose I'm rushing you about a paperback of *Sawbones*, but of course I wasn't thinking about next month. I don't know anything about these things, but I imagine planning and producing a paperback is a fairly protracted business. By January '76—you say the earliest, and I certainly hadn't thought of an earlier date myself—I'll be 68; no time to lose; I want to be able to step out and *spend* my big royalty cheques.[1] In the meantime I certainly hope it does sell a few hardback copies. What worries me, I must admit, is the price. Yes, I know about costs, but as I said in a letter just the other day to your Greg Gatenby $7.95 is such a lot of money for a novella—who's going to fork out? Needless to say I'll be delighted if I'm wrong.

As to *Whir of Gold*, I suppose I'll have to make up my mind that as a novel it doesn't amount to much. In my letter to Gatenby I said what a hopeless judge of writing I must be: to me it has so many things better than anything in *Sawbones*. All right, don't say it—a case of arrested development—all those Saskatchewan dust storms...Still, I keep my fingers crossed that a paperback house may yet be interested.

Thank you for sending along the reviews. That's 9 now I've seen, 7 from you (McClelland's) and 2 from a friend in Calgary. Nothing yet from BC or Montreal but, so far, friendlier than I expected. One of those with your letter (by Pat Barclay, name of the paper doesn't show on the clipping) says I'm mellower.[2] Slander! As an old (expletive deleted) so-and-so I'm barely getting under way.

I appreciate your efforts to place *Sawbones* in London and New York; apparently, like certain wines, I don't travel...I don't know who Dennis Weaver is—high time, in other words, I came back at least briefly to brush up on the Canadian scene—but I assume he's somebody with the CBC.[3] Well, fingers crossed again...

Yes, I do indeed like *Sawbones*—the book. As I wrote to Miss Miller, it pleases both hand and eye. It's almost an "abstract"—the magnificent expanse of golden wheat and black sky—and at the same time, especially for a westerner, so movingly "real." I've also had a couple of letters commenting on it.

Sincerely,
Sinclair Ross

1.   *Sawbones Memorial* was published as a paperback in the New Canadian Library series in 1978.
2.   Pat Barclay's review of *Sawbones Memorial* was syndicated across the country. The copy Ross received from the Canadian Press Clipping Service (no source or date) is titled "The Doctor Comes Home" and includes a photo of Ross in Málaga taken by William French for the *Globe and Mail*. The same review appeared in the *Peterborough Examiner* on 30 October 1974 with the title "A Bit of Hope Helps Hard Medicine Go Down."
3.   Dennis Weaver has not been identified.

To Margaret Laurence

Lakefield, ON
14 December 1974

Dear Margaret:
Your letter and review[1] arrived just at the right time to help dispel my annual attack of old expatriate-pre-Christmas blues. (Nothing but memories—not many of them good.) I wrote *Sawbones* as an experiment—something that has been rolling around in my head for years, that is to say, the technique—and I'm surprised that so far the response has been mostly good. (I expected to be mowed down.) I say so far because there's still time for me to get hell. I've seen nothing from BC or Maritimes. The only really "sour" review they've sent me is in the Regina *Leader-Post*, and while I'm sorry that of all places it's

Regina, at the same time I can't help chuckling: Ross leaves it up to the readers to figure out who is talking...and "readers shouldn't have to engage in that kind of mental activity."[2]

It is a good discipline—tougher even than writing a play (not that I've ever written one) for you can give stage directions and say what an actor should wear, what movements he should make and the actor himself with gestures, tone of voice etc. can express a great deal more than the actual words, and this way you have the naked words only. A good discipline especially for me—I have to admit I like writing for its own sake—but it is terribly restrictive; and although I'm working now on another using practically the same technique I doubt whether I would want to do more. Perhaps the next one, which I hope will be a sequel to Sawbones. I think, in fact I'm almost sure, that I once told you and Adele about it—it's idle talking about the future. Hell, I'm almost 67 and looking every minute of it—frequently feeling it too.

Yes, I would like to visit Canada for a month—I should come for a number of reasons—but at the moment everything is in the air. Here, as in the rest of the world, there are a great many economic problems with some political rumblings thrown in. I may be coming—that is to say, returning—in any case. With a week in New York I probably couldn't do it on less that $1,500, which for me is a lot of money, and while prices are soaring here I daresay I'll find living, apartments, etc., even steeper in Canada. But if and when I come I would like very much to come out at least for the day. (Of course, I would expect a good Canadian lunch.) You say that at heart you're small town, which is probably not a bad way to be. Myself, I like the anonymity of a big city (yes, I know, I must be guilty, wanting to hide) although I don't always like the big city itself. I would also like the countryside, but that is increasingly difficult. At least I know my label: outsider. Canada or Spain or sitting on a flag pole—I doubt it makes much difference.

I haven't read The Diviners but have it on order. Along with Buckler's The Mountain and the Valley and The Apprenticeship of D.K., which tells you what a disgrace I am to the Canadian literary scene. In fact I read St. Urbain's Horseman only this last summer. When I have read The Diviners I will write again.

Thank you again for your generously kind review of *Sawbones*. I
hope I see you in '75.

As ever,

Jim

P.S. *Say hello for me to Adele if you see her. Hers is another on my "must" list.*[3]

---

1. Laurence's laudatory review of *Sawbones Memorial* was titled "Sinclair Ross Looks at
   the Prairies, His Time and Place," and appeared in the Montreal *Gazette*, 9 November
   1974, 58.
2. This negative, unsigned review appeared in the Regina *Leader-Post*, 25 October 1974.
3. Ross is referring here to Adele Wiseman's second novel, *Crackpot*, also published
   in 1974.

To Margaret Atwood

Alliston, ON
Christmas card, 1974

Dear Margaret:

Your letter and review is the Christmas gift of my life. Feel I could step
off the balcony, 12 floors up, and go right on walking all the way to
Africa...Would like very much—enormously—to meet the ducks and
geese, and a ghost to curl what's left of my hair is just what it needs...
Writing soon.

Best wishes for an old-fashioned snowy turkey and cranberry
Christmas and a "productive" 1975.

Jim Ross

Literary
Forefather | *Letters 1975–1986*

THE WIDENING INTEREST in Sinclair Ross is reflected here in the number of Canadians who started writing him letters. Of special importance are the letters from young writers such as Keath Fraser, Ken Mitchell, Andy Suknaski, and Guy Vanderhaeghe, who expressed their indebtedness to him for creating a literary tradition out of the western experience. These late letters reveal him engaged in the academic debates surrounding his famous novel and, confronted with chronic illness, making his own assessments of his life's work. Many of the letters here are from Ross's private collection, including carbon copies he sometimes made when answering his mail.

To Kenneth M. Glazier

University of Calgary Library, AB

3 January 1975

Dear Dr. Glazier:

I have your letter of December 13th and I am more than gratified that you are interested in my manuscripts.

Unfortunately, however, I have very little to offer you. It was not until about ten years ago, when I was still working in Montreal—and long after I had thrown away the manuscript of *As for Me and My House*—that an enquiry from someone in Queen's made me aware that old manuscripts, however disreputable-looking and scribbled over, are sometimes valuable. Then and there, of course, I resolved not to be so foolish in the future, but it was a little like locking the stable door etc. In any case, all I have are the manuscripts of *Whir of Gold* (1 early version) and *Sawbones Memorial* (5 versions, including the first draft).

To say they are scribbled over, incidentally, is anything but an exaggeration. Deletions and corrections; notes and amendments in the margins; notes to turn over and see other amendments on the reverse; amendments scratched out and re-amended. A mess, in other words; and the notes, moreover, are often difficult to decipher because of my habit of using a mixture of longhand and shorthand.

I say this in order to help you decide whether it would be worth your while seeing them. If you think you might still be interested—and I won't be in the least surprised if you are not; I feel somewhat guilty, in fact, that my remarks to Keath Fraser may have led you to expect considerably more—I will send the manuscripts for your appraisal, with the understanding that there is no commitment on either your part or mine, other than that you will return them if you decide their place is not in your Library or if we are not successful in working out a satisfactory arrangement.

As a preliminary, however, I wonder if from the foregoing you could give me a rough idea of their probable value in the event that you should have a place for them in the Library—again, of course, without commitment on your part. I make the suggestion because I haven't the faintest idea of prices. I might be more than willing to turn the manuscripts over to you; again I might not. And if I was not, then we would at least save ourselves, both your office and myself, the trouble of packaging and mailing the manuscripts.[1]

Yes, *Sawbones Memorial*—at least from the reviews I have seen so far—seems to be receiving a better press than I expected: Toronto *Star*, Montreal *Gazette* (Margaret Laurence), CBC (Margaret Atwood), *Maclean's* (George Woodcock), *Books in Canada*, *Winnipeg Free Press*, all very good. On the other hand, the *Ottawa Citizen* was rather vicious and the Regina *Leader-Post* seems to think it is anything but a credit to Saskatchewan.[2] Well, I suppose it takes a while for a book to find its level—or to disappear. As to sales, I have heard nothing from McClellands, but I'm not shopping round yet on the strength of my royalties for a villa or a yacht.

Yours sincerely,
Sinclair Ross

1. Ross subsequently decided that neither the size of his collection nor the price offered were worth the trouble of sending his papers to Calgary. On 23 May 1978 Sheila Kieran, speaking for herself and also on behalf of Timothy Findley, Margaret Laurence, and Margaret Atwood, wrote to Kenneth Glazier urging that he make another offer to Ross of no less than $10,000, stressing how important he was to Canadian literature, but Glazier replied 29 May 1978 wondering if the Library would really be justified in spending $10,000 for two novel manuscripts and no correspondence. He concludes his brief note by quoting a letter from Ross dated 8 July 1977, which says "I have decided, however, after considerable thought, to retain the manuscripts." Ross's few papers were eventually sent by his friend and secretary, Irene Harvalias, to the National Archives (now Library and Archives Canada).
2. For a fuller account of the reviews of *Sawbones Memorial* see Stouck, *As for Sinclair Ross*, 230–33.

To Margaret Laurence

Lakefield, ON

5 February 1975

Dear Margaret:

I groaned when *The Diviners* came—My God, why do people write such long books, it's going to take me a month! But in fact I went through it in a few days, absorbed all the way. And it's not just long, it's big. Morag is fine—human, believable. Her early years in Manawaka impressed me especially, the pain and embarrassments and gawky pride. Part of your achievement, it seems to me, is that while you always understand Morag you don't always like her, just as you don't always like Hagar. And yet Jules, I would say, in a different way, is even better—the hard, strong, wild streak, contrasting with the pathetic compromises to survive. It's the blank places that haunt the reader. There's so much you don't know—as you say, so much pain. As I read I kept wondering about him, rather resenting Skelton, for instance, wondering if you were going to bring him back; for from his first appearance he was, so far as I was concerned, "her man." Of course I didn't like the way he died, but I thought it was especially fine the way she slipped out while he was still sleeping and left him to die alone. I don't know how it would be in real life, but I was so glad she respected the Indian in him and didn't hover over the ignominy of his death, humiliating him with kindness.

And of course it's such a good prairie book—all the fascinating "little" things, such as 40 below, never 40 below zero, and *bluff* meaning a grove or clump of trees...Enough said—I liked it, was impressed. It's on the shelf for now, but I'll be dipping in again.

After such a long, sustained effort I daresay you're still enjoying a well-earned breather; all right, but don't forget to eat your porridge and take your vitamins so you won't be too long mustering energy for the next one.

As ever,

Jim

To Roy St. George Stubbs[1]

Winnipeg, MB
4 March 1975

Dear Roy,

Your review of *Sawbones Memorial* in the *Free Press* has given me a tremendous lift. There's no one whose good opinion of my efforts could please me more. Yes, my performance over the years has been disappointing—especially so to me—but there are blocks, hang-ups and limitations for which one is not always responsible. Ironically, I feel I could do better now, but 66 is an age which brings new limitations. In other words, I hope you continue to "root" for me but I wouldn't urge you to stake much money. One of the things I hope to do, incidentally, is a sequel to *Sawbones*, in which the principals will be Nick and Caroline—but at the present time I'm at work on something else.

I'm not sure—there are so many uncertainties everywhere these days it's hard to make plans—but probably I shall be in Canada for a month next spring, as far west as Saskatchewan, and I hope I will have a chance to see you. In the meantime my warm thanks again for your sympathetic reading of *Sawbones* and best wishes for the New Year.

Sincerely,
Jim Ross

---

1.   When *As for Me and My House* was published in 1941, Roy St. George Stubbs (1907–1995), a Winnipeg lawyer and author, wrote the first feature-length article about Ross. It was titled "Presenting Sinclair Ross" and appeared in *Saturday Night*, 9 August 1941. Ross and St. George Stubbs became good friends, often meeting in company with another published writer, Dyson Carter, to discuss the latest books and their views of writing.

SINCLAIR ROSS - AS FOR ME AND MY HOUSE

A caricature of author and book by cartoonist Isaac Bickerstaff. When it appeared in Tamarack Review, October 1975, Ross exclaimed: "Now I'm famous." [Isaac Bickerstaff files, University of Calgary Library]

To Ken Mitchell[1]

University of Regina, SK

28 March 1975

Dear Ken:

How I envy you your energy. I suppose it's a matter of the glands you're born with but if you've hit on some special vitamins for Heaven's sake give me the details. My own "petty pace" shames me.

A "country opera" called *Cruel Tears*[2] sounds good. Questions spring up: you say you got the idea in Greece, so is it Greece or Saskatchewan? *Lysistrata* in Gull Lake—*The House of Atreus* in Saskatoon? Are you involved in the score, or just the libretto? Full length or for a double bill? I wish I was there to hear it....The dramatic workshop idea raises questions too—"the materials which will be largely *improvised*" you say—but it also opens wide a few doors. The rise and fall of a Saskatchewan town certainly has possibilities, both moving and funny. I didn't realize, in fact, that there are so many prairie towns winding up their days until I read Person's book.[3] I must say it jars me a bit—there's still enough dust and Russian thistle in my blood....No, I don't mind in the least if you call the town Horizon—on the contrary—although it makes me think of the passage in *As for Me and My House* about the "grasshopper" towns that grow old but *can't* die. In other words, I didn't see far enough into the future. (Damned if I can think of the name of the goddess I talked about who asked the gods to give her lover immortality but forgot to mention youth.[4] An old man's memory—drives me up the wall sometimes.) As to the drama of a dying town, you bring out some of the poignancy in *The Train*[5]—although from reading the play what I picked up was *their* plight—the characters'—not the town's. It has power—right at the end Rose's desperate loneliness hits hard. (You mention Meadowlark—is this the town of *Meadowlark Connection?*[6]) After *Wandering Rafferty*,[7] which has such lusty, walloping vigor, I was surprised by the starkness. In other words, more than one string to your bow—that's good. A great many strings, it seems—a one-man band....I don't know enough about poetry to comment on *The Village Idiot*[8] except to say that I *liked* it. Especially the no-nonsense—"turned his eyeballs back so far he shuts off from view and watches his demons"—so many would probably put in an "as if he were watching." Keep the good work up and do keep me posted, if only briefly, how everything comes off.

Delighted to find myself making statements about the human condition along with Faulkner and Conrad. At least so far as I am concerned, Faulkner is the best of company. I have great admiration for him, especially *Light in August*, *As I Lay Dying*, *The Sound and the Fury*—also, to a somewhat lesser degree, *Absalom, Absalom* and some of the short stories. It's years and years—I'm telling myself it's time to start again.

No plans at the moment to come to Canada. As I may have told you in an earlier letter, I'm stalling to see what happens here: I may be coming anyway. I also have some health problems and right now I'm a bit dubious about a long trip, on the go steady for at least a month. My ruptured disc bothers me and the last year another disc lower down has also been cutting up—pinching a nerve and causing a pain, sometimes crippling, in the foot. I was in Paris last fall for a couple of weeks, walked too much of course, and although I have been taking treatment and injections, it's not completely gone. Serves me right for getting so damned old....

Surprised to hear you met Mavis Gallant[9] in Edmonton; is she back in Canada now, or just on a visit? It must be at least ten years since I last saw her in Montreal. If you run into her again say hello for me.

All the best,
Jim

---

1. Ken Mitchell (1940–), prolific author and creative writing professor, initiated a correspondence with Ross in 1974. He became one of Ross's most vocal champions, publishing a valuable study of his work titled *Sinclair Ross: A Reader's Guide* and, in the mid-1980s, producing a radio documentary for CBC titled "The Ross File," and a dramatized version of *Sawbones Memorial*.

2. Mitchell's opera, based on the folk music of Saskatchewan, was first performed in 1975 and featured the bluegrass band "Humphrey and the Dump Trucks." Inspired

according to the author's account by *Othello, Cruel Tears* is a story about waitresses and truck drivers. A text version was published by Talonbooks in 1977.

3. Ross is referring here to *Growing up in Minby*, 1974 by Saskatchewan author Lloyd Person (1918–1985).

4. Ross is referring here to the story of Aurora, goddess of the dawn, who fell in love with Tithonus, son of the King of Troy. This myth is recounted in the 9 July entry of Mrs. Bentley's diary in *As for Me and My House*.

5. Mitchell's *This Train* was published by the Playwright's Co-op in 1973.

6. This novel by Mitchell, subtitled "A Saskatchewan Thriller," was published by his own imprint, Pile-of-Bones Publishing, in 1975. It was reprinted in *Ken Mitchell Country*, an anthology of Mitchell's work edited by Robert Curries and published by Coteau Books in 1984.

7. *Wandering Rafferty*, one of Mitchell's most popular works, adapts the conventions of the picaresque novel to a Saskatchewan setting. It was first published by Macmillan in 1972.

8. This poem appears as "The Village Idiots of Greece" on page 387 in *Ken Mitchell Country*.

9. Ross and Mavis Gallant became friends in the late 1940s when they were both living in Montreal. They continued to see each other occasionally afterwards, even as late as 1993.

To Margaret Laurence

Lakefield, ON

14 April 1975

Dear Margaret:

Thank you for your generously long letter....Yes, I know what you mean—I don't have nearly so many letters to write as you, but some of them nevertheless—the necessary ones—are a damned nuisance. Some students are writing their M A theses on me—one I think is finished now, I hope—and they ask the damnedest questions. For you, I imagine it's a real problem, unless you've done as the writer in Updike's *Bech: A Book*[1] and had a card printed—"It's your thesis, you write it." At the same time I'm always pleased to make contact with the youngsters—and do write; it's a sort of compensation at my age, and I was of course very happy to read in your letter about the boy who has read *Sawbones* and liked it. I'm into the sequel—*Price above Rubies*; maybe I told you—and although there are a lot of problems I *think* I see my way. In his review in *Maclean's*, Woodcock said Nick, never on stage, is as important as the old doctor—right; and in this one, although he plays a much bigger role, he is still never on stage. Foolish perhaps, throwing drama away. It's bad luck, they say, to talk about work in progress but I will say just this: I jump forward 20 years; Robbie, the English war bride's baby is a medical student, home for old Sarah's funeral. Same technique as for *Sawbones*, trying to put the bits and pieces together so that at the end it will all be there. Robbie is perhaps as important as Nick. Ironically, he's had problems very similar to Nick's.

A visitor to Málaga looked me up recently: a Mrs. Janet McPhee,[2] an organizer of adult classes in Cdn. Lit. at some college in Toronto—the name has slipped me—and she's very much a Jules fan too. Also a Margaret Laurence fan—especially *The Stone Angel* and *The Diviners*. One of the lecturers is or was Clara Thomas who, she says, has just finished a study of Margaret Laurence.[3] From bits I've read in the *J. of Cdn. Fiction* I imagine she's done a perceptive job.

It's heart-warming that you still find good things to say about *As for Me*…. It surprises me how it holds its own. Students still read it and it still maintains modest sales—65/70,000 in the paperback which is, I suppose, for such a quiet book, not bad…My trouble when I write is that I never know what I'm doing—is it fair, or out and out terrible? As I wrote someone the other day, when I finished *Sawbones* I felt I hadn't done as well as with *Whir of Gold*. I see the faults in *Whir* but I still have a soft spot for Mad. For me, she's alive…Speaking of my damned women, *Price above Rubies* is supposed to be principally about Nick and Robbie—despite the title—but as I work I wonder if Caroline isn't nosing in and trying to upstage them.

Margaret, I have a favor to ask you and I hope you will understand. In your review of *Sawbones* in the Mtl. *Gazette* you mentioned the Royal Bank, and if you are ever writing or talking about me again I would be grateful if you would slip around them.[4] I appreciate your being so staunchly "for" me of course, but they *could* cut off my pension. It hardly seems likely they would but apart from that they have been my bread and butter most of my life — Mother's too for many years — and looking back I see that I owe them a great deal. The last thing I want to do is embarrass them. If they did cut me off it wouldn't be the end of the road but it would be damned inconvenient. I don't make much from writing — *Sawbones* they tell me has sold only 2,000/2,500 copies — but I have, I think a fairly strong Scotch-Canadian-Russian-thistle survival instinct. I have some savings and with the Old Age Pension I would manage. It might even be an incentive to put in longer hours at the typewriter. However, it's a bridge I haven't come to yet...

Speaking of working hard, an old friend wrote me recently, "Why don't you get busy and write a really dirty book that will make you some money. *Sawbones* convinces me you could." I suppose he was thinking about what went on at the Happy Haven country school... And speaking of dirty books, the Sask. Fed. of Teachers said — I don't know in what publication; McClelland's sent a Xerox of the typescript: "The spicy language will cause raised eyebrows." And it was a rather nice review; I had a feeling that the person who wrote it was genuinely distressed. It ties in with your friend Lowella from Texas who was incensed by your "obscenities." I suppose it's that we who read novels and about novels forget that all the battles haven't been won. We read of the *Ulysses* and *Lady Chatterley* trials, read *Portnoy's Complaint* or maybe *St. Urbain's Horseman*, and then are surprised that the old prudishness is up and around and hale and hearty. Well, let's be cheerful and say it all adds to the zest of life.

No definite plans to come to Canada — the way I'm doing *Price above Rubies* a Saskatchewan refresher course isn't necessary — but if and when I will certainly get in touch with you...Apartado, by the way, is P.O. Box. Ha ha — fooled you!

As ever,
Jim

1. A short story cycle, published in 1970, by American author John Updike (1932–2009).
2. Janet McPhee has not been identified.
3. Clara Thomas (1919–), a prominent educator and author, published *The Manawaka World of Margaret Laurence* in 1976.
4. In her review of *Sawbones Memorial*, Montreal *Gazette*, 9 November 1974, 58, Laurence referred disparagingly to Ross's life being wasted in a bank.

To Roy St. George Stubbs

Winnipeg, MB
28 June 1975

Dear Roy:

I'm very grateful for your help.[1] Just what I needed—left to myself I would have had the trial held in a district court house instead of in Regina. Another question if you are in good humor and can spare a minute: the crime or killing takes place early in September—when would the trial probably be held? I want the lady home as soon as possible.

Don't concern yourself about it, however, if this finds you "up to the eyes." I can slip around it; the story is twenty years later, and the events come through as they are discussed and mulled over by the woman's son, who wonders what really happened. (He's the 3-month-old child in *Sawbones*, Robbie, son of Duncan and Caroline.) While there's no trial scene, a great deal hangs on the verdict, that is, the acquittal. I don't lean on it too hard, but Robbie's childhood and adolescence, (psychologically at least) roughly parallels that of Nick. In due time—I hope—you will see.

I am nearing the end of the first draft and won't know until I start revising whether it has possibilities or—as I sometimes fear—it is just a lurid melodrama awkwardly told. I'm using the same technique as in *Sawbones*, and while it's a good discipline for the writer—no off-stage noises or atmospheric effects, no signals to the reader as to the charac-ter's attitude or state of mind, such as "her eyes flashed," or "his tone was withering," the naked words having to do the whole job—it has its serious limitations, and at the moment I'm not sure that I would want to experiment with it further. I do see it, though, as a way to write a travel book—unlimited possibilities. An excursion to an archaeological site—I have Crete in mind—and the passengers on the bus talk. Travel talk, prices, bargains, food, the trips they took last year to Mexico and Egypt; and informed, scholarly talk, archaeology, history, mythology (Crete is especially evocative), democracy in Greece, ancient and modern, democracy in general, survivals from ancient times, Greece and Russia, Greece and Turkey, etc. etc.—unlimited, as I say. Whether I am up to it, of course, is something else again.

I'm pleased to hear that *As for Me and My House* is still holding its own in Winnipeg and grateful that you are putting in a good word for *Sawbones*. As I may have said before, the response to *As for Me...* continues to surprise me. Someone wrote me a few months ago, for instance, that she had just finished reading it again after an interval of several years—her third reading—and had found many things she had missed before. A young Saskatchewan-Ukrainian poet (I think he's young, probably 30), Andy Suknaski, writes about Saskatchewan; *Wood Mountain Poems, Leaving Wood Mountain*—I don't know anything about poetry but to me he is a fine, authentic voice—tells me *As for Me...* and the short stories have been an important influence and that *Sawbones* started him on some new things. He brings out his own chapbooks—he has had one, perhaps two, Canada Council grants—and during the summer works in a hotel in Lake Louise...But when *As for Me* came out, 34 years ago, there were only a few like Roy Stubbs and Doris Saunders and Miss Preston[2] who gave it much time or attention. I suppose I should say it hasn't been bad luck all the way.

I'm just back from five days in Sevilla—a relief from, and a contrast to, Upward. Still a fascinating old city, but construction, traffic and outdoor advertising are taking their toll. And *hot*—they call it the frying-pan of Spain. My little apartment in Málaga, overlooking the sea, is in contrast almost chilly.

I look forward to the book which you say you are sending...Again my thanks for troubling to answer my questions so carefully.

Sincerely,
Jim

1. In an undated letter (but probably within a month of this one) Ross asked St. George Stubbs, his Winnipeg friend and court judge, for some legal advice pertaining to the situation he was writing about in the sequel to *Sawbones Memorial*. He wanted to know if a woman who murdered a man for attempted rape could possibly be free after the trial and, if not, what the minimum sentence would be. Was bail possible? He also wanted to know if the trial could take place at the District Courthouse.

2. Manager of Eaton's bookstore, Winnipeg, who promoted *As for Me and My House*.

To Ken Mitchell

University of Regina, SK

5 September 1975

Dear Ken:

To say I enjoyed *Meadowlark Connection*[1] is an understatement. It's a wonderful romp—with a bite. I'll never see RCMP again without thinking of Jimmy and his toothbrush. When I finished it I was at first rather disappointed that nothing happened between Jimmy and Sharon—girl *didn't* get boy—but of course you're right, to have him continue on his bumbling, priggish way, beyond the reach of either intelligence or woman. It *moves* at a good clip; in other words, you have what I think could be called a "suspense-narrative" gift. Despite the utter absurdity of Jimmy's predicament at the end, chained to the rocket—and not for one moment believing it—I nevertheless was caught up in the race to rescue him—very good indeed. It's a shame it wasn't brought out by one of the eastern publishers—I know from experience what a nerve-racking time they can give you—but don't worry, you're young and have a great many others under your belt.

I was interested to read the review of *Genesis*.[2] It sounds interesting—and brand-new. I mean I've never heard of a play being done that way before and am wondering if you're thinking of more like it, or if it was a one-shot experiment. In any case as I've said before probably, you seem to have an enormous amount of drive and imagination and will probably make your way both with plays and novels.

As to the novel you're having trouble with—my own experience is that when there's a bit that doesn't seem right, that worries you, the best thing to do is cut ruthlessly; and if it's a chapter or scene that's necessary, re-write. What I mean and I hope you don't think me presumptuous for saying this—is that if something isn't *basically* right in its structure or psychology or probability, no amount of doctoring, no changes in the writing or atmosphere, will help. And I think it's for the author to decide—to trust "the feeling in his bones." Myself, I have two novels abandoned half-way; when I finish with *Price above Rubies* I'm going to look them over again, because in both there are "things" I like. Perhaps, though, thrifty old Scotchman that I am, I can fit those "things" into something else. As to *Price above Rubies*—well, the axe fell with a thud on three pages yesterday. At the moment, I don't know what it amounts to—can't *see* it yet.

You said probably the poor sales of *Sawbones* might be the result of adverse reviews, but no—there were a number of very good ones: Margaret Atwood (CBC), someone else CBC Halifax, Margaret Laurence in Mtl. *Gazette*, Woodcock (*Maclean's*), *Books in Canada* (a rave), Toronto *Star*; and others not enthusiastic but favourable; Mtl. *Star* was frosty, *Time* ditto and the *Ottawa Citizen* incredibly vicious—"at least it may serve as a warning to other Cdn. writers." So I don't know; McClelland's will probably be wary of *Rubies*. They promised a paperback of *Sawbones*—sometime—but I've heard nothing more....As to *As for Me...*, yes it was originally published in New York (Reynal and Hitchcock) and distributed in Canada by McClelland's, but only the one edition. Some polite reviews, but no enthusiasm. Of course it was a poor novel for 1941—the war was on.

I still have no plans—as I've said before, it's hard to predict what's going to happen here. Next spring if you come back to Greece we may be able to get together. Hope you have an enjoyable and profitable time at Victoria...and that word of *Meadowlark Connection* gets around.

Sincerely,
Jim

1. See letter to Ken Mitchell dated 28 March 1975, note 6.

2. *Genesis* was the first title for a historical drama that changed into a musical titled *All Our Yesterdays*, produced by Regina Summer Stage. It has not been published.

From Margaret Laurence

Lakefield, ON
17 November 1975

Dear Jim—

As we are now approaching the second month of the postal strike, the longest in our fair country's history, and we are all totally fed up with both sides (a plague on both their houses), I do not know when I will be able to post this. But am writing because I want to get it off to you when (if ever) Canada once again has a Post Office.

Several people (this is a small and—believe me—kindly literary community now in this country; we do care) have told me that you were thinking you'd like to return to Canada on a visit. I was in Ottawa not long ago, for the Writers' Union of Canada yearly conference, and Naim Kattan[1] of the Canada Council phoned me up about something or other, so I took the opportunity to make a few enquiries about how the Council could get some money to you quickly, if you want to come back. Naim said the best thing would probably be for you to apply for a Short Term Grant, which would be your airfare *to* Canada, although not back to Spain again, and a maximum of $600 per month for three months. This could, upon application to the Council, be put through without the whole application-delayed bit which accompanies a request for a Senior Arts Award. That is, you could probably get it pretty quickly. I talked, also, to Lloyd Person[2] of Univ. of Sask. recently, who would really like you to come back for a visit (wouldn't we all!). Anyway, if you feel so inclined, you could simply write the Council and apply for a Short Term Grant, for 3 months (it doesn't matter if you don't stay 3 months)...travel expenses to Can, plus $600 for 3 months, namely $1800 plus travel. The address: The Canada Council, Awards

Section, P.O. Box 1047, 151 Sparks Street, Ottawa, Ontario K1P 5V8, Canada. HOWEVER, Jim, I think you should also give serious thought to applying for a Senior Arts Award, to help you with writing your present novel. I would guess you have never had a Can Council Award, and this is ridiculous. To do this, you do not need to be resident in this country, just to be a Can writer, and who in hell is more Canadian than you?? You write to the Council, get the forms, outline what you are doing (you don't have to outline very much, just tell them you're working on a novel which will be a kind of sequel to *Sawbones*), and ask for $12,000. You may not get twelve thousand, but you'll almost certainly get between $8,000 and $10,000. You then get three referees to write letter of ref. for you (crazy, but there it is). I would be honoured to be one, and also, any serious writer in this goddamn country would be honoured to be one, to write a letter for you. More than 3 letters never hurts—I would suggest Hugh MacLennan, me, Ernest Buckler,[3] Robert Weaver (CBC), George Woodcock (ed. of *Canadian Literature* and a great man of letters), and possibly a younger writer such as Margaret Atwood. It would be a privilege for any of us. If you don't feel like coping with all this bureaucratic nonsense, could you let me or some of us (Adele Wiseman would be also terrific) do the spadework?

This is not money for jam. You have earned it a thousand times over. It is the only way that we can get for you the kind of help you ought to have had many years ago. Will you let us try? When I think of all the people who have had grants (many of them deserving, some not, and some deserving but also on full professors' salaries, which most writers have never earned) I think you should give serious thought to this. Please don't let your old prairie pride get in the way. I would not presume to take any definite steps unless you felt you wanted to do this. But if you give the go-ahead, I know it can be done. Naim Kattan, of the Can Council, was really talking just about what could be done quickly. The Senior Arts Award takes longer, because you apply mid-October and don't hear until April. Please let me know. It is absolutely ludicrous that you have never had a Can Council grant.

Love,
Margaret

1. Naim Kattan (1928–), author and later professor, was head of the Writing and Publication Division of the Canada Council from 1967 to 1990. Ross enjoyed a short friendship with him in the mid-1950s and later contributed a few paragraphs to an essay Kattan published in *Tamarack Review* 40 (Summer 1966) titled "Montreal and French-Canadian Culture: What They Mean to English-Canadian Novelists."

2. See note 3 of letter to Ken Mitchell dated 28 March 1975.

3. Ernest Buckler (1908–1983) was a major writer in the 1950s and 1960s. His first book, *The Mountain and the Valley*, is still regarded as a classic work of fiction from this period.

To Margaret Laurence

Lakefield, ON

15 December 1975

Dear Margaret:

Thank you for your letter of November 17 and your suggestions regarding a Canada Council Grant to help me write a sequel to *Sawbones*. This sequel, however, is already written and pretty well revised. It needs another run or two through the typewriter, of course, but I've put it aside for a few weeks hoping that when I pick it up again I will be able to "see" it better. It should be ready to show McClellands about March.

Whether it will be worth showing is another matter. I don't know at this time what I've got. As I wrote to someone not long ago, I loathe it and I like it. It's all *about* Nick, but he's never on stage and I'm not sure that it works—that is to say, that he comes through as I want him. In any case, *Sawbones* having been such a flop—2,600 copies—it's unlikely McClellands will be interested. And even if they are—another 2,600 copies, what the hell—

Your letter sounds, Margaret, as if what you call "the Canadian literary community" is concerned about me, and that is the last thing I want. I have my pension to live on, comfortably enough, and to get in some travelling. I'm getting along fine; nobody owes me anything. If I haven't "made it" as a writer, I have only myself to blame. No one ever put the pressure on and said I *should* be one. But the 2,600 copies tell the story. I haven't made it myself, and well-wishers such as you can't make it for me.

When I finish the sequel to *Sawbones* will I try again? At least right now I'm inclined to say probably not, it's not worth it. Sometimes I think of a book on Greece and another on Spain, but rather as something to do in my old age—an excuse to go places and poke around—than as a project. Or perhaps try a few articles I don't know. I'm not only 68 (at least damned close to it); I'm also beginning to *need* my afternoon siesta.

A trip to Canada? Yes, I keep thinking of it but I don't know exactly when. I nearly came this fall, but my back was bothering me for a couple of months, easier now although it still grinds, and I decided to get on with the book so that I could forget it and be free again. There's uncertainty everywhere these days; I don't plan very far ahead. This coming spring I hope to go back to Greece for a month—providing, of course, things in that area haven't blown up by then.

Thank you again for your interest—and all the best for 1976.

As ever,
Jim

To John Moss
Sir George Williams University, Montreal
2 December 1975

Dear John:
You no doubt think me ungrateful, but far from it. In fact, the generosity of what you suggest overwhelms me.[1] But apart from being a colourless old man with a poor voice who would not help things along, I don't measure up. A two-day symposium in my honour, everybody saying what a fine writer I am, while all the time, in what we might say "practical terms," I am such a dud! *Sawbones Memorial*, despite a

number of favourable reviews, has sold 2,600 copies; *Whir of Gold*, 1,100. I have never been translated: apart from 3 short stories on TV, I have never been filmed. I'm not complaining; I have my own reservations about Ross; but what I would hear in Montreal, with the "facts" of my literary career staring me in my face, would have a hollow ring.

It is hardly for me to make suggestions—and I am not campaigning—but since you are concerned, and obviously very much "for" me, I will say that a paperback of *Sawbones* would help. I mention it because I learn from David Stouck of Simon Fraser that he wrote McClellands urging it so he could use it in his Can. Lit. courses, but they haven't answered. He says W.H. New[2] also wishes it were available, for the same reason. A few expressions of interest from professor-critics such as yourself and New might persuade McClellands that a paperback would not be a financial loss. They promised it when they accepted the book, but hard-cover sales having been so poor, it wouldn't be surprising if they have had second thoughts.[3]

But I repeat, John, I'm not campaigning. It's late; next month I'll be 68. At the moment I am at work on a sequel to *Sawbones*, but not, I'm afraid, with much enthusiasm. Even if it stands up as a novel—and at this stage, revising, I'm not at all sure—McClellands will no doubt think of those 2,600 copies and be wary. Revising, of course, is a depressing chore, and later I may feel the urge to scribble at something else; but right now I'm ready to call it a day and for the rest of the time left me try to relax and enjoy myself. Some make it; some don't. There's no use pretending. At least I can give myself an A for effort.

My warmest thanks for *your* effort. And I'm sorry.

Sincerely,
Sinclair Ross

---

1.   In this letter Ross is responding to an invitation to appear at a symposium about his work in Montreal. This event did not take place, but Moss's concern that his work be carefully analyzed and celebrated by academics was realized when he organized the Ottawa Symposium on Ross in 1990.

2. W.H. New (1938–), professor, author, and anthologizer, taught English at the University of British Columbia for more than thirty years.

3. McClelland & Stewart eventually brought out a paperback version of *Sawbones Memorial* in 1978 with an introduction by Lorraine McMullen. It was available in this edition for approximately twelve years. In 2001 it was reissued in paper by the University of Alberta Press.

From Andy Suknaski[1]

Regina, SK

5 March 1976

dear jim,[2]

sorry about this long silence. i've been absolutely selfish about my time and depleted energy (what remains of it to do anything creative) in the last couple months. unanswered letters have piled up in the last few months — now that I've quit my job and am on easy street, i can answer some of them. anyway — in the last month I've harvested and honed my winter wheat. what I call THE GHOSTS CALL YOU POOR[3] — about a 100 pages. Will no doubt add to it while omitting some poems in some future version that'll be another book.

   i know your discouragement re SAWBONES MEMORIAL — know it in the light of what people are going to have to pay for a paperback of WOOD MOUNTAIN POEMS. MACMILLAN'S spring catalogue lists it for $6.95 — for a paperback (128 pp) ! i don't think SAWBONES was a flop at all. it's just that people i think aren't buying the books the way they used to. i know i buy about half the books i used to buy — simply refuse to pay some of the prices. it's not the contents — it's the abysmal prices now that are going to be the signature of our defeat if these turkeys we call our publishers don't twig onto cheap newsprint and a simple attractive cover for books at a decent price people can afford. i think the day of the beautiful hardback is gone — unless it's done like kroetsch's BADLANDS[4] (newsprint paper with a cheap hard cover for $5). as far as I know BADLANDS has sold out. donno. donno. i don't even want to think of what a MACMILLAN book of poetry will cost two years from now.

the last few months working with the ole prairie men who wound up in pile o' bones[5] was trying at times—the stories, however, were a consolation and redeemed everything. a section of the GHOSTS is called *the orange lunchbox*—the best stories became poems, sometimes interwoven with the men's lives. finished work last friday. my co-workers gave me a present when we arrived, and then for the next hour we turned to the LIL BROWN JUG—finished work two hours earlier (10pm) and headed for the BUKORIA (the happy place in romanian) for beer...ole hanowski ending all goodbyes with "well, like I say, the world is not so big we cannot find ourselves again...we'll no doubt run into you sometime somewhere."[6]

happy to hear you've discovered purdy. very fine poet. it's sad to read that interview with him in CV II.[7] purdy deadset on the belief that he's all washed up. the power gone. a man can feel that at times about himself and believe there's a lull in the energies...but to admit it and dwell and mope about in beersteeped disillusionment is very sad very sad—turns one into a very piteous person.[8] i do hope the hell he gets out of that state of mind—i fear for him if he doesn't. he'll also have to stop all his yammering about dying and all that crap...always affirming "oh i'm all washed up...i'm gonna die soon."

i have about 5 readings to do by the end of the month. also want to read some things here in the archives—things about dumont, riel, and others. after that I head to wood mountain to my shack to heal from winter urban disasters. sometime in april I have to go to toronto to help publicize WMPS. in may i return to the mountains—leaving behind all books, typewriter (will take a couple books). a notebook and a pen. will take all my fishing equipment. and a sketchbox and my guitar—if possible, poems will have to go fuck themselves...i want to reclaim something of a mountain innocence i had once long ago when nothing mattered more than rainbow trout and love, in that order.

address end of march / WOOD MOUNTAIN eternal forwarding address—will write a decent letter from there.

Love,

Andy

1. Of Polish and Ukrainian descent, Andy Suknaski (1942–) was born in Wood Mountain, Saskatchewan, which he made the centre of his poetic world, examining the history and ethnic heritage of the people of the Canadian prairies. Suknaski initiated a correspondence with Ross in 1974. See Ross's letter to Roy St. George Stubbs dated 28 June 1975 for his view of the poet.

2. Like American poet E.E. Cummings, Suknaski insists on his own typographic trademarks—in this letter no capitalization is used except for occasional place names, publishers, and book titles wherein the whole of each word is capitalized.

3. *The Ghosts Call You Poor*, published by Macmillan, won the Canadian Authors Association Poetry Award for 1978.

4. *Badlands* by Canadian novelist Robert Kroetsch (1927–) was published by New Press in 1975 and proved to be one of his most important and popular novels.

5. Wascana, translated as Pile of Bones, was the aboriginal name for a creek where Regina, named for Queen Victoria, developed in the late nineteenth century.

6. Suknaski is presumably describing a drinking spree that includes a workmate named Ole Hanowski.

7. Al Purdy was interviewed by S.G. Buri and Robert Enright on 11 November 1975 in Winnipeg. The interview was published in *CV II*, Vol. 2, i (January 1976): 50–58.

8. In this statement about Purdy, Suknaski anticipates something of his own fate as a writer. His last book, *Silk Road*, was published just nine years after this letter was written. Except for the republication of *Wood Mountain Poems* with a new introduction by Tim Lilburn (Regina: Hagios Press, 2006), he has remained silent since that time.

To Andy Suknaski

Regina, SK

29 March 1976

Dear Andy:

Thank you for letting me see the two poems from *The Orange Lunchbox*. Yes, I remember the shamrock lard lunch pail—brings a world of things back to me. The lines "where hanowski's sad eyes will become a northern lake / when the sun finds a hold in the clouds above it" are memorably lovely and "spinning round that drive shaft like a wind wrapping a blanket round a clothesline"—well, I've seen a wind doing just that. Right on, as they say. All the best for *The Ghosts Call You*

Poor—although wishing you luck is not at all necessary. Both this and the orange lunchbox, incidentally, are fine titles. A friend in Winnipeg sent me *Leaving*[1] not long ago—a few pieces I recognized, many I hadn't see before. One of the lines—just one of many—that caught my eye and memory is "the budding willows that seemed to stitch the sky to the prairie at the horizon." I learn in this collection you are a traveller—that you went to the Tate to see Moore's drawings of the sleepers in the subway (I remember them in an exhibit during the war). I was in London—the Tate of course was closed, and everything removed from the National to a mountain hideout in Wales (I believe) but there was a show in the National of wartime artists. I remember the sleepers in the subways too and I wonder if in "Mirages"[2] you are thinking of Debussy when you write "to hear tolling bells of buried cathedrals." You give the impression of being very outgoing, and I—always tied in knots—think how fortunate you are—giving yourself, seeking and accepting contacts without reserve.

Yes, I agree that the prices publishers put on books are for many of us prohibitive, and I can't see why they can't put out cheaper editions. And yet they are no doubt shrewd businessmen concerned about making a profit—they *must* know what they're doing. No doubt about it, $6.95 for a paperback is going to scare buyers off. Hans Jewinski sent me a copy of his *Poet Cop*[3] in paperback, the usual newsstand style, which I see is marked $1.95—now why the hell can't Macmillans do the same. Yes, it's gratifying to have your first book in what I daresay will be a more attractive, better quality edition, but after all having your work *read* is the most important....Incidentally, Andy, I would like very much to have a copy of *Wood Mountain Poems* signed by you know who, which means I can't order it myself, and therefore—now no backtalk, you work hard and need your money—I enclose my cheque to cover cost and mailing. I already have wmp but that is beside the point. *I want the new one.*[4]

I didn't know about the interview with Purdy you mention. Fits of depression are part of the artistic temperament, I suppose, and as you say it would probably have been better not to talk about it publicly—but of course, interviews are quickly forgotten and he'll write it down. I admire some of his things—intellectually tough and at the same time sensitive.

I hope the trip to Toronto is successful and that you have a good summer in the mountains. Fishing equipment, sketchbook and a guitar—sounds wonderful, although I suppose there's plenty of hard work too. Myself, I feel a bit ragged—some health problems and *Price above Rubies* not going as smoothly as I would like. I *thought* it was finished, but then after it was all typed out for the *last* time I decided it needed more work. (Why the hell did I ever get mixed up with those damned Ukrainians!) But will take my time, letting it rest a bit. I have plans to spend the month of May in Greece and unless things blow up in the meantime I'm going ahead....Spain a bit tense these days—as always, nobody knows what's going to happen, although as yet it hasn't bothered me. Went to see a riot squad lined up with all their equipment, tear-gas throwers and shields etc. to meet a parade, but nothing happened. Frightening, though.

All the best,
[JSR]

1. Suknaski's poetry collection titled *Leaving* was published in 1974 by Repository Press in Alberta.

2. "Mirages" is one of the poems in *Leaving*. Ross refers to Claude Debussy's 1910 prelude entitled "The Sunken Cathedral," often cited as an example of musical Impressionism.

3. Although cheaply produced, Jewinski's collection of poems was nominated for the Toronto Book Award in 1976.

4. *Wood Mountain Poems* was originally published as a chapbook by Anak Press in 1973. Ross is presumably referring to this earlier edition when requesting the new one from Macmillan.

To Lorraine McMullen[1]

University of Ottawa, ON
18 July 1976

Dear Miss McMullen:
(This is probably not the correct way to address you, but there's no clue
in your letter.)

I'm delighted to hear you are doing a book about me and—although
you may find me frequently vague in my answers—I will do my best to
be helpful.

Influences—well, here's where the vagueness begins. I suppose
that to some extent, and more often than not without our knowing
it, we are influenced by everything we read. I started reading when
I was 7 and I'm still going strong, but I think I can truthfully say I
have never been a "disciple" of anyone. I have often been impressed
by a book or author, but it has been my way to wish I could do it and
pass on. When I was 9 or 10 I used to read the *Boy's Own Paper*[2] (now
folded, I believe) in an annual volume—the event of the year—and I
was out and out "crazy" about the Tarzan books. Perhaps they influenced me, I don't know. Moving on, I read Tolstoy and Dostoyevsky
and have gone back to reread *The Brothers K* and *Crime and Punishment*;
but while *As for Me and My House* and some of my short stories have
their share of gloom I feel, without pretending to be analytical, that it is
not Russian gloom. Then there was Faulkner, especially *As I Lay Dying*,
The Sound and the Fury and *Light in August*, and he's on my "to be reread
shelf." (Although I must admit I was always a bit afraid of him—those
endless serpentine sentences—afraid I might pick up the lilt and go
on endlessly too.) Also Hemingway—of course—especially *The Sun
Also Rises* and *Farewell to Arms*. Somewhere along the way there was a
"French period"—Sartre, Camus, Gide, Malraux, Mauriac[3] (strange that
someone from Saskatchewan with a Scottish-Presbyterian background
should have responded to the dark torments of his Catholic world). And
also somewhere along the way of course I read *Ulysses*—twice, with
many dips—but I think it would be correct to say (I still read as a child,
not a critic) that it was what he does with language that fascinated me,

the dazzle of his technique, if you like. I never "liked" Stephen or the Blooms, always remained on the outside.

Now the man who interests me is Gabriel García Márquez; *Cien Años de Soledad* is, I think, a really great novel, and at the moment I am reading an earlier one, *La Mala Hora*;[4] but if I ever get around to writing another story about a Saskatchewan village I am sure it will have slight resemblance to the Colombian one of *Cien Años*.

Probably it's because I don't read very well. I'm absorbed at the time, then pass on and forget. It's disgraceful how I forget. I would never make a teacher or critic.

You ask about Grove — no, I don't know him. I remember many years ago when I was living in Winnipeg and *Queen's* were publishing some of my stories, a friend went to the trouble of bringing me *The Master of the Mill* from the public library — it was out of print at that time — but for some reason I resisted it. I didn't like the style — that at least was what I told myself — but the real reason may have been deeper. A Canadian novel I read with great enjoyment in those days was Martha Ostenso's *Wild Geese*. It certainly made an impression, but I don't know about "influence."

Hardy, yes, in the interview[5] I mentioned him, although it was probably because I was extremely nervous and had to say *somebody*. I did, though, have great admiration for *The Return of the Native* — less, perhaps, for the story, than for the sombre mood and presence of the landscape.

A novel which impressed me tremendously when I was about 20, awed me, in fact, with the new intellectual world it spread before me — remember I was a Saskatchewan bank clerk with a Grade XI education — was Huxley's *Point Counter Point*;[6] but while it was still I suppose what you would call my "formative period" I think you'd have to look long and hard for traces of it in *As for Me...* and *The Lamp at Noon*.

None of which is very helpful, I know. Well, there's one strong influence at work in *Sawbones Memorial* — although not in the sense of absorbing through the pores a style or atmosphere. I mentioned Mauriac above, meaning François, Mauriac père. Well, his son Claude wrote a book, probably 20 or 25 years ago, called *Dîner en Ville* followed by *La Marquise Sortit à Cinq Heures*. No introduction, no descriptions, people just talk and think and the reader has to watch for clues and decide who is talking and thinking. (The Regina *Leader-Post* in its review of *Sawbones Memorial* complained that "Ross makes you figure out who's talking and readers shouldn't have to engage in that kind of activity.") For some reason the manner or technique appealed to me and I thought I saw possibilities, although with some concessions to the readers so that the amount of figuring out required wouldn't discourage them. I thought of a new building as a setting — the Royal Bank in Montreal where I worked had just completed an impressive new Head Office — with people wandering through remembering and reminiscing. However, I never got down to work on it — too difficult, no story — but I still kept thinking, at least occasionally, that a book centred on a new building might not be a bad idea. I don't know exactly when, or how my mind was working, but years later instead of a bank's Head Office it was a new village schoolhouse, teachers and pupils reminiscing etc., then a new village hospital, and as I already had a village doctor in mind ...

There, talk about long-windedness — but if you write again I promise to be concise and, allowing as always for a certain amount of vagueness, to the point. Yes, of course, if you come to Spain I should be very happy to meet you.

Yours sincerely,
Sinclair Ross

1.   A professor of English at the University of Ottawa, Lorraine McMullen (1926– 2002) wrote to Ross 18 June 1976 to say she had recently "signed an agreement with Twayne publishers to write a critical-analytical study" of Ross's works and asked if he would give her an account of the influences on his writing.

2.   *Boy's Own Paper* was published in England from 1879 to 1967, the first publication of its kind for young male readers. It was conceived of, and initially sponsored by, the Religious Tract Society of London to ensure that boys of all backgrounds were exposed to Christian moral teachings in their formative years.

3. From this list, Ross has identified in other letters and interviews his specific interest in reading Albert Camus' *The Stranger* and André Gide's *The Counterfeiter*.

4. Ross refers here to *One Hundred Years of Solitude* and *In Evil Hour* by Gabriel Garcia Márquez (1928–).

5. Ross made a taped interview with Earle Toppings in 1970 for the Ontario Institute for Studies in Education Series.

6. Aldous Huxley's novel, *Point Counter Point*, was first published in 1928. It shocked and delighted its readers with frank depictions of sexual infidelities and with the highbrow capers of its intellectual and bohemian artist characters.

To Ernest Buckler[1]

Bridgetown, NS
3 September 1976

Dear Ernest Buckler:
Just to say how pleased and grateful I am for the inscribed copy of *The Mountain and the Valley*.

I must confess that while of course I knew about it I finally got around to ordering it only five or six months ago, after seeing Chambers' book[2] and deciding it was high time. And it is truly a "mountain" of a book, impressive and moving; and, as I have just finished writing to Al McGuire,[3] I feel very close to it, despite the distance between Saskatchewan and the Maritimes. It "rang bells" for me all along the way.

A poignant and beautiful picture of a family, the ties and loyalties and tensions, and above all the silences. It is the measure of your achievement, of the insight and compassion with which you bring your people to life, that its dissolution hurts so much.

I look forward to settling down to it again — to read and to explore.

Sincerely,
Sinclair Ross

1.   See note 3 of letter from Margaret Laurence dated 17 November 1975.

2.   Ross is referring here to Robert D. Chambers's joint study titled *Sinclair Ross & Ernest Buckler*.

3.   Not identified.

To Ken Mitchell

University of Regina, SK

18 November 1976

Dear Ken:

Wrong church, wrong house—what a sleuth you turned out to be! I'm ashamed of you.

No, Horizon in *As for Me...* is not patterned after Arcola.[1] It's 43 or 44 years since I left Arcola, but even then it was relatively old and settled, with tree-lined streets (a few), a courthouse, and a land titles' office; whereas Horizon is bare, wind-swept, gritty. Arcola had a dozen or so houses which, by Horizon's standards, could be described as palatial.

What surprises me is that the old house where we lived is still standing. It must have been "reformed," as the Spanish say—places here are always being closed for "reformación"—for even in those days it was old and run down, with heaving floors and a leaky roof. It was too large for us, just Mother and myself, but when we arrived it was all that was available. Fifteen dollars a month. Later, I think about a year and a half, we found another, more satisfactory place, for which we paid a reckless eighteen. The good old days.

I'm sorry you aren't likely to be in Europe for a while, but I understand the financial problems—I myself keep putting off a visit to Canada because I doubt if I could do it, a month say, for much less than $2,000. I would suggest you make a list of hard questions when you are ready, and while I may not be able—or willing—to answer everything, I will certainly do my best to be co-operative.

I was very happy to read the enthusiastic review of *Cruel Tears* and hope it helps stoke the engine. The Greek story that you mention—

about Mrs. Mitchell's family—of course you must write it. The Greeks are a wonderful people, complex, maddening, astute, big-hearted, with a Hermes and an Odysseus still on every street corner. I have no quarrel with Spain—except the 20% inflation; that's official, it's no doubt closer to 25%—but there are days when I feel "homesick" for Athens and the islands.

No word from McClellands yet about *Price above Rubies*—which I assume is not good. They've had it over three months.

All the best to yourself and family,
Jim

---

1.   Ross always insisted in conversation that physically Horizon was based largely on Abbey, Saskatchewan, though he resisted drawing too close a comparison with any one town. Certainly Abbey is located in a more arid, treeless part of southern Saskatchewan. Horizon was in fact the name of an actual village, but it was a ghost town by the time *As for Me and My House* was published.

To Alvin Goldman

Montreal, PQ
10 May 1977

Dear Alvin:

Yes, I understand that you don't want to spend time and energy making contacts and then have the script[1] written by someone else, but I'm afraid I don't see a solution. It seems to me that tying you in would mean that I authorize you to offer producers a sort of "package deal," my book and your script. In other words, I endorse a script I haven't seen to the exclusion of all other scripts. It's not by any means that I am shying away from you as a script writer, but it would in effect give you practically complete control of the film rights. Granted I know nothing about the business, but it seems likely that many producers already know a writer whose work they like, or one to whom they are committed, and all those producers would be lost to me as potential purchasers. I know, as it is they aren't purchasing and business has to be drummed up, but I think I would rather leave the rights open and take my chances.

Not that I think my chances are good: I rather think that *As for Me...* is not good film material, especially today, with the pictures getting sexier and more violent. To a considerable extent, Philip is the trouble. In the book he's "there," brooding in the background, a presence making himself felt, but bring him onstage and he's a stick. Important: his hypocrisy is the motor which runs the book, the gnaw and anguish of having to live with himself as a liar and fraud, when, by nature, he is frank and honest—he's in a trap—but to make telling drama from his tight-lipped silences would take an awfully good director and an awfully good actor. And if his anguish is not revealed he is just a miserable bastard who needs a good boot up his ass.

And it has been around. Ted Kotcheff[2]—I think that's his name— "expressed interest" twice through McClellands, with details of his offers, and twice I "expressed agreement" but the contract never came. Peter Pearson, who had an option on it for 4 years, tried hard in both Canada and USA to no avail.[3] When the option lapsed he offered to buy the rights outright—his own money, he said—for $5,000. Not an exciting figure, so I countered yes, but what about 2% of the net profits as well, and what about giving me back the rights after say 5 years if the film isn't under way? He didn't deign to answer. Of course if someone came up with a good offer, real money, I wouldn't mind if he shelved it till Judgement Day.

I'm getting old, Alvin—hell, I'm already old, 69—which is one of the reasons I don't want the rights tied up. Probably no one is going to be interested, at least not in my time—I've been resigned to that for years; but just in case someone comes along, I want to be in a position to say yes.

Sorry to be negative. I repeat it's not because I have doubts about you as a script writer.

As ever,
Jim

P.S. If you have any ideas, or if I haven't understood what you intend, don't hesitate to come back.

1.   A screenplay for *As for Me and My House*.
2.   Ted Kotcheff (1931–) is a successful Canadian director whose features include film versions of Mordecai Richler's novels, *The Apprenticeship of Duddy Kravitz* (1974) and *Joshua Then and Now* (1985).
3.   See letter from Sheila Kieran to Peter Pearson dated 30 November 1972.

To Geoff Hancock[1]

Toronto, ON
1 October 1977

Dear Geoff Hancock:
I appreciate your suggestion that I give you an article on the writing scene in Canada 35 or 40 years ago, but I am not the one to do it. I was too isolated to be representative. There was, I am sure, even in those days, a great deal of literary activity of which I knew nothing.

A few years ago I was asked what it was like to be an author working in a bank during the depression years: I replied that I never thought of myself as an author working in a bank, but as a bank clerk trying to do a little writing on the side. A farm boy—incredibly "backward"—with Grade XI and responsibilities, I was lucky to have a job. Making my living as a writer was out of the question. *Queen's Quarterly*, where my stories were published, paid about $3.00 a page. (I suppose it was an honorarium rather than payment.) I remember it was $25.00 for "A Field of Wheat" and "The Lamp at Noon" and $50.00 for "The Painted Door." When *As for Me and My House* came out in New York I received an advance of $300, less an agent's fee of $30.00. And that was all. The edition sold out so perhaps the agent forgot to get in touch with me again. Or perhaps it was a very small edition.

The trouble, of course, was with me and the kind of story I wrote. It's hardly fair to blame Canada. There were markets in the States—and good ones, *The Saturday Evening Post*, for instance—if you could give them what they wanted. In Winnipeg, in fact, a woman had something like 50 *True Confessions* to her credit at $1,000 a seduction. She also had a class and taught writing.[2] (I met her once: a grey, prim, pleasant little woman whom you might take for the wife of a Methodist parson. After *As for Me...* was published, one of her pupils lamented to me, "If only you'd let me see the manuscript—half an hour and I could have turned it into a best-seller."[3]) But what could *Chatelaine* or *The Grain Growers' Guide*—or, for that matter, *Sat. Evening Post*—do with a story like "The Painted Door"? Just as I was lucky to have a job I was lucky to be published by *Queen's*. (Such was my hickish "backwardness," it was a long time before I understood that appearing in *Queen's* was something of a distinction.) To my knowledge, there were no "little" magazines to give fledgling writers a home, and of course no government grants.

Encouragement? Perhaps too much. By that I mean the occasional word of approval kept me going, and I understand now I might have had a better, more satisfying life if I had put writing behind me as something I wasn't up to and given my time to other things. Sir Andrew Macphail, for instance, wrote me of "A Field of Wheat" and "September Snow," "Two of the best stories ever written in Canada. The lamented Kipling could not have done better."[4] Naturally I was elated, even though I hadn't the foggiest idea who Sir Andrew Macphail was. (My mother's comment, incidentally, innocence itself, was, "Now wasn't it nice of him to say that, even if he didn't mean it." She knew who Kipling was.)

Which has nothing to do, of course, with Mavis and is simply a response to your letter....I hope your interview went well. She is indeed a fine writer and, as I have told her, she always makes me green with envy. I look forward to your special issue.

You speak of Canadian exiles: I never think of it that way. At least I never *feel* an exile. ("Breathes there a man with soul so dead etc."[5]—I'm afraid that's me. If it's not dead it's at least moribund.) I have a ruptured disc which is easier to live with in a mild climate, and apart from that I like it here. As I also liked it in Greece, I was back for a month's "holiday" in June—last year as well—and both times it was a sort of homecoming. If inflation here continues—it was 30% last year and is now running considerably higher—I may return. The recent devaluation of the peseta, 25%, has eased things for the time being. But the Canadian dollar has also slipped again lately, and if it keeps on falling I may have to come back to Canada. There would be compensations, I know, but I would leave Spain reluctantly—the sunshine, the Prado[6] etc. Just a few days ago I had a letter from a young Greek[7] who gave up his job in Athens last spring and went to work in Jeddah, Saudi Arabia. He's not very happy—he misses his wife and two-year-old daughter—and says, "The life is bad but good the pay so I stay until I can." Well, that's about how it is with me—I stay until I can.

I'm two-thirds of the way through *Rayuela* and in places find it tough going. Have *Libro de Manuel* waiting and it looks even tougher.[8] I envy you your youth and enthusiasm. You'll get back to South America all right.

Sincerely,
Sinclair Ross

1. Geoff Hancock, editor of *Canadian Fiction Magazine*, was putting together a special issue on Mavis Gallant and asked Ross if he would contribute an essay describing what it was like trying to get published in Canada in the 1940s.
2. Ross is referring to Lillian Beynon Thomas (1874–1951), a former suffragist and moderately successful short-story writer who taught creative writing classes in Winnipeg in the 1930s (one of her pupils was Gabrielle Roy).
3. Nellie Anderson, a magazine writer, made this comment to Ross. He knew Anderson as a member of the Phoenix Club, Winnipeg's creative writers association.
4. Andrew Macphail to Ross, 22 January 1936.
5. From Sir Walter Scott's "Lay of the Last Minstrel," canto VI, verse 1.
6. Spain's foremost art museum, located in Madrid.
7. Not identified.
8. Ross is referring here to two works in Spanish by Argentinean novelist Julio Cortázar (1914–1984). They have been translated into English with the titles *Hopscotch* (1966) and *Manuel's Book* (1974).

To Andy Suknaski
Regina, SK

14 November 1977

Dear Andy:

Sorry for the long silence. Not forgetfulness: in fact, you've been on my mind often, but the last year I have been somewhat depressed, poor health one of the reasons, and no letter is better than a gloomy one. Coming out of it however. Maybe next year will be better.

No work done—almost none. I wrote a sequel to *Sawbones Memorial* which the publishers didn't like—and they were right: it's put together awkwardly—but lately I have been revising and begin to think it's maybe not hopeless after all. I want to get rid of it—out of my mind, I mean, published or not—so I can get on with something else. I'm lazy about writing, need a good boot, but I realize I'm in better spirits—probably better health too—when I have something under way. Good therapy, no matter what it amounts to....[travel plans and finances excerpted here]

Yes, Andy, I know what you mean about certain people wearing masks. And how I know! When I was young there wasn't much of the coyote about me, but I have a fairly sharp eye now. It's one of the little ironies of life that if you start out starry-eyed, wanting to trust everybody, you're likely to end up a sour old bastard. The smart boys spot you as an easy mark and you get taken so often you begin to be suspicious of everyone. I've never mixed much with the "literary crowd" and while it must be interesting and sometimes stimulating to rub shoulders with the good ones, I imagine there's a lot of bitchiness and friction too. Artists and writers are a thin-skinned lot, I suppose that's the trouble. I'm sure I miss a lot but, especially at my age, I'm just as well to be out of things. I could never hold my own. I have one of those slow minds that think of the bright retort when the part's over; *esprit d'escalier* I think they call it.

More important, how are things with you? And *Ghosts*? That's the one I want to hear about. Warmest wishes for its success—both dollars and cheers — for in Canada, except for the lucky few, being a writer is not economically a bed of roses. Myself, I'd have starved long ago if I'd had to live on my royalties, and poetry, I'm sure, is even less remunerative than fiction.

I hope you had a good summer and caught your quota of trout. I hope too this letter reaches you, for I don't suppose you are still in Camrose. In future will try to do better.

As ever,
Jim

P.S. I nearly forgot: I liked Almighty Voice.[1] A good poem — the last six lines especially appealed to me. Keep them coming.

1. "Almighty Voice" appears in Suknaski, The Ghosts Call You Poor, 16–17. Based on an incident in La Ronge, Saskatchewan, where a three-year-old boy was killed by a pack of dogs in January 1975, the poem concludes with these lines: "small prairie child / almighty voice / the wild dog pack hunts us all / while we dream of those sweet fabled bitches / freedom / and justice."

To Kathren Mattson[1]
[no address on letter]

12 July 1978

Dear Kathren Mattson:

Thank you for your letter of June 20th. Your interest in As for Me and My House, after 37 years, is heart-warming.

I am afraid, however, it is beyond me to give you satisfactory answers. My approach to a character is not intellectual — nor even analytical. I try to "get inside" and then more or less go with the current. I say to myself—in Mrs. Bentley's case, did say—"Supposing I were a woman married to someone like Philip, devoted to him, burdened with a sense of guilt because marriage has clipped his wings—how would I think and feel, how would I try to work things out." Writing blind, I suppose you would say, not sure that a woman would think or feel that way, making no claims that I am right. You call her "a lost cause" and speak of her "tragic failure of the imagination." Well, I see her differently. At least, she has enough imagination to see and understand Philip's predicament. Possessive, of course; but isn't every woman in love possessive?

It is bewildering; many women who have read the book are militantly *for* her—poor soul, married to that terrible man; on the other hand, John Moss in one of his books describes her as petty, vindictive, jealous, possessive, catty, etc., etc., etc.[2]

As to Philip, the same. Supposing I entered the Church without conviction or faith and then found myself trapped? Perhaps he came out wrong—I make no claims for him either. When you say "his ultimate salvation" I assume you mean his finding himself as an artist. Well, *his* sense of guilt—his hypocrisy—has been weighing on him, shackling him. Out of the Church, I like to think he might begin to grow again, "get back on the rails." A happy future? No, probably not. In this world are there many happy futures? To sum up, I have great respect for both of them, and great compassion. To me they are both very human, and if you say then I must have some weird ideas about humanity, I make no defence. I am finished with them; such as they are, they are out on their own. I think it was Eliot who said somewhere—and I am probably not quoting him exactly—"For us there is only the trying. All the rest is the business of others."[3]

Needless to say how gratifying it is that others such as yourself continue to make the Bentleys their business. As you probably know, *As for Me…* was first published in New York in 1941. This fall it is being brought out again in the U.S. by the U. of Nebraska Press.[4] A very small publishing event, I know. Still, it gives me a little lift.

Yours sincerely,
Sinclair Ross

P.S. No, I have dipped into Blake several times, but my knowledge of his poetry is superficial. If I remember right, I became lost in Jerusalem. *He had no influence whatever on* As for Me...

1. Addressee unidentified.
2. See note 3 of letter to John Moss dated 15 May 1973.
3. In "East Coker" V (*Four Quartets*) T.S. Eliot writes "For us, there is only the trying. The rest is not our business."
4. *As for Me and My House* was published as a Bison Book in 1978 and introduced by David Stouck.

From Margaret Laurence

Lakefield, ON
31 July 1978

Dear Sinclair Ross,[1]
Some of us have decided it is time that writers try to achieve some input regarding Canada Council grants in the Senior Arts Award category. We would like to be able to apply from time to time on behalf of a writer whom we feel has made an outstanding contribution to the literature of our country, for an award which would express at least in some way our gratitude for this contribution. We have discussed this project, and in searching for an ideal candidate your name was the obvious first choice.[2] You have never had a Canada Council award. You have made an enormous contribution to Canadian literature, both in your own writing and through the fact that you have been mentor (whether you realized it or not) to so many of us. We would like to ask your co-operation, therefore, with this pilot project. You have pioneered in other areas. We ask you now to pioneer in this—in order to clear the field for those who will follow you. Will you allow us to apply on your behalf for a Senior Arts Award? We will do all the paper work as far as the application is concerned. We will obtain all the letters of reference. All you will have to do is sign the completed form,

a necessary procedure because of Canada Council regulations. After debate, we have unanimously chosen you as the writer we would most like to have as the recipient of a Senior Arts Award in which the candidate was nominated by a group of his peers. With your name we think we have the best possible chance of success — therefore, if you will, you can help us to establish what we believe is a vital new granting procedure in behalf of Canadian writers.

With every good wish,

Margaret Laurence	*W.O. Mitchell*
Adele Wiseman	*Jack Ludwig*
Timothy Findley	*Mordecai Richler*
Margaret Atwood	*Jane Rule*
Graeme Gibson	*Robert Kroetsch*
Gabrielle Roy	*Pierre Berton*
Marie-Claire Blais	*June Callwood*
Sylvia Fraser	*Charles Taylor*
Harold Horwood	*Gwendolyn McEwen*
Alice Munro	*Silver Donald Cameron*

1. Laurence uses the formal salutation because she is writing on behalf of a group.
2. The idea of trying to get Ross a financial award of some kind was not new in the writing community. Sheila Kieran had written to Laurence 15 February 1975 hoping the latter would use her influence to secure for Ross a Molson Award.

To Margaret Laurence

Lakefield, ON

21 August 1978

Dear Margaret:

I have been in Greece for four weeks and received your letter a few days ago on my return.

My warmest thanks for your interest and concern. It's good to know that you, Adele and so many others have been thinking about me. After careful thought, however, I find I must say no.

As I understand it, the purpose of the Canada Council is to help writers on their way, make it possible for them to write their books. If the Council were to extend its program to cover out-and-out awards for books already written, that is to say, for recognition, not aid, and if my name were brought forward and approved by the Selection Board, then surely an announcement would be made, a cheque mailed, and that would be it. There would be no question of references, paper work or forms to sign. I have read and re-read your letter, and every time it comes out the same: in effect I would be applying for financial aid, if not for a particular project, then no doubt to "further my writing career." If I had a project in mind requiring, say, travel or research, I wouldn't hesitate five seconds in applying, and you would be the first I would turn to for a reference. But at the present time I have no such project.[1]

As you know, I'm retired from the Royal Bank on pension. That is to say, my time is my own, my living assured. Not one damned thing stands between my typewriter and a best-selling G.G. winner but *me*. I know—poor old Ross and Mrs. Bentley, we've been around such a long time and never had a G.G.—but whose fault is that? The last thing we want is Canada's writing community to feel under an obligation to arrange something by way of compensation for all those dust storms and Russian thistles.

Sorry to sound so churlish. I understand and am grateful for the generous goodwill which has prompted your letter.

Yours sincerely,
Sinclair Ross

1.   Ross never did receive financial assistance of any kind for his writing. And except for the story "Spike," he never sought nor was offered payment in advance for any of his work. He felt it would be like a farmer taking a loan against next year's harvest.

From Robert Weaver
CBC, Toronto, ON
29 September 1978

Dear Jim:

I've been intending for months to write to you, and now that I have an additional reason for a letter I find myself nervous about writing because I don't want to seem to be interfering in your business.

It's a small world here, as you know, and this week I discovered that Margaret Laurence and some other writers have been trying to persuade you to apply for a Canada Council grant. I told Margaret that I would write and add an editor's support for the idea, but that I also knew that you were perfectly able to make up your own mind and unlikely to be influenced by me. If you could bring yourself to apply for a grant, I'm sure you know that you could have a lot of support from your fellow writers—and from me as an editor, if you wished. I still have a letter you wrote to me three or four years ago, and at that time you did seem to be interested in doing some more writing, so you really have every justification for accepting a grant.

I can understand that you may find it almost impossible to make yourself apply. It's curious that when the Ontario Arts Council was being established I went to see their first literary officer, Ron Evans, who was a friend of mine, to try to persuade him that the Council should put aside some money every year that would be offered to certain writers, painters, musicians who, for one reason or another, might find it unbearable to have to have to go through the whole application procedure. Ron, who has been very flexible in his dealings with writers, magazines, and book publishers, understood what I was getting at but said that he was sure the Council would draw back from any procedure that liberal and that demanding on their own judgment—and they have. With politicians to answer to, all the arts councils demand applications, supporting letters, etc, etc. My annual applications for *Tamarack Review*[1] always turn out to be the most difficult thing I have to do for the magazine, and I guess it says something about the system that in the twenty-two years we've been publishing, I've never been able to persuade any of the other editors to do this job for me—so I do it to keep the magazine alive and continue publishing poets and fiction writers.

Anyway, if you do decide to apply for a grant, and if I can help in any way, please let me know. There's a new development at the Canada Council: an annual grant to a writer (one English, one French) of $18,000.00 a year for a three year term. But again, an application is required.

Since I'm writing after such a long time, I'll try quickly to bring you up to date about my life. I had some years as a reluctant, and not very good, administrator. I can handle budgets and such matters with no difficulty (a hangover from my three years in the bank?), but I was too sympathetic to do well with staff problems, I hate meetings, and I'm not ambitious enough—or in the right way—for the administrative world that has grown in the CBC. So I finally stepped down in the midst of internal wars. I had six months last year negotiating for the CBC with ACTRA (the radio and television writers and performers union), a job I quite liked. Now I'm back in programming in a period of budget restraint, and since I had appointed someone else to run "Anthology" when the administration became too pressing, I haven't got that series any longer. I'll enclose a brochure that describes one thing I'm working on right now. However, it's boring not to have enough to do or as much involvement with writers as I'm used to. I may be joining you in retirement in a couple of years—but only to get some other work because my family is still young.

The children are fine, by the way, except that David had the misfortune to become a teenager too fast. He's as tall as I am at thirteen, and in fact grew so quickly the bones and muscles in his knees didn't knit properly (not an uncommon problem, apparently, but usually not at age eleven); so he had to give up hockey and track, and is just getting back to sports this fall. Not much of a student, and school is depressingly not much changed from our day in some respects. My daughter—eleven—is untroubled by the world, school, and such matters, and a chore for her brother.

I've just edited a short story anthology—writings of the past ten years or so—due out in about two weeks, and I have two other anthologies I'm planning to work on this winter: not short story collections, I really think I've done my last of those.[2] Best of all, I review mystery novels for the Toronto *Star*—there are only two of us in Canada! Now that I've broken silence—with real apologies, Jim: the CBC did get to me in the past two or three years—I hope you'll break silence too. At least think once more about the Canada Council, and forgive me if I'm interfering.

Would there ever be a new story for *Tamarack Review*?[3]

As ever,
Robert Weaver

1.   *Tamarack Review*, edited by Robert Weaver, was published for 28 years beginning in 1956. Chiefly a magazine of poetry, it also included some short stories and non-fiction essays and featured early work by writers such as Leonard Cohen, Alice Munro, and Margaret Atwood.

2.   Weaver refers here to *Canadian Short Stories*, 3rd series (Toronto: Oxford University Press, 1978). No further anthologies appear under Weaver's name until *Small Wonders: New Stories by Twelve Distinguished Canadian Authors* published by CBC Merchandising in 1982.

3.   In his reply to Weaver of 14 October 1978, Ross repeated what he had written to Laurence—that he no longer had a writing project on his desk and was therefore not eligible for an award. It would be ten years before he submitted another piece of writing for publication and that would be a family memoir, "Just Wind and Horses," rather than fiction.

To David Stouck

Simon Fraser University, Burnaby, BC

30 January 1979

Dear David:

Yesterday 4 copies of the U. of Nebraska Bison Edition arrived. I have been waiting to write so I could give you a piece of my mind if the Introduction didn't suit me.

But it's all right—you get an "A." Not only because you are kind in what you have to say, but also because you are discerning. I am especially pleased that you take a balanced view of Philip and Mrs. Bentley. Myself, as I have no doubt written you, I have always felt they were both in a trap, both victims, and as you correctly say, "The novel's deepest pattern is rooted in the psychology of Philip." You of course made the point in "The Mirror and the Lamp"[1] that it was his story more than hers. I particularly like, near the end, "[Its] optimistic ending is erected like a false front that will soon topple in the wind." I hadn't thought of it before. Very good.

As to the appearance of the book, I gather from your card you don't like the way the title has been handled. Yes, I know what you mean—it doesn't stand out, you have to look, but on the other hand, to my eye, it has been fitted into the picture so that it becomes an integral part of it; and it also serves to break up the flat expanse of tracks and gravel. A wonderful photograph, incidentally—at least for prairie specialists.[2] Rings many bells. I agree, too, that the book is easier to handle and read than the NCL editions....But you also mention *my* picture—not a sign of it. The contract covered both a hardback and paperback; possibly they have brought out both and you have the hardback—I assumed they had brought out only one.[3]

Not knowing what to expect in the way of American response, I am playing safe and expecting nothing. I do hope, though, it does well enough to justify Nebraska's faith in it.[4]

A few days ago I had a letter from the Canada Council to tell me *As for Me...* has been selected for publication and translation—should be the other way round—in French. What happens now, I have no idea—all they say is "Congratulations." I suppose they find a translator and then a Quebec house to bring it out—probably a matter of 18 months or 2 years.[5]

In a letter last fall you asked about my mother, and what she thought of my writing. Well, to answer truthfully, not much. She thought it was a good thing to write, she had a Scottish respect for books and "things of the mind," but she also had respect for success and used to shake her head and say, "Why don't you write something cheerful that people will read?" She liked "Cornet at Night" and "A Field of Wheat" and that was about all. As for Me—no—but she had what is probably a sound criticism of it: They have been married too long. Mrs. B's devotion would not have stood up to his aloofness and lack of response for so many years. Two or three at the most, and she would have lost patience and told him off. Well, it all happened a long time ago.

More another day—

Best 1979 wishes for you and your family, and another thank you both for the Introduction and the missionary work that preceded it.

Sincerely,

Jim

1. See David Stouck, "The Mirror and the Lamp in Sinclair Ross's *As for Me and My House*," reprinted in Stouck, *Sinclair Ross's* As for Me and My House: *Five Decades of Criticism*, 95–103.
2. The black and white photograph, taken by Wayne Wiens, is of a weather-blistered train station in Miami, Manitoba.
3. The Bison edition of *As for Me and My House* was published in both hardback and paper format, but the hardback had no dust jacket. Neither version included a photograph of Ross.
4. The first printing of 5,000 copies sold slowly. A second printing of 5,000 in 1989 sold more quickly, but in the mid-1990s University of Nebraska dropped the Canadian paperback title from their list.
5. *As for Me and My House* was translated into French by Louis-Bertrand Raymond with the title *Au service du Seigneur?* and published by Montreal's Éditions Fides in 1981.

Ross with friends in Vancouver, 1992. L – R : *John O'Connor, Irene Harvalias, David Stouck, Sinclair Ross, Mary-Ann Stouck.* [Private collection; David Stouck]

To Alvin Goldman
Montreal, PQ
5 February 1980

Dear Alvin:

I was pleased to have your card and message. Myself, this year I didn't send cards. Not feeling very energetic, I delayed until it was too late. It's good that you are embarked on a novel. I'll have any number of questions when I see you. In the meantime, fingers crossed.

Something may happen in the meantime, but my plans are to return to Montreal the end of March. I feel *fairly* well. I'm on a drug which is pretty well controlling the tremor in my hand, but I tire easily. I probably told you earlier I had vascular sclerosis, but all three doctors I saw were wrong; which is to say that for five or six months I was taking drugs which were of no help and in fact gave me headaches and nausea. My problem is Parkinson's disease. It's something you don't die of—so I believe—but you never recover from it either. The neurologist I'm seeing now assures me I won't lose my mind, although in ten years' time I may be somewhat forgetful. (God bless him!) Exercise, keep active and I should remain *fairly* well—all the time, of course taking my pills.

I plan to have Iberia reserve a room at the Laurentian for a couple of nights and then see if I can find a room in one of the rooming-houses on Sherbrooke. I think I'm going to try to find an apartment in the same areas as when I lived in Montreal: McGill to Park, Sherbrooke to Pine—a number of reasons; but if there's nothing, I'll have to go farther. As soon as I'm installed—at least have a bed and a few dishes, so I can live, I will have to see a doctor, not only for an examination but for a prescription for drugs. I'll probably be turning to you for advice and suggestions, but I promise not to overdo it.

One liberty I'm taking concerns the 14 or 15 cartons of books I'm bringing. I have to put an address on them, of course, but as yet I haven't one so I'm saying c/o of Alvin Goldman. There's no danger of their being dropped at your door, however, as they have to go through Customs. They will send an advice of arrival and I'll be in touch. The damned things are a lot of work, but I'm going slowly. Douglas was over the other day to see if, among my discards, there is anything he wants, and he and Dallas are coming tomorrow to look again.[1] With what they're going to cost me I could buy a lot of new ones, but that's the way we're made.

Douglas and Dallas are both well and seem to be settling into Málaga contentedly. A big apartment with a fine view of Málaga Bay, all their furniture and books etc., installed to their satisfaction. The middle of March they're away again for a couple of months to Italy....I'm going to miss Málaga, of course, but I'm beginning to look forward now to Montreal again. I'll probably have some bad moments with my French and get mixed up with Spanish, but I'm not worrying about it.

All the best to you both. Looking forward to seeing you again and catching up on Canada.

As ever,
Jim

1. Douglas Tunstell, whom Ross had first met in Winnipeg through Roy Daniells, had worked for a time alongside Alvin Goldman at the National Film Board in Ottawa. He and his partner, Dallas Thorston, retired to Málaga in the late 1970s.

To Keath Fraser
Vancouver, BC

3433 Durocher St. Apt. 803, Montreal, PQ

1 August 1980

Dear Keath:
As you see I have finally made the move. For the last 2 years my health has been going down—Parkinson's disease—and I decided it was a bit risky living in a foreign country. Getting money, signing etc.—as

you probably know, one of the symptoms of Parkinson's is a trembling hand and some days it's a problem to write. (And to type; this letter tells the story.) There are drugs, but the problem is tolerating them. The neurologist here says he can't improve on what they prescribed in Málaga, so I shuffle and shake and tell myself it could be worse.

Yes, I miss Málaga, although I've been here only 4 months so I haven't had to stand up to winter weather yet. I find Montreal changed, of course, but so far at least I have encountered no hostility—on the contrary—and there seems to be as much English spoken as in the old days. I think it's a little cheaper than Spain, and as to taxes, I don't know yet but they probably will not be as steep as the flat 25% no exemptions I paid as a Non-Resident. Travel? I don't know—the trip from Málaga to Montreal left me winded and unenthusiastic—but I'm thinking guardedly of New York, Mexico and perhaps next summer the West Coast.

Glad to hear of your writing activities and hope there are encouraging results. Keep me posted. It's a long, uphill climb and from what I hear things are getting more difficult in Canada. I suppose you know how drastically McClellands are cutting their lists; I was one of their 85—I believe—whom they squeezed. Both *Whir of Gold* and *Sawbones Memorial* have been dropped. They commissioned a ms about me for their Cdn. Writers Series, then without taking the trouble to let me know, dropped it. Somebody else, the author tells me, a small house in Saskatchewan, is bringing it out.[1] Ken Mitchell—you may have run into him. He's interested in the theatre too.

All the best to you both. If ever you're in Montreal be sure and call me. I don't do too badly at the table providing I don't try soup.

As ever,
Jim
Telephone—unlisted 845 0678

1.　McClelland & Stewart encouraged Ken Mitchell to prepare a short monograph on Ross for their series of critical introductions to Canadian writers, but when they stopped adding new titles to the series in 1980, Mitchell signed a contract for his study of Ross with Coteau Books of Moose Jaw, Saskatchewan.

To Ken Mitchell

University of Regina, SK

5 August 1980

Dear Ken:

I'm sorry to hear of the rough time Roula has been having. It's a terrible cloud to have hanging over her—and you. Perhaps going to China is the best thing that could happen to her—she'll be distracted from herself.[1]

No, I can't imagine how you go about teaching Eliot and Shakespeare to the Chinese; it's certainly a challenge—a "pedagogic adventure."[2] Good luck!

Sorry you feel I unbosomed myself more to McMullen than to you.[3] I don't think there's much more in the way of biography in her book than in what you knew—except that, as I'm sure I wrote you in a previous letter, she was interested in my "religion" and asked a number of questions. How come that I, something of a Unitarian, should have read so much of François Mauriac, father of Claude, one of France's most Catholic writers etc. In fact, I wasn't particularly co-operative. She brought a tape recorder with her and I refused, absolutely, to work with it. Instead, we had lunch and dinner a few times—the most dangerous way, from the interviewee's point of view—and I suppose she was a good listener.

As to a play of *Sawbones*, I'm interested of course, but am a bit vague about rights—I'll have to ask McClelland's. They have dropped it from their lists—also *Whir of Gold*—as so much dead wood. Their cuts have been drastic, about 85 authors, I believe; "in order to survive," Jack McClelland wrote me 8 or 9 months ago. What happens, so far as rights go, when a publisher drops a book, is what I'll have to find out. Yes, someone is interested in a film of *As for Me...*, but at the moment, so far as I know, nothing is happening. It's a matter, presumably, of finding financial backing. Re: U. of Nebraska edition—I haven't seen or heard a thing. Flat on its face again, no doubt—typical Ross.

My own health is about the same—not very good. The damned drug I take for it gives me ear trouble and hives, and nobody, not surprisingly, is remotely interested. 72 and itchy—so what? Nobody is remotely interested either in my apartment problems. They promise to do things and don't; yes, yes, we'll get around to it.

Have a good time in China. You'll likely be a terrible pain in the neck when you get back, showing off how well you handle chopsticks. And all the best for Roula—

Jim

1.   Ken Mitchell's wife, Roula, was seriously ill with cancer. She died in 1982.
2.   Mitchell had arranged to teach at a university in Nanking for a year.
3.   Ross is referring here to Lorraine McMullen's book, *Sinclair Ross*, in the Twayne World Authors Series, 1979. In a letter to Ross 31 July 1980, Mitchell expressed surprise that Ross had given McMullen considerable biographical information when Ross had previously told Mitchell that he "thought biography was not interesting and unnecessary."

To Keath Fraser

Vancouver, BC

3463 Ste. Famille St., Apt. 704, Montreal, PQ

21 January 1981

Dear Keath:

My warmest thanks for your handsome card. I'm delighted that someone should know my birthday and be thinking of me. Tomorrow—73. Must admit that The Golden Years aren't all they're cracked up to be.

I envy you the mild weather in Vancouver. Here it's been polar— better the last few days but still cold. I find I can't take it—several times started out and had to turn back. I think the Parkinson's has something to do with it. I'm starting to think of Vancouver, but read in the paper that it's very expensive—especially rents. Here I'm paying $260 plus water tax, roughly $25 a month, for 2 and a half rooms—could I find something adequate for the same money in V.? I think—at my age and with my health problems one must always add a rider to his plans. I will come to V. in May for a look around—and then perhaps move in September. I'll be in touch and if I come in May I will be very grateful if you can make a reservation for me in a modestly priced hotel or rooming house.

You sound as if you are living an ideal life—writing, reading, enjoying a mild climate and getting in some travel. I hope the writing is coming along....I don't mean to be nosey but I'm curious to know if you're working on a novel—how's that for a hint?

Yes, I was pleased that Woodcock had so much to say about *As for Me and My House* and *Sawbones*.[1] And yes, it might have made a difference if there had been a little enthusiasm 40 years ago, but there's no use thinking about it or brooding. Intermittently I am working on a novel which common-sense says will go nowhere: a 40-year-old widower with a 17-year-old son who has the mental age of 3. Can you imagine anyone picking a worse subject. In plain English, I'm nuts.[2]

I've also been having apartment trouble—noise and more noise. The neighbours object to *my* noise, the electric typewriter, so I have to keep it to a minimum.[3] The apartment house looks fine but it is fairly new and you hear everything. And the damned electric typewriter, I can't get used to it—my left hand is in rather poor shape—and I'm forever getting capitals when I don't want them. Well, enough griping—as the doctor says, I'm an old man, and old people always have something wrong. Compared with many, I'm not too badly off.

Hope to see you about May.[4] Say "hello" to Lorraine for me—her job sounds fascinating.

All the best,
Jim

1. George Woodcock wrote very positively about Ross in "Rural Roots," *Books in Canada* 9 (October 1980), 7–9.
2. Ross titled this manuscript "Teddy Do." It did not survive with his papers, but to Keath Fraser he gave a verbal account of this story wherein the father is a pedophile and abuses his handicapped son.
3. Friends reported that on his return to Montreal Ross became paranoid, a condition sometimes experienced by those afflicted with Parkinson's disease.
4. Ross didn't make the trip to Vancouver until the following year.

To Wilfred Cude

R R # 2, West Bay, NS

11 November 1981

Dear Wilf Cude:

Thank you for your generously long letter.

As to poor Mrs. Bentley, it's a long time ago—the book came out in 1941, which means the actual writing took place at least two years earlier—and it's impossible to recapture my thoughts and problems as I "wrestled" with her. I do remember, though, deliberately making her a little hard and bitter where Judith was concerned just so she would not turn out "pure gold." Apparently I felt I had room, just as I deliberately roughed up old Sawbones to make sure he didn't emerge as "pure gold" either, a stereotype of a bland and benevolent old country doctor. Back to Mrs. B., I *think* I was aware of the basic problem of having her tell the story: part of the time she is giving the reader "the facts" of their lives and situation, and part of the time she is giving her version of them but—apparently, again—I was satisfied it didn't matter and that the reader would "see through" her and find his way. Very sloppy work on the author's part. Off with his head!

I have been reading and enjoying what you have to say about *Fifth Business*, *Lady Oracle* and *St. Urbain's H*. I have read all of them, but now am telling myself I must reread them; in other words you are the right kind of critic.[1]

I wish you many years and many battles.[2]

Sincerely,
Sinclair Ross

1. Ross is referring to Cude's book of criticism titled *A Due Sense of Differences: An Evaluative Approach to Canadian Literature*. Two of this book's chapters focus on *As for Me and My House*.

2. Wilfred Cude, an independent scholar, has recorded his "battles" with the academy in *The PHD Trap* (1987), in which he describes the formidable obstacles and frustrations preventing a PHD candidate from successfully completing a degree.

From Ken Mitchell

University of Regina, SK
15 December 1981

Dear Jim,

Here is a "wee giftie" for Christmas.[1] I hope you can enjoy looking it over. Perhaps Coteau Books have already sent you a copy. Anyway, we'd be pleased to get your comments, even if they're critical. A rather handsome publication, I thought, for a small press. And I believe that with the inclusion of your two stories, it may attract some national critical interest.

I do expect to be in Montreal sometime in the second half of March, doing workshops on a couple of new plays. And I'd like to get together with you very much, for as long as you might wish, and wherever you like. Just to chat, really. I'd like to persuade you of the value in coming to see the opening of "The Hunter Memorial" (a change of title suggested by the adaptation to stage) in Edmonton.[2] I recently finished the second draft, and it's more exciting than ever. I'm never very objective about these things in progress, but I swear it's the best play I've written. The dialogue, of course, is already there—brilliantly—and that makes a big difference. But it's in the dramatic structure, a sort of prairie *Our Town*,[3] that my contribution will be apparent. Benny is on stage almost completely throughout, providing a musical counterpoint to the conversations. If it comes off (theatre is always a dodgy operation), it will be in July or August, and I guarantee you will enjoy it. You must come, even if disguised as a Trappist monk. Doc Hunter is a monumental character.

Anyway, I hope to see you in March. All my plans are tentative at the moment. My poor Roula is in very bad health, none of the treatments have worked finally, and she is dying. She has a terrible fear of hospitals, needles, pain, etc., so we are trying to look after her at home as long as possible. I was able to finish my semester of teaching, touch-and-go at times, and we're all determined to have a good Christmas. I hope you will be having company; do you have friends in Montreal who are able to help out?

I am considering another "Ross" project, as my other two appear to be going so well. I'd like to propose to a publisher—Coteau perhaps—a volume of your previously uncollected stories. That is, I'd like to edit the volume; by editing I mean putting together, introducing, arranging an order, providing notes, etc.—not changing them. I count eight uncollected stories (including "Spike"), and if that isn't enough, I think we could also include the two articles we've listed in the bibliography. What do you think? Can I put together a proposal? It may not be a really hot-selling item (though then again it might), but it would be of great importance and interest to the growing "Canadian Literature" community, especially on the Prairies. Please consider it.[4]

Now I must go. Best wishes for the season and the new year,

Ken

1.   This letter was accompanied by a newly published copy of Mitchell's *Sinclair Ross: A Reader's Guide*.

2.   "The Hunter Memorial" is Mitchell's stage adaptation of *Sawbones Memorial*. It was workshopped by Northern Lights Theatre in Edmonton in May 1982 and was scheduled for the Lennoxville Festival later that summer, but the festival folded mid-summer before the play was produced. The cast of fifteen characters made it a

potentially expensive production and the only other presentations it received were workshop performances by the Saskatchewan Playwrights Centre in Regina and the Stratford Festival in Ontario, both in the mid-1980s.

3.   Thornton Wilder's immensely popular *Our Town* (Pulitzer Prize for 1938) is a sombre story of birth, life, and death in a small American community.

4.   Ross wrote to Mitchell 23 December 1981 explaining that Lorraine McMullen had already taken up the idea of bringing out the uncollected stories. They were published by University of Ottawa Press in 1982 as *The Race and Other Stories*.

To Alvin Goldman
Montreal, PQ

2060 Comox St. Apt. 501, Vancouver, BC

19 March 1982

Dear Alvin,

A very brief note for the moment to let you know I arrived a bit tired but in one piece. Furniture not here yet and am still in the hotel. The apartment—well I hope and think it will work out, location very good, a step from Stanley Park and not very far from the sea. Vancouver—at least this part—looks wonderful, with impressive mountain backdrops but it's *cold* despite the spring sunshine. Well, more thermals.

I hope the script is progressing satisfactorily and that you *won* in the Rental Board dispute.

All the best to you both—
Jim

P.S. As yet, no telephone.

From David Williams

University of Manitoba, Winnipeg, MB

29 October 1982

Dear Sinclair Ross,

I wouldn't presume to bother you with an academic piece if the basic narrative facts of *As for Me and My House* were better known. But since no one has ever identified Paul Kirby as the father of Judith West's child, I take encouragement from the thought that you might have been waiting for us to read back the novel you actually wrote.[1] Philip, as I recall, was maturely disillusioned and unexpectant about his drawings too, but still hankered for a little recognition behind his front of resignation.

If you have indeed been keeping Goethe's rule of silence[2] these past forty years while your readers stumbled, then I am both humbled and amazed. There's an artistic chastity here which rivals Philip's own silence about the child he adopts. I don't mean to embarrass you in this, but I'd like you to know what you mean to younger writers like me, how you've made it so much easier for a kid from North Central Saskatchewan to believe in his community's need of an artist to paint the soul. I grew up on the other side of Prince Albert, Lac Vert, south of Melfort. We were hidebound fundamentalists; I didn't know there were writers from our own place till I got to University in the mid-sixties with an evangelical pastor's diploma in hand. It was "Cornet at Night," from Carlyle King's *Saskatchewan Harvest*, that first made me feel a writer had stood on my ground.[3] That story continues to haunt me, to touch a lot of deep hurts and longings from my own growing up in the Fifties. I'm very grateful to you for "proving up" the land, for making it artistically inhabitable. Because your family (I assume) were there first, you might not share the same farm-boy experience of calling each quarter by the name of the homesteader. But when my grandfather took his five boys out of the valley of dry bones down by Nokomis and moved up to the shower-belt of Lac Vert in 1929, he bought his first quarter from Great West Life[4] who'd foreclosed on the John Wullum family who homesteaded in 1907. There was a kind of magic in the memory of those who had been there first. The difference with books is that they are still with us.

I know too that Bob Kroetsch has told me that *As for Me and My House* is the first book in our literature, the great text that stands at the beginning, as does *The Scarlet Letter* in American literature (my adopted, academic specialty). Somehow I doubt that the relation is coincidental, even though your handling of "sin" and the relative sufferings of women and men and the mode of redemption are almost completely opposite to Hawthorne. Even if I'm wrong in my reading here, please understand that you've made my own novels possible, and I only wish you well.

Sincerely,
David Williams

1. Professor David Williams is referring here to his article, "The 'Scarlet' Rompers: Towards a New Perspective in *As for Me and My House*."
2. Williams may be referring here to the fact that Johann Wolfgang Goethe (1749–1832) defended his privacy, particularly holding himself aloof from his younger contemporaries.
3. *Saskatchewan Harvest*, edited by Carlyle King, was published by McClelland & Stewart in 1955.
4. The Great West Life Assurance Company was founded in Winnipeg in 1891 and has functioned both as a life and health insurance company and a financial securities investment company.

To David Williams

University of Manitoba, Winnipeg, MB

30 November 1982

Dear David Williams—

Thank you for your letters of Oct. 29 and November 22. It is gratifying to know that my stories made a favourable impression on you when you were growing up.

I have health problems, however, and am not up to commenting on your article in detail, nor, I'm afraid, in entering into a correspondence regarding it.

To be brief: so far as I am concerned, Paul Kirby is not the father of Judith West's child. He is a mild rebel thoroughly rooted in the conventional small-town morality of 40/50 years ago. Is it surprising that when he realizes his feelings have run away with him and that he is in love with a respectable married woman—with the preacher's wife—is it surprising that he should feel awkward and constrained in her presence? Especially after the woman's husband has made it clear that he, the husband, knows or suspects the way the wind is blowing and is anything but pleased about it?

Mrs. Bentley of course is not all of a piece. Few human beings are. Ironically—as I wrote Wilfrid Cude a year ago in response to his book—I remember deliberately "roughing her up" a bit so she would not seem too patient and long-suffering. (Even so Roy Daniells in his Introduction described her as "pure gold.") Perhaps I have a warped understanding of human nature but it seems to me that a woman in love is more likely than not to be jealous and possessive—even irrationally so, in the presence of competition or threatened by encroachment. Indeed, I simply cannot imagine her tolerating such encroachment with equanimity. What a dead stick she would be! Unless, of course, tolerance was her strategy. Give him a little line and he'll tire himself.

As to the ending of the book, the last couple of lines, to me it is very simple; she has lost Philip and she knows. But there is the son and so as a reflex to fill the void—a reflex of desperation, if you like—she turns to him as something to live for, lose herself in.

What kind of mother would she make? Perhaps a very bad one, possessive and pampering. But she is not without intelligence and may get her bearings, come to see herself and work things out. What about the bookshop she is opening? Prospects not very good—6 months or a year—but again she knows the value of a dollar and with so much at stake, the future of the 2 Philips, she may, by hard work and determination make a go of it. Supposing she does...I'm sure that when *As for Me and My House* comes out in paperback she'll look it over with a wary eye and, prudently sales-minded, be careful never to order more than one copy at a time.

I'm sorry to disappoint you but what can I do? If it's a bad book because Paul didn't sleep with Judith, then it's a bad book. It all happened over 40 years ago; I can only be as honest about it as memory permits.

Canada's first novel? I have never concerned myself about such things, what they will say about me when I'm on the other side, or will they say anything at all, and now, almost 75, I'm not tempted to begin guessing? Gradings are for others.

Thank you for your interest. As to your own writing career you have my warmest wishes for success.

Sincerely,
Sinclair Ross

P.S. *May I keep your article? If you need your copy back, drop me a line.*

From Guy Vanderhaeghe

Saskatoon, SK

29 January 1984

Dear Mr. Ross:

Please forgive my lateness in replying to your very kind letter,[1] but I was out of town for a time.

You cannot possibly imagine what your note meant to me; there is no one who has meant more to Saskatchewan writers than you, Mr. Ross. I recall a writer here placing a short story with *Queen's Quarterly* and saying, "That's who published Sinclair Ross's short stories." That fact gave the whole thing an added lustre in his eyes.

It has always seemed to me that *As for Me and My House* is a kind of historical document as well as being a great work of art. I can think of no Canadian writer who told the painful truth with the honesty you did and shaped that truth into a shining work of art. No one will equal your noble achievement.

I am so sorry to hear that you have Parkinson's disease; I only hope it does not prevent you from writing. I would like to think you will give us another book.

This poor letter is a confused attempt to express my gratitude to you for your kindness and your books. They are both great gifts.

All the very best to you Mr. Ross,
Guy Vanderhaeghe

---

1.   Douglas Gibson at McClelland & Stewart sent Ross a complimentary copy of Vanderhaeghe's first book, *Man Descending*, 1982, and Ross sent the young author a letter of praise.

To Ken Mitchell

University of Regina, SK

From Keath Fraser

Vancouver, BC

27 September 1985

Dear Ken Mitchell,

Jim Ross has asked me to reply to the recent request he received from CBC in Regina to do a program with you about his writing. Mischievously (I think) he misplaced the CBC letter from—was it Wayne Schmaltz?— possibly to avoid having to respond directly but also because he feels more comfortable in letting *you* know that he doesn't feel up to it (you, he believes, are more likely to understand his characteristic reluctance to decline such invitations). Would you, he wonders, kindly thank Mr. Schmaltz (I apologize if this isn't his name) for his interest? He assumes you and he have spoken about the matter.

Perhaps I should add that Jim fell and broke his hip in July and has been in the hospital ever since. The hip has mended fairly well since his operation—he has started to get around a little with canes—and right now he's biding time in what's derogatively known as the holding tank in the hospital, waiting for his name to come up on a nursing home list. Over the summer he decided to give up his apartment because of his inability to cope entirely on his own. The problem, as you know, isn't so much his recent injury as the enervating effects of Parkinson's. The hospital has been good for him at least because he eats regularly and receives the assistance he requires to get in and out of his clothes, etc. And, too, he isn't so isolated.

Unfortunately, before he lands in the nursing home that he has chosen he will have to bide more time in another place about as attractive as the one he's in at present. It could be up to a year before he is more or less permanently settled. Please don't let that stop you from writing to him c/o the address above. He apologizes for not being the best of correspondents.

> With all good wishes. Yours sincerely,
> Keath Fraser

P.S. By the way, the CBC Cities series—your contribution on Moose Jaw, that is—was thoroughly delightful. Jim missed it, I discovered, but seemed to relish my inadequate recapitulation.

To Dorothy and Alvin Goldman
Montreal, PQ

Brock Fahrni Pavilion, Shaughnessy Hospital
4500 Oak Street, Vancouver, BC

21 November 1986

Dear Dorothy and Alvin,
Thoroughly ashamed of myself for my long silence. I have finally got around to asking a friend to write a few lines of explanation. My hand-writing has become unreadable (Parkinson's) and I am in hospital a little over a year and am pretty well immobilized with a fractured hip. Prognosis, I'm afraid, not very good. At that, things could be worse. The food isn't bad and I still do a fair amount of reading, although my eyes are a long way from what they used to be. A hospital, smile as one will, is a hospital.

You, however, have had your share of troubles and then some, and I often think how brave you both are to carry on as you do.

Well, let's all cross our fingers and look forward to a better 1987. In the meantime, Season's Greetings...and a letter, however brief, would be appreciated.

> Sincerely,
> Jim

Ross in his room at the Brock Fahrni Pavilion, Vancouver. [© Suzanne Ahearne]

P.S. I've heard nothing from Douglas and Dallas since their card a year ago.

With the assistance of Irene Harvalias, his friend and voluntary amanuensis, Ross sent short thank you notes in reply to some of the letters he continued to receive while living in hospital, but they were rarely more than three or four sentences. Perhaps most telling of these was one he sent to Alan Twigg, the publisher of *BC Bookworld* and of several volumes about literature in British Columbia. For his book *Vancouver and Its Writers* (1986), Twigg requested an interview. Ross's original reply has been lost, but part of it was reproduced in Twigg's book, a grim envoi to his readers and career:

> I would be grateful if you would ignore me. You see, I have Parkinson's disease. I don't speak well. There are things that enter my mind to say but I don't trust myself to say them. If you came to see me, I'm afraid it might be unpleasant for you.
> For a long time I've felt that *As for Me and My House* never amounted to much. It was alright at the time. But I feel the world has changed so much....If I was starting out again I think I'd concentrate on the novella. Ideas enter my head from time to time but I no longer think of myself as a writer....If you wrote about me in your book it might make some people want to visit me. And I don't want that....

Recalling that letter a few years later, Twigg said most striking was that Ross had turned so resolutely against his craft, had insisted "*the writing life wasn't worth the candle.*"

Sinclair Ross | *Canadian Writers on Tape*, Toronto, 1971

SINCLAIR ROSS'S PUBLISHING CAREER spanned more than fifty years, but during that time he agreed only once to a formal interview. Remarkably in an age when Canadian artists were regularly being brought into the media spotlight, Sinclair Ross never appeared on radio or television, and his image was never caught on motion picture film. Instead, as Robert Kroetsch has observed, Ross embraced his historical moment with a kind of invisibility that forces his readers to see themselves instead of the author and to examine the world they have created around them. The scarcity of personal material makes the glimpse we have of Ross in this interview that much more valuable. But especially interesting here are his views of what it meant to be a writer from western Canada in the early and middle years of the twentieth century.

EARLE TOPPINGS: "The most important body of fiction written about the Canadian west. In Sinclair Ross, we may, through indifference and neglect, have permitted a fine artist to perish." Those two lines were written by novelist Edward McCourt in 1949. Sinclair Ross is with us, and I'd like to ask him if we in Canada have allowed him to perish.

SINCLAIR ROSS: Well, writers and artists are often neglected, and I don't think that the Canadian public should be rapped over the knuckles too hard because they didn't respond with more enthusiasm to *As for Me and My House*. I'm inclined to put it the other way and say that the trouble is I didn't make enough—I didn't make sufficient impact. In fairness to myself, however, probably my failure to make the impact is because I am a western Canadian. Western Canada is a little apart from the rest of the world and probably the rest of the world isn't particularly interested in it. For instance, I remember reading once that Pearl Buck said—I'm not sure of the exact words, but the gist of it is something like this—she said, "A writer should be very careful in the choice of his birthplace." And of course she wasn't being funny when she said that. She was born in China, grew up in China, and when she started writing, apparently for a long time all her stories came back, and sometimes she would get a note from an editor: "We like this story, it's well written, etc., but we're not interested in China." Well, I think that's true, that literary decisions in the English language are made in New York and London and, to some extent, in Toronto, and I don't think they're particularly interested in Saskatchewan.

ET: There is, though, something universal in what you've written, in that it has relation, surely, to times of drought, anxiety, poverty, and hardship in almost any nation of the earth. I'm wondering too if *As for Me and My House*, your best-known book, which was published in 1941, if it was, like many good books, a bit ahead of its time, in that the vogue for the Thirties, and the vogue of Depression studies did not come until a great deal later.

For example, it's only now that it's become fashionable to do mixed-media kits on the 1930s.

SR: Yes. When *As for Me and My House* came out, of course it fell flat on its face. And it was out of print from about 1942, I think, until it came out in the New Canadian Library in 1958. Ah, speaking of neglect, probably if it had come out earlier in that edition, and Canadians had become more aware of it, I might have been encouraged, because by that time, the years had gone on and it was much more difficult to break away from what I was doing to become what you might call a professional writer, to make my living as a writer.

ET: It's hard to send a book out into the world and find that there is no response. I can see that it could be disheartening. Could you tell us a bit about what moved you to write *As for Me and My House*? Why did you feel motivated to write that book, which is a book about the dust-bowl period in the Thirties in Saskatchewan?

SR: That's something I never thought about.

ET: Had it been something that had been in your mind and in your soul for a long time?

SR: Probably, but it's a long time ago, and when you do these things you don't keep notes. And it would be pretty hard to go back and trace the development of it. But I might, just speaking of *As for Me and My House*—where the idea for the story came from—I was living in a small town, and a United Church minister, he thought that I might make a better minister than I would a banker. So he made the suggestion which was made to Philip: "Would you like to go into the church?" And of course I said no. It didn't tempt me at all, but—and probably this is what they mean by having a writer's mind—I started thinking, "Well, supposing somebody did accept that offer and then he finds himself trapped."

ET: And it got you started on—

SR: That was the idea. The United Church minister, who was a kind fellow and meant well, but he wasn't a very good judge of human nature, of human character.

ET: You were working in a bank on the prairies.

SR: That's right, yes.

ET: What are some of the vivid experiences you had then? What do you feel really formed your roots and background in Saskatchewan?

SR: Well, just that I lived there all my life. I mean it was the life I knew. I didn't know any other life. It never occurred to me to write, at that time, of anything else. This was my background and the people I knew.

ET: What themes and ideas have continued to interest you?

SR: Well, of course, man's struggle with the land and the elements—that's the most obvious thing. One other theme, which isn't very apparent so far in what I've done is that I'm interested in crime. Not the actual crime but the mind, by the criminal mentality, and the motivation for the crime. In a book I did called *The Well*, I dabbled at that, and I wasn't able to do what I wanted to do. I failed, and that's really why it isn't a very good book.

ET: If you were interested in a criminal's motivation, or in the psychological distortion that makes him a criminal, do you feel that you are able to get insight into it as you write a book, as you write a character?

SR: Well, I try to, but that is where I failed in *The Well*, because I didn't succeed. I wanted the character to be a fairly sympathetic character, and I wanted to get inside him and follow him right through to carrying out a crime, to carrying out a murder, and I couldn't do it.

ET: Do you have some kind of basic intuition about the criminal mind, as you put it? Do you feel that the criminal is just any one of us, only he happens to be the one who commits the crime?

SR: Probably. It's a mystery. It puzzles me. I don't pretend to know the answers. And you asked if I have intuition. I don't know. Probably I haven't. But it fascinates me.

ET: Have you continued exploring criminality in your new book called *Whir of Gold*?

SR: Yes, yes. I try but whether I've come up with the right answers or not, I don't know. The chief character takes part in a very stupid crime, and he puzzles himself over why he did it. And he makes plausible suggestions—probably they're not right. As I see it, it's a self-destructive urge and he himself is not aware of this. I'm hoping that, while he isn't aware of it, that the reader will be.

ET: Mr. Ross, why do you write? What do you really want to accomplish? Is it basically something for yourself?

SR: Well, you know, that's another question that I don't know, that I never ask myself. I don't know whether writers do ask themselves. I suppose it goes back to—it goes back to "Look!" You know when we see something, and we're with somebody and we say, "Look!" You're walking along the road, and you round the corner and there's a beautiful scene before you, or maybe a garden or an animal or something, and you say, "Look!" It isn't necessary because the other fellow has good eyes too—he can see it. But we seem to have that urge, and if there's no one to whom we can say it, probably we feel just a little bit disappointed. And I think that's the beginning of all writing. Things impress you and you have this urge that, well, you feel it, this sounds a bit pompous, but you feel it so intensely that you must get it said and so you write it. I think probably that's the basic urge behind all writing.

ET: So that someone else can see it as well as you.

SR: That's right, yes. You have something to communicate. And I suppose it's a form of conceit and arrogance. You feel that—the way I feel it, that's the right way, and I must communicate the way I feel it.

ET: Do you have any opinions on commercialism? There's a line in your book, Philip's work in *As for Me and My House*, to the effect—instead of trying to make his story popular and saleable, he pushed it on sombrely the way he felt it ought to go. Now, Philip, of course, had made his living in the church, which he disliked and wished to leave. He was a frustrated artist who couldn't buy the free time to paint. And secondly, I'm wondering, is there a parallel with yourself in that you spent much of your life in a bank, with little time to write?

SR: No, there's not really a parallel. It's not the same. I worked in a bank to make my living, but there was nothing disgraceful or shameful about that. Many people who want to become artists and writers, at one time in their life, they work in an office or a factory or all sorts of jobs. But it's perfectly all right. But with Philip, he was in the church making his living, and he was preaching a gospel which he didn't believe. So in other words, he was a hypocrite. That was something to be ashamed of. And that is the key of course to Philip, because he was big enough, honest enough, to look at himself squarely in the eye and say "You're a heel, you're a hypocrite," and that takes some courage to do that. He never tried to rationalize. He never said "Well, if I don't do the job, somebody else will. Maybe I'm doing just as well as the next fellow." He was too honest for that. But he wasn't big enough to do something about the trap he was in. He never got out.

ET: You don't feel, then, that having spent your life in a bank has hindered your writing or prevented you from writing?

SR: Ah well, yes, probably it has, because you have only so much time, you've only so many hours a day. But I mean the parallel. There's not the parallel—Philip was ashamed of what he was doing, while I was never ashamed of working in a bank. It was just my way of making a living. So that's what I mean—there's not the parallel.

ET: I'm interested in the conflict between the simple and the complex. For example, Roy Daniells, Canadian literary scholar, in introducing As for Me and My House, said, "Simplicity is the keynote of Ross's artistic achievement," and concerning the stories he said, "These brief narratives of pioneer settlers, their burdened wives and imaginative, isolated children move the emotions as do few of our more recent and more complex studies of character." I rather take issue with what he says about complex studies because I think that you have written characters infinitely more complex than he seems to be giving you credit for. For example—there's nothing simple at all about the Bentleys, I don't think, about their personalities.

SR: Well again, that's something I never thought of in terms of simple or complex. I was just trying to reveal these people and, yes, probably they were complex. Philip is complex. But I never thought of it in terms of simple or complex.

ET: There are many conflicting wants—

SR: That's right.

ET: —and aspirations, I think, impeding all the time, especially with Philip, and with his wife too.

SR: Yes, probably the characters in the stories, in the short stories, they are more simple because their needs are more simple, and their urges and drives. But it's a little difficult to say just what is simple and what is complex.

ET: Would you comment on some of the other characters that are in all of your stories, such as the land, and some of the more ghostly elements, such as feelings of loneliness and striving for survival, the hard training of the hard-work ethic and Puritanism? It seems to me that there's a real flavour of what it's like to live on the prairie, and to be part of that people, in your stories.

SR: Well, if that comes through, that is just because probably I wrote honestly of the life that I knew. This is the background I knew. For instance, you speak of Puritanism. I'm sure that that is correct, but I never thought of it as Puritanism. The word "Puritanism" never crossed my mind. I wrote about these people and that's what they were. For instance, you have a colour film in your camera and you snap a girl with a blue dress. Well, you get both the girl and the blue dress. You describe people, you get the people plus their religious beliefs, plus their moral attitudes. You can't separate them. So there was nothing conscious or deliberate about that when I did it. It was just describing the people, and what they are came through. It's the same way if you're writing about Canadians. You don't set out to write a Canadian novel, but if you write about Canadians, you've got a Canadian novel.

ET: When you write, you start with what you see. You start with the visual and when you see these people, as you say, you *see* them in their entirety and it doesn't strike you that they are necessarily fundamentalists or Puritans or hidebound.

SR: No, but again that's something you don't think about, and where you start on a story, it's that needle under the skin where you get the shot of something which makes you—which grows and becomes your story. It's pretty hard to pin it down because, when you don't take notes, as I say, at the time and then by the time you do look at it, it's grown considerably. The actual beginning you probably don't pay any attention to. I've often tried to run down a story. For instance, "One's a Heifer"—all I can remember of that is that I was out on horseback and a woman waved to me and, when I got to the door, she said they had lost two calves. And she asked me if I'd seen them, and she said, "One's a heifer and the other ain't." Well, that's a long way from the story, but that's the only—that must have been what stayed in my mind.

ET: Do you find that you have many other givens that way? Either you hear a phrase, or you see something memorable and then you have to write about it sometime, even if it's much later?

SR: I don't think it works that way with me. I think probably something happens and then it becomes embedded in my mind, as it were, and then later I come back to it. But at the time I don't say, "Well, this is something I must write about." I think it grows and then reaches the stage where, well, it may be somewhat urgent. But that's later on. It may be months later or years later.

ET: What literary influences have you felt in your life? What books do you like to read? What authors have moved you?

SR: Oh, I've read all over the place. I've always read a great deal. I don't know of any that have influenced me. I suppose they have but I'm not aware of any particular influence. For one thing, when I started writing over thirty years ago, there wasn't very much western Canadian literature to influence me. But as a youngster I read Scott and Dickens and all sorts of things—Conrad at one time, Hardy. Probably Hardy, if anyone influenced me, probably Hardy and a book like *Return of the Native* might have. But I'm not aware of the influence.

ET: What do you like to read now? Do you read current American and English fiction? Do you read biography, or history?

SR: Everything, everything—whatever. I have no reading patterns but I read a great deal.

ET: Are you part of some kind of fast-moving literary scene? And do you write reviews for fashionable journals? Do you lunch with book people all the time? Or do you live rather more by yourself, doing your own thinking?

SR: No, I know very few literary people. I'm completely out of the swim, as it were. And of course now that I'm living in Europe I don't know anybody at all.

ET: Do you think this is for you a positive feature?

SR: Well again, that's something I never think much about because, as I say, I have always lived apart and that's part of life now. If I knew more literary people, they might be stimulating. I don't know.

ET: But then also you come back to what you have to work with, which really is your own mind, your own senses. And that's still what you have to train and—

SR: Well, that is the important thing, yes. Other writers, as I say, might be stimulating, but you can't feed off them. They can only stimulate you and you, if you listen to them talking and know what they're doing, well, you might have a little spurt of rivalry sometimes and you might feel, "Well, I can do this too." I don't know because, as I say, I'm out of the swim.

ET: There is a good deal of rivalry and that's probably a very healthy thing to stay out of. Probably a great waste of time. Could you sketch in, chronologically, a bit of your life story?

SR: I was in several small towns in Saskatchewan working in the bank, and then I went to Winnipeg when I was about—oh, I would be about twenty-two or twenty-three—and then I stayed there for about twelve or fourteen years, and then I was four years in the Army and then I was about twenty years in Montreal. And I've been retired for two and half years now. At the present time I am living in Greece, but I don't expect to be there much longer.

ET: I see. What encouraged you to go to Greece?

SR: Health was the principal reason. I have a sort of arthritis and I feel much better in a warm, dry climate.

ET: Is there a stimulus for your work in Greece that you wouldn't have found in Montreal?

SR: No, I don't think so. The only thing is that, living in a foreign country, I think it makes you more aware of yourself as a Canadian. You have a sense of Canadian identity which probably you wouldn't have here. But whether that will make any difference in what I write, I don't know.

ET: Yes, it may make you recall. Are you able to see Canadian things, and aspects of Canadian memories in a sharper way than you would if you were right on this soil?

SR: Probably. I'm not sure. As I say, I don't stop to think about these things, but I think these do have an effect on you, on your subconscious.

ET: Mr. Ross, could you tell us about your new book, *Whir of Gold*? When did you begin writing it? Something about the basic structure of the book and the impulse you had in writing it?

SR: Well, I started — oh, a great many years ago — to write. I wrote a long short story, and nothing happened. It was an awkward length. It was too long for a short story, and not even a novella length. Well, I forgot about it. But, still, in a way I forgot about it, but one character in particular always stayed with me. Well, finally I got around to thinking that I could expand it and make a novel of it. And I spent quite a time working on the novel because there was one version which didn't go, and then I finally had made another version. But it's Saskatchewan. The principal, one of the principal characters is an out-of-work musician in Montreal and the other is a girl from Nova Scotia. Speaking of my interest in the criminal mind — he takes part in a very stupid crime.

ET: Is this part of your thinking about crime, that it's a kind of lapse of the moment or a kind of stupid choice that one makes, that could have been avoided?

SR: Well, in this case I think that it's a self-destructive urge. He wanted to be a musician, and he became a popular musician, instead of a serious musician. And he — it was a logical choice to make, because at his age, and with his lack of background and training, it would have been impossible for him to become the musician he wanted to be. So it was a very sensible choice to take up popular music. But he, within himself, always felt guilty. Well, again there was the guilt of the Puritan conscience, I suppose, although again, I never thought of it as the Puritan conscience because he'd had a fairly strict upbringing and then he'd broken with that. Well, he tries to analyze himself, why he took part in this crime, and he never hits the nail on the head, but I'm hoping that the reader will see the reason for it, which is self-destructive. He feels guilty and from that flows this urge to, not exactly to destroy himself, not suicide, it doesn't go that far, but it is self-destructive.

ET: A very strong feature in your books and stories is human survival. And one quotation from Margaret Laurence, who wrote the introduction to your collection of stories, is: "In counterpoint to desolation runs the theme of renewal. Tomorrow it may rain. The next spring will ultimately come. Despite the sombre tone and the dark themes of Sinclair Ross's short stories, man emerges as a creature who can survive, and survive with some remaining dignity against both outer and inner odds which are almost impossible." Would you comment on this quality of survival?

SR: Well, survival is important to all of us. It's basic. Probably, in a story about the land in conflict with nature, it stands out in relief. But the problem of survival is just as acute for a man in an office or a factory. No matter what your job is — it's still survival. But it's probably more dramatic when you see man fighting against nature, against the land. Survival, for rural people, is a matter of holding their own against nature, against the elements. Survival, for people in a city, is more often a matter of holding their own against the neighbours. Now I don't know whether this has any effect on the nature, on the character, of the people. It seems to me if we followed it through that it might be. This is just speculation. If your enemy is the land, and the seasons, it seems to me it gives you more room to have faith in basic human nature, in the basic good in your fellow man, whereas if you're up against — if your enemy is your neighbour — well, you may become more wary and suspicious. I don't know whether that's true or not but it's something to think about.

ET: Did you find this in your personal life, that survival was an important theme in your own life?

SR: No, I've never thought of it. But I don't think we do think of it as survival, but it's an instinct and one way or another we all are struggling for that. It's part of life. Only in the case of a man on the land, it's thrown up in relief so that you see it and are aware of it as a struggle for survival.

ET: Allied with that is the hard-work ethic, and this is something you have said yourself about some of your people: "They were compelled not by labour, but by the spirit of labour, a spirit that pervaded their lives and brought with idleness a sense of guilt."

SR: Yes, I think that's probably true. I don't know whether it would be true of the people in Saskatchewan today, because this was written of people thirty and thirty-five years ago. But I think it certainly was true then. Probably they've changed, yes.

ET: Yes. They really hated even to have Sunday an idle day.

SR: That's right, yes. I think there was a feeling of guilt if they rested, yes.

ET: I think you are a writer who has a really—really an ethical position against selling out. This is very strong in the character of Philip in *As for Me and My House*. Have you in your own work striven not to make it commercial, not to make it popular, or not to make it saleable, but to let the writing go the way you think it should go, even if it means it doesn't have a great audience?

SR: Well, I suppose I have. I feel that a story should be done a certain way and I do it that way. At the same time, I don't know whether—probably if I could write the other kind of story, I would, but I don't think I can. That is—I'm not adaptable enough for it. Because often what you might call light fiction—I don't think we should turn up our nose at it—it calls for great skill sometimes. It isn't everybody who can do it. You say, "Oh well, there's nothing to it, it's of no importance." But still it calls for great skill to turn it out. Because everybody can't turn out a popular bestseller which is of no importance. Otherwise, we all would be doing it.

ET: Mr. Ross, what books have you not written yet—or stories—that you would like to write, or are planning to write?

SR: Well, I have another novel about Saskatchewan coming up. I think it's coming up. I haven't done any work on it, but I have it pretty well completed in my mind. I know what's going to be in it, and I know what it's going to be about. That's the next thing I want to do.

ET: Are you superstitious about talking about a book before it's written? Do you think if you talk about it you won't write it?

SR: Not superstitious, but I think that you dissipate the urgency if you talk about it. I think it's wise not to talk about it.

ET: Have you found it possible to go ahead, to still have a stimulus to write, and to still derive satisfaction from writing, although your books don't sell in very large quantities?

SR: I suppose it's a compulsion. I always scribbled and I suppose I—yes, I suppose it is a compulsion. I can't help it. I'm always getting something in my mind that I should write it down and I want to write it down, even although it does seem hopeless sometimes, and all along it has often seemed hopeless. But I like to keep on scribbling.

ET: In what ways does it seem hopeless?

SR: Well, I have written so little, and I've had such little success, that I suppose that has had its effect on me. But I'm not too optimistic about the future, about my future as a writer.

ET: I think it was Scott Fitzgerald who said that nothing fails like success and it's really a great North American lesson, and sometimes not to succeed in the cheap, popular term of success is perhaps a blessing. I think there are much deeper ways to succeed. In other words, if the story really means something deep, and lasting, and personal to the reader, I think that's the greatest success you could have. But you will probably never hear from that reader.

SR: That's right. That's right.

ET: There won't be any way that he can get in touch with you in Athens, Greece or Montreal, Quebec. And what is a marvellous feature about writing, I think, is that it is preserved, it's on the record. People can go back to it. It may not be well received, no notice may be taken in 1941, but 1971 might be the big year. They might begin to rediscover your books. Mr. Ross, as a writer, what do you most want to be remembered for?

SR: Ah, that's something else I never think about, because that would mean thinking about when you're dead, and I never go that far. But to answer your question, I suppose I would like people to say, if they talked about me after I'm dead, "Well, what he wrote was well written." And I would like to think that the people in my books were human, and that they rang true. Oh, I'm wanting quite a lot now. And probably that I had said something revealing about human nature, human conflicts, the human predicament. That's enough.

Archival Sources

A FULL ACCOUNT of primary and secondary sources until 1990 appears in David Latham's "A Reference Guide to Sinclair Ross" in *From the Heart of the Heartland: The Fiction of Sinclair Ross*, ed. John Moss (Ottawa: University of Ottawa Press, 1992): 125–39. Subsequent bibliographical information can be found on the website for Professor Andrew Lesk, University of Toronto. Given below are abbreviated descriptions of primary sources, an updated account of archival materials, and a list of secondary sources specific to this volume of Ross correspondence.

Sinclair Ross's Published Works

BOOKS

As for Me and My House. New York: Reynal and Hitchcock, 1941. Toronto: McClelland & Stewart, 2008.

The Well. Toronto: Macmillan, 1958. Edmonton: University of Alberta Press, 2001.

The Lamp at Noon and Other Stories. Toronto: McClelland & Stewart,
  1968; 1990.
Whir of Gold. Toronto: McClelland & Stewart, 1970. Edmonton:
  University of Alberta Press, 2001.
Sawbones Memorial. Toronto: McClelland & Stewart, 1974. Edmonton:
  University of Alberta Press, 2001.
The Race and Other Stories. Ottawa: University of Ottawa Press, 1982.

SHORT STORIES

Listed here are first publications, with current printings in *The Lamp at
Noon and Other Stories* (LNOS) and *The Race and Other Stories* (ROS).

"No Other Way." *Nash's-Pall Mall Magazine* 95 (October 1934): 16–17,
  80–84. ROS, 23–36.
"A Field of Wheat." *Queen's Quarterly* 42 (Spring 1935): 31–42. LNOS,
  67–76.
"September Snow." *Queen's Quarterly* 42 (Winter 1935): 451–60. LNOS,
  54–61.
"Circus in Town." *Queen's Quarterly* 43 (Winter 1936): 368–72. LNOS,
  62–66.
"The Lamp at Noon." *Queen's Quarterly* 45 (Spring 1938): 30–42. LNOS,
  7–17.
"A Day with Pegasus." *Queen's Quarterly* 45 (Summer 1938): 141–56. ROS,
  37–48.
"The Painted Door." *Queen's Quarterly* 46 (Summer 1939): 145–68. LNOS,
  93–112.
"Cornet at Night." *Queen's Quarterly* 46 (Winter 1939): 431–52. LNOS,
  29–45.
"Not by Rain Alone." *Queen's Quarterly* 48 (Spring 1941): 7–16. LNOS (as
  "Summer Thunder"), 46–54.
"Nell." *Manitoba Arts Review* 2 (Winter 1941): 32–40. ROS, 49–59.
"One's a Heifer." *Canadian Accent.* Ed. Ralph Gustafson.
    Harmondsworth: Penguin, 1944, 114–28. LNOS, 113–28.
"Barrack Room Fiddle Tune." *Manitoba Arts Review* 5 (Spring 1947):
  12–17. ROS, 61–68.

"Jug and Bottle." *Queen's Quarterly* 56 (Winter 1949): 500–21. ROS, 69–85.

"The Outlaw." *Queen's Quarterly* 57 (Summer 1950): 198–210. LNOS, 18–28.

"Saturday Night." *Queen's Quarterly* 58 (Autumn 1951): 387–400. ROS, 87–97.

"The Runaway." *Queen's Quarterly* 59 (Autumn 1952): 323–42. LNOS, 77–92.

"The Unwilling Organist." *The* [Royal Bank] *Teller* (December 1958): 12–16.

"Spike." Trans. Pierre Villon. *Liberté* 11 (mars–avril 1969): 181–97. In English in Ken Mitchell, *Sinclair Ross: A Reader's Guide*. Moose Jaw: Coteau Books, 1981, 95–107. ROS, 99–110.

"The Flowers That Killed Him." *Journal of Canadian Fiction* I (Summer 1972): 5–10. ROS, 119–34.

"The Race." *The Race and Other Stories*. Ed. Lorraine McMullen. Ottawa: University of Ottawa Press, 1982, 111–17.

ARTICLES AND MEMOIR

"Why My 2nd Book Came 17 Years Later." *Toronto Daily Star*, 13 September 1958, 32.

"Montreal and French-Canadian Culture: What They Mean to English-Canadian Novelists." *The Tamarack Review* 40 (Summer 1966): 46–47.

"On Looking Back." *Mosaic* 3 (Spring 1970): 93–94.

"Just Wind and Horses: A Memoir." *The Macmillan Anthology I*. Ed. John Metcalf and Leon Rooke. Toronto: Macmillan, 1988, 83–97.

Archives and Unpublished Manuscripts

ARCHIVES

Sinclair Ross and Irene Harvalias donated items to establish a Ross collection at Library and Archives Canada in Ottawa, but most Ross materials are still scattered throughout the country in private holdings and in the publishing archives of Macmillan and McClelland & Stewart at McMaster University.

PUBLIC COLLECTIONS

LAC: Library and Archives Canada
  Myrna Kostash Papers
  Robert Weaver Fonds
MUL: McMaster University Library
  Macmillan Company (Canada) Papers
  McClelland & Stewart Collection
QUA: Queen's University Archives
  Grant Macdonald Collection
  Queen's Quarterly *Archive*
TFRBL: Thomas Fisher Rare Book Library, University of Toronto
  Earle Birney Collection
  W.A. Deacon Papers
UBCL: University of British Columbia Library, Rare Books and
  Special Collections
  Roy Daniells Papers
UCL: University of Calgary Library
  Rudy Wiebe Collection
URL: University of Regina Library
  Ken Mitchell Collection
USL: University of Saskatchewan Library
  Ralph Gustafson Collection
YUL: York University Library
  Margaret Laurence Collection

PRIVATE COLLECTIONS

In private collections there are letters to the following individuals: David Carpenter, Wilfred Cude, Harriet Duff-Smith, Keath Fraser, Alvin Goldman, Sheila Kieran, Lorraine McMullen, John Moss, John O'Connor, Audrey Peterkin, Roy St. George Stubbs, Doris Saunders, David Stouck, and Andy Suknaski. Copies of some of these letters were also kept by the author with his private papers, which include the letters to Kenneth Glazier, Geoff Hancock, and Kathren Mattson, reproduced in this volume of correspondence.

UNPUBLISHED MANUSCRIPTS
"Old Chippendale" (short story), Grant Macdonald Papers, QUA
"The Troopship Story" (incomplete war memoir), Sinclair Ross Papers,
    LAC

Secondary Sources

Atwood, Margaret. *The Edible Woman*. Toronto: McClelland & Stewart,
    1969.
———. *Survival: A Thematic Guide to Canadian Literature*. Toronto: Anansi
    Press, 1972.
Buckler, Ernest. *The Mountain and the Valley*. New York: Henry Holt,
    1952. (Reprinted in the New Canadian Library, 1961.)
Camus, Albert. *The Stranger*. New York: Alfred A. Knopf, 1946;
    Harmondsworth: Penguin, 1964.
Chambers, Robert D. *Sinclair Ross and Ernest Buckler*. Toronto: Copp
    Clark, 1975. 1–52, 99–105.
Cude, Wilfred. "Beyond Mrs. Bentley: A Study of *As for Me and My
    House*." *Journal of Canadian Studies* 8 (February 1973): 3–18.
    Reprinted in *A Due Sense of Differences: An Evaluative Approach to
    Canadian Literature*. Washington, D.C.: University Press of America,
    1980, 31–49.
Daniells, Roy. "Introduction." *As for Me and My House*. Toronto:
    McClelland & Stewart, 1957. v–x.
Deacon, William Arthur. *Dear Bill: The Correspondence of William
    Arthur Deacon*. Ed. John Lennox and Michele Lacombe. Toronto:
    University of Toronto Press, 1988.
Dickinson, Peter. *Here is Queer: Nationalisms, Sexualities, and the
    Literatures of Canada*. Toronto: University of Toronto Press, 1999.
Djwa, Sandra. "No Other Way: Sinclair Ross's Stories and Novels."
    Canadian Literature 47 (Winter 1971): 49–66.

———. *Professing English: A Life of Roy Daniells.* Toronto: University of Toronto Press, 2002.

Fraser, Keath. *As for Me and My Body.* Toronto: ECW Press, 1997.

———. "Futility at the Pump: The Short Stories of Sinclair Ross." *Queen's Quarterly* 77 (Spring 1970): 72–80.

French, William. "Too Good Too Soon, Ross Remains the Elusive Canadian." *Globe and Mail*, 27 July 1974, 25.

Fulford, Robert, David Godfrey, and Abraham Rotstein. *Read Canadian: A Book about Canadian Books.* Toronto: James Lewis & Samuel, 1972.

Goldie, Terry, *Pink Snow: Homotextual Possibilities in Canadian Fiction.* Peterborough, ON: Broadview Press, 2003.

Harrison, Dick. *Unnamed Country: The Struggle for a Canadian Prairie Fiction.* Edmonton: University of Alberta Press, 1977.

Kattan, Naim. "Montreal and French-Canadian Culture: What They Mean to English-Canadian Novelists." *Tamarack Review* 40 (Summer 1966): 46–47

King, Carlyle. *Saskatchewan Harvest.* Toronto: McClelland & Stewart, 1955.

King, James. *The Life of Margaret Laurence.* Toronto: Knopf, 1997.

Klinck, Carl F. and Reginald Watters. *Canadian Anthology.* Toronto: Gage, 1955.

Kostash, Myrna. *All of Baba's Children.* Edmonton: Hurtig, 1977.

———. "Discovering Sinclair Ross: It's Rather Late." *Saturday Night* 87 (July 1972): 33–37.

Laurence, Margaret. *The Diviners.* Toronto: McClelland & Stewart, 1974.

———. "Introduction." *The Lamp at Noon and Other Stories.* Toronto: McClelland & Stewart, 1968.

Lecker, Robert. *Making It Real: The Canonization of English-Canadian Literature.* Concord, ON: Anansi Press, 1995.

Lesk, Andrew. "On Sinclair Ross's Straight(ened) House." *English Studies in Canada* 28 (March 2002): 65–90.

———. "Something Queer Going on Here: Desire in the Short Fiction of Sinclair Ross." *Essays on Canadian Writing* 61 (Spring 1997): 129–41.

Lucas, Alec. *Great Canadian Short Stories*: An Anthology. New York: Dell, 1971.

McMullen, Lorraine. *Sinclair Ross*. Boston: Twayne, 1979.

Mitchell, Ken. *Sinclair Ross: A Reader's Guide*. Moose Jaw: Coteau Books, 1981.

Moss, John. Ed. *From the Heart of the Heartland: The Fiction of Sinclair Ross*. Ottawa: University of Ottawa Press, 1992.

——. *Patterns of Isolation in English-Canadian Fiction*. Toronto: McClelland & Stewart, 1974.

Raoul, Valerie. "Straight or Bent: Textual/Sexual T(ri)angles in *As for Me and My House*." *Canadian Literature* 156 (Spring 1998): 13–28.

Ricou, Laurie. "The Prairie Internalized: The Fiction of Sinclair Ross." In *Vertical Man/Horizontal World: Man and Landscape in Canadian Prairie Fiction*. Vancouver: University of British Columbia Press, 1973. 81–94.

Rimanelli, Giose and Roberto Roburto, *Modern Canadian Stories*. Toronto: Ryerson Press, 1966.

Rose, Marilyn. "Sinclair Ross's 'Foreigners'." *From the Heart of the Heartland: The Fiction of Sinclair Ross*. Ed. John Moss. Ottawa: University of Ottawa Press, 1992. 91–101.

St. George Stubbs, Roy. "Presenting Sinclair Ross." *Saturday Night*, 9 August 1941, 17.

Stouck, David. *As for Sinclair Ross*. Toronto: University of Toronto Press, 2005.

——. "The Mirror and the Lamp in Sinclair Ross's *As for Me and My House*." *Mosaic* 7 (Winter 1974): 141–50. Reprinted in Stouck, ed. *Sinclair Ross's As for Me and My House: Five Decades of Criticism*. Toronto: University of Toronto Press, 1991.

——. "Notes on the Canadian Imagination." *Canadian Literature* 54 (Autumn 1972): 9–26.

——. "Introduction." *As for Me and My House*. Lincoln: University of Nebraska Press, 1978. v–xiii.

Suknaski, Andrew. *The Ghosts Call You Poor*. Toronto: Macmillan, 1978.

———. *Wood Mountain Poems*. Toronto: Macmillan, 1976. Reprinted with a new introduction by Tim Lilburn. Regina: Hagios Press, 2006.

Toppings, Earle. *Canadian Writers on Tape: Mordecai Richler/Sinclair Ross*. Ontario Institute for Studies in Education, 1971.

Twigg, Alan, *Vancouver and Its Writers*. Madeira Park, BC: Harbour Publishing, 1986.

Williams, David. "The 'Scarlet' Rompers: Towards a New Perspective in *As for Me and My House*." *Canadian Literature* 103 (Winter 1984): 166–74.

Index

Canada Council for the Arts
  proposed applications, xxiv,
    113, 208–09, 210, 231–35,
    236n3
  translation funding, 237–38
Canadian Accent, 24n3, 39n1
Canadian Anthology, 66n1
Canadian Authors Association,
    29n1, 29n2, 46
Canadian literary canon, ix–x,
    xxii, xxv, 110n2, 251, 253
Canadian literature
  As for Me and My House
    significance, ix, xx, 10n1
  Canada's need for, 36
  popularity of, xx, 143n7, 248
  SR's influence on, xxv, 231–32
  SR's status in, ix, xx, xxii,
    xxiii, 112, 143n7, 159n1,
    207, 210, 248
  supporters of, xx, xxi, 54n1,
    82n2
  See also Canadian literary
    canon; Canadian
    publishing; young writers
Canadian nationalism. *See*
    nationalism
Canadian publishing
  decisions in, x
  difficulties in the 1950s, 41
  expansion of, xxii, xxiv, xxv,
    103, 143n7
  financial pressures on, xix
  and nationalism, xx
  reception of SR's works, xi

See also Canadian literature;
    nationalism
Canadian Short Stories, 113
Canadian Writers on Tape, 130n1,
    259–72
Carr, Emily, x
Carter, Dyson, 197n1
Cather, Willa, 162
CBC (Canadian Broadcasting
    Corporation), 235, 236,
    256
  invitation to SR to submit
    works, 63
  possible interviews on,
    102n1, 143n7
  publicity about SR's works
    on, xxiii, 146–47
  reviews of SR's works on,
    105n2, 187, 195
  SR's works broadcast on, 61,
    113, 120
  SR's works rejected by, 62–
    64, 63n3
  television adaptations, 105n5
  works on SR, 200n1, 255
Chambers, Robert D., 221, 222n2
Chatelaine (magazine), 160, 226
Chesley, Stephen, 133, 135n2
Chesterton, G.K., 69n2
Chinese immigrants, xxviii n34
Chopin, Frederic, 4
"Circus in Town," 52
Clarke, G.H., xxvii n25, 60–61
Clay, Charles, 25, 26n3, 27–28
climate change, x

Foster, Malcolm, xxvii n29
Fowlie, Irene, 170n7
Fraser, John Foster (uncle), xi,
    1, 2–5
Fraser, Keath, xi, 127n1, 193
    CBC program on SR, 255
    letter from to Mitchell, 255–
        56
    letters to, 126–27, 140–43,
        171–72, 241–42, 244–46,
        255
    SR on Fraser's works, xxvi
        n12, 141
    works on SR, xxvi n12, 127n4,
        141, 143n1
Fraser, Sylvia, 232
French versions of SR works,
    237–38
French, William, xxviii n32,
    190n2
Fry, Pamela, 91
    letters from, 109, 113–15,
        129–30
    letters to, xxvi n2, xxvii n27,
        106–07, 110–13, 116–18,
        121–23, 128–29
    relationship with SR, xxi,
        107n1, 113
    and Whir of Gold, xxi, 110–11,
        113–17, 133, 173
Frye, Northrop, 156
Fulford, Robert, 142, 143n5, 158,
    159n2, 175

Gallant, Mavis, 200, 201n9, 226
García Márquez, Gabriel, 219
Gaskell, Eric, 27, 29n1
Gatenby, Greg, 179n1, 189
Gazette (Montreal), xxvii n29, 88,
    192n1, 195, 202, 204n4
gender, xxv, 101. See also women
    in SR's works
Gibson, Douglas, 254n1
Gibson, Graeme, 152, 154n1, 160,
    232
Gide, André, 218, 221n3
Glazier, Kenneth M., 194–95
Globe and Mail, xv, xxviii n32, 42,
    43n1, 190n2
gloom, xiii, xx, 43n1, 65, 92, 112,
    139, 169, 218, 238, 269
Godfrey, Dave, 142, 143n6
Goethe, Johann Wolfgang, 250
Goldie, Terry, xxvii n12
Golding, Louis: Magnolia Street,
    36, 37n3
Goldman, Alvin, x, 99, 100n2,
    104, 105n5, 109, 131–32,
    223–25, 240–41, 249, 256
Grain Growers' Guide, 226
grants. See awards; Canada
    Council for the Arts
Gray, James, 172, 173n3
Gray, John, xi, 54n1, 99
    about, 54n1
    and agents, xix, 68, 69n1, 77
    depicted, 58
    inviting SR to submit
        manuscripts, xx, 92

musicians
  SR as, xxxi, 4
  in SR's works, xiv, 15n2, 38,
    113–14, 268–69

Nash's-Pall Mall Magazine, xii,
  xxxii
National Archives of Canada,
  195n1
nationalism, xx, xxii, xxv, 146,
  159n2
nature (as literary subject),
  105n2, 138–39, 165–66,
  262
Nelson, J.C., 9
New Canadian Library
  about, 82n2
  As for Me and My House, xix,
    xxxii, 81, 82n2, 102, 149,
    175, 237, 261
  effect on SR's reputation,
    82n2
  royalties from, 149
  SR's works in, xxii, xxxiii,
    102–03, 190n1
New, W.H., 212, 213n2
"New Writing" series, 34n2,
  37n3
New York
  market, 189
  SR in, 8
  SR's attempts to be published
    in, 65, 66–67, 69n1–2, 78,
    82

SR's works published in,
  xxxii, 225, 230
New Yorker, xii
Newlove, John, 179n1
"No Other Way," xii, xxxii
Northern Lights Theatre, 248n2
"Not By Rain Alone," 52, 103n2
novellas, 172, 174, 189, 258

O'Connor, John, 239
Odets, Clifford, 95
Oedipal themes, xviii
O'Kelly, Audrey, xiv, xv, 25–26,
    30–33, 35–37
"Old Chippendale," 49, 50, 52,
    52n2, 55, 57n1
O'Malley, Martin, xxiii
"On Looking Back," 126n4
"One's a Heifer"
  in collections, 65, 66n1
  comments on, 59, 162
  earnings from, 24n3
  origin of, 266
  proposed illustrated
    collection, 52
  publication of, 39n1
  quality of, xvi
  revisions to, 18n3–4
  search for a publisher, 18n3,4,
    22, 24n3
Ontario Institute for Studies in
    Education, xxv, 130n1
Order of Canada, xxxiii
Oro Films, 157, 158n5
Ostenso, Martha: Wild Geese, 219

origin of, 56, 57n3

plans for, 152, 154n7, 177, 184-85, 191, 197

plot, 151-02, 184-85

publication plans, 210, 223

rejected by McClelland & Stewart, xxiii, xxxiii, 228

research for, 107n2, 184, 188n2, 203, 204, 206n1

revisions to, 228

writing process, xxxii, 202, 204, 207, 210, 212, 217, 228

prizes. *See* awards

Protestantism, 149, 151

Proust, Marcel, 124

prudishness, 203

psychiatry, 151, 153

psychology, xxii, 237

public readings, x

public taste, 72

publicity photos, 12, 186, 238n3

publishing. *See* Canadian publishing

Purdy, Al, 214, 215n7, 216-17

Queen's Quarterly, 1, 7n1, 9, 10n1, 21, 219, 254

works in, xii, xvi, xx, xxii, xxxii, 6-7, 52, 52n1, 52n3, 60-62, 225, 226

works rejected by, xxi, 63n3

works on SR in, 127, 141

Queen's University, 47n3, 194. *See also* Queen's Quarterly

The Race and Other Stories, xxxiii, 249n3

race in SR's works, xxv

Raddall, Thomas H.: *The Nymph and the Lamp*, 170n5

radio. *See* CBC

Raoul, Valerie, xxvi n12

Raymond, Louis-Bertrand, 238n5

re-use of material, xx, 39n2, 63n3, 113, 133, 152, 177, 184, 204, 268

reading

influences on SR, xvii, 138-39, 181-82, 218-21, 266

miscellaneous books, xvii, 26, 28, 38, 97, 104-05, 141, 143, 156, 157n1, 158, 159, 162, 164n2, 166n4, 191, 200, 203, 206, 227, 266-67

poetry, 22, 166, 172, 205, 214, 215-17, 232

as research, 172, 173n3, 199

SR's book collection, 240-41

Realism, 32

regionalism, x, xxii

Reid, Kate, 154n1

rejection, 73, 81, 83, 104, 114, 177

religion

SR on, 38, 150, 151, 243

and SR's culture, 218, 220n2

in SR's works, xxii, 139, 150, 230, 261, 264, 265

revenue. *See* earnings

writing process, xxii, 163,
171–72, 174–75, 190, 191,
194, 246
Scott, F.R., 80n1
Scott, Sir Walter, 266
screenplays
for *As for Me and My House*,
139, 140n2, 223–24, 225n1
for *The Well*, 87–88, 131,
132n4, 132n6
Senior Arts Award (Canada
Council for the Arts),
231–33
"September Snow," 7, 103n2, 226
sex, 72, 110–11, 154n10, 221n6
sexual assault, 153
sexuality
SR's, xvi, 47n3
as theme in SR's works, x, xiv,
xviii, xxv, xxvi n12, 15n1
See also bisexuality;
homosexuality
Shakespeare, William, xv, 31, 35,
36, 38, 51, 52n5, 243
Sharp, Mitchell, 152, 154n9
Shaw, George Bernard, xv, 31, 36
short stories. *See* stories
Simon Fraser University, 212
Sinclair Ross Symposium, xxxiii,
170n1, 211, 212n1
Smith, A.J.M., 16, 23, 24
"Sonny and Mad," xxi, 63n3
Spain
plans to write about, 211

SR in, 144–46, 148–54, 155,
157, 191, 202, 205, 217,
226–27
SR's move, xxxii, 132, 134
SR on, 104, 146, 223
travels in, 140–41, 172
"Spike," 234n1, 248
Stendhal, 138
Stevenson, Robert Louis, 5
stories
awards for, xii
collections of, xx, xxi, xxxiii,
24n3, 57n2, 59, 65, 66n1,
100n4, 102–03, 113, 175,
248
on curriculums, xiv, 175
earnings from, x, xi, 24n3,
112, 225, 229
in literary journals, 147
lost manuscripts, 63n1
Margaret Laurence on, xxii
plots, xii, xv
re-editions of, 6, 247
revisions of, 102, 103n2
as SR's medium, 83, 172, 174
style of, 59, 60
subjects of, 47, 57n1, 64
uncollected, 248, 249n3
works about, 127n4
See also works by name
Story (magazine), 17, 18n2, 18n4,
21
Stouck, David
conversations with SR, xxvii
n14, 17, 19

film rights, 84, 86–87
John Gray on, 70, 71, 78,
  80–81
Maclean's Novel Award, 71–76
payment for, 84
publication of, xvi–xvii, xxxii,
  66–68, 81, 82–84
publicity for, 85
rejections of, 73, 76, 79, 81, 82
reviews of, xxxii, 87n1, 92n1
· plot and revisions to, xvii–
  xix, 68–70, 72–75, 77–84,
  131–32
sales of, 87n1
screenplay for, 87–88, 131,
  132n4, 132n6
setting of, 70, 88
SR on, 84, 88–89, 92, 131, 262
W.K. Wing on, xix, 70
West, Rebecca, xii
western Canada
  history, xiv, 15, 172, 173n3,
    199, 254
  literature, ix, xxii, xxv, 36,
    254. *See also* prairie life
Whir of Gold
  characters in, xx, 113–14,
    116–17, 121–23, 131, 133,
    139, 202, 268
  commercial appeal of, 112–13
  contract for, 15n6, 173, 175
  crime in, 262–63
  earnings from, 133
  film potential of, 149, 158n6

and Macmillan Canada, 92,
  94n1, 111n1
manuscripts collections, 194
Margaret Laurence on, 133
and McClelland & Stewart,
  xxi, 106, 107n3, 110–11, 115,
  133–34, 158n6, 243
McClelland & Stewart list,
  242, 243
origin of, 15n2, 39n2, 63n3,
  268
plot, 113–14, 116–17
production problems, 128–
  30, 133–34, 158n6
proofreading of, 129n1, 130,
  133, 134
publication of, xx, xxi, xxxii,
  119, 129n1, 130, 134
publishers' internal reviews
  of, 94–95, 112–13
rejections of, 65, 94–95, 110,
  111, 111n1, 113
reviews of, xxi, xxv, xxxii, 131,
  132n2, 133, 140
revisions to, 95–97, 106, 110,
  115, 116, 117, 121–23, 268
sales of, 185, 187, 212
SR on, xxi, 65, 96, 106, 111–12,
  139–40, 149, 189, 202
title of, 130
voice in, 139
writing process, xx, 65–66,
  66n2, 121, 268
Whitefoot, John, 8
Whitman, Walt, 138

Wiens, Wayne, 238n2

"The Wife of Peter Guy," xiv,
15n2

Wilder, Thornton: *Our Town*,
248, 249n3

Williams, David, xxiii, 250–51,
252–53

Williams, Oscar, 37n3

Wilson, Ethel, 54n1, 78n1, 100n1,
170n5

Windsor Star, 140

Wing, W.K., xviii–xix, 69, 70,
76–77, 79

Winnipeg, xii, xxxi, xxxii, 2, 4,
5n5, 8, 14, 26n1, 36, 38,
43n2, 125, 205, 226

Winnipeg Free Press, 25, 99,
100n3, 132n3, 195, 197

Wiseman, Adele, xxii, 101–02,
104, 105n6, 109, 110n1, 118,
191, 192n2, 209, 232, 233

women in SR's works, 62–64,
101, 202, 230, 251, 252

Woodcock, George, 195, 202,
209, 245, 246n1

Woolf, Virginia: *To the
Lighthouse*, 26

Wright, Richard B., xxi, 94–95

writers' groups, xii, xxxii, 208,
227n3

writing full-time, x, xiii, 99, 109,
261

the writing life, 140, 258

young writers
SR encouraging, xxiii–xxiv,
193, 213–17, 229, 247, 253,
254
SR as inspiration, ix, xxiv, 112,
193, 205, 231, 250–53

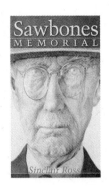

Sawbones Memorial

SINCLAIR ROSS

KEN MITCHELL, *Introduction*

On the eve of his retirement, Doctor "Sawbones" Hunter reflects on his career as a small-town physician.

152 pages | 5.25"x 9" | $16.95 paper | 978-0-88864-354-4
A volume in (cuRRents), a Canadian literature series

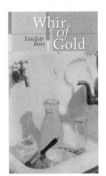

Whir of Gold

SINCLAIR ROSS

NAT HARDY, *Introduction*

Sonny, an aspiring musician, and Mad, a young woman down on her luck, struggle to survive in the mean streets of Montreal.

256 pages | 5.25"x 9" | $16.95 paper | 978-0-88864-355-1
A volume in (cuRRents), a Canadian literature series

The Well

SINCLAIR ROSS

KRISTJANA GUNNARS, *Introduction*

A petty criminal eludes capture by becoming a hired man on a prairie farm, only to discover deception and betrayal.

260 pages | 5.25"x 9" | $16.95 paper | 978-0-88864-359-9
A volume in (cuRRents), a Canadian literature series

Order these books from your local bookseller or from www.uap.ualberta.ca